EVERY CHILD CAN FLY

An Early Childhood Educator's Guide to Inclusion

➤ JANI KOZLOWSKI, MA ◄

Gryphon House
www.gryphonhouse.com

Copyright

© 2022 Jani Kozlowski

Published by Gryphon House, Inc.

P. O. Box 10, Lewisville, NC 27023

800.638.0928; 877.638.7576 [fax]

Visit us on the web at www.gryphonhouse.com.

Library of Congress Control Number: 2021946057

Bulk Purchase

Gryphon House books are available for special premiums and sales promotions as well as for fund-raising use. Special editions or book excerpts also can be created to specifications. For details, call 800.638.0928.

Disclaimer

Gryphon House, Inc., cannot be held responsible for damage, mishap, or injury incurred during the use of or because of activities in this book. Appropriate and reasonable caution and adult supervision of children involved in activities and corresponding to the age and capability of each child involved are recommended at all times. Do not leave children unattended at any time. Observe safety and caution at all times.

This book is not intended to give legal advice. All legal opinions contained herein are from the personal research and experience of the author and are intended as educational material. Seek the advice of a qualified legal advisor before making legal decisions.

TABLE OF CONTENTS

Preface	**iv**
Acknowledgments	**ix**
Introduction	**1**
Chapter 1: Inclusion: What, How, and Why	**9**
Chapter 2: Understanding Early Intervention and Special Education	**29**
Chapter 3: Working with Families	**48**
Chapter 4: Screening, Evaluation, and Assessment	**67**
Chapter 5: Working on IFSP or IEP Goals	**84**
Chapter 6: Inclusive Learning Environments	**98**
Chapter 7: Inclusive Teaching Practices	**130**
Chapter 8: Inclusive Practices to Foster Social-Emotional Development	**151**
Chapter 9: Culturally and Linguistically Responsive Practices	**180**
Chapter 10: Self-Care for the Early Childhood Educator	**194**
Appendix A: Glossary of Terms	**211**
Appendix B: Online Resources to Support Inclusion	**223**
References and Recommended Reading	**238**
Index	**261**

PREFACE

Inclusion is a passion for me. I have dedicated my professional career to early childhood education, and I care deeply about all children of all abilities. Early childhood educators and other staff are central figures in the lives of children and families. We have the privilege of being able to offer a helping hand to children and families during a critical period of development. I am passionate about inclusion because I have experienced disability from many different perspectives.

I am an early childhood professional with a disability.

I am the daughter of a parent with a disability.

I am the mother of a son with a disability.

I was born with a rare orthopedic impairment called *Spondylometaphyseal dysplasia* or SMD. It is a form of dwarfism, and I stand at four feet six inches tall. I am a "little person," which is the preferred term for many people in the United States who have the medical condition of dwarfism. SMD is a relatively "tall" form of dwarfism. Many little people have shorter arms and legs, but my arms and legs are proportional to the rest of my body. People typically regard me as just a petite lady, albeit a *very* petite lady. In addition to being a little person, I have significant curvature in my spine and have dealt with pain in my joints throughout my life. Many months of my childhood were spent in recovery mode

from more than twenty orthopedic surgeries. As an adult, I now have artificial joint replacements in my hips, knees, and ankles. My legs are bionic. My spine is fused from the base of my skull to the middle of my back. I cannot turn my head from side to side or up and down. I use my torso to turn my head. Sometimes I feel as though my skeletal system is a jigsaw puzzle with pieces that don't quite fit together. I'm kinda funky on the inside, in ways that you would know only from looking at an X-ray.

SMD is a condition that I have, but it is not who I am. It has been significant in my life, though, because of all of the surgeries and because it affects my height and my joints and my spine. I have had some very difficult experiences living as a little person in this world, mainly because I look different from everybody else. Even though I have achieved a great deal of success in my life as an early childhood professional, as a wife, and as a mother, the truth is that people still stare at me in the grocery store. Out in public, people judge me by my size and my disability.

This was especially difficult as a teenager and young adult. During my senior year of high school, I had a type of surgery called a spinal fusion. Due to the curvature in my spine, the doctors had to "fuse" vertebrae together so my spinal cord would be protected. As a result, I spent several months of my senior year wearing a medical device called a halo as I recovered.

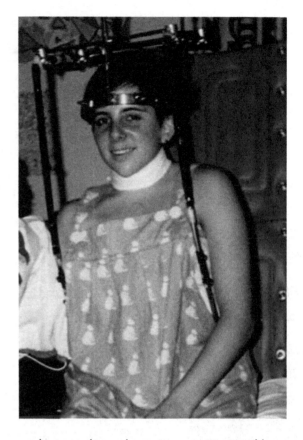

It would be a difficult recovery to go through at any time but especially during the self-conscious teenage years! In college, I had my first hip-replacement surgery and used crutches for a time as I walked around on campus. I refused to use a handicap sign in my car because I didn't want people to think that I was "handicapped." I struggled a great deal to be seen the same as everyone else, as most children do. These experiences shaped me as a person, and I am proud of the fact that I have been able to overcome many challenges. Over time, I have even learned strategies for coping with the stares. Being a little person with a big smile is very powerful. My size makes people look at me, and my smile disarms them. They mostly smile back. Children almost always smile back.

I inherited SMD from my father. He dealt with many of the same struggles as I have and overcame many challenges. My father was born and raised in Buenos Aires, Argentina. In the Latin culture it is especially difficult to be a short-statured man, but my father didn't let his height affect his dreams. My dad was a motivated student and successfully graduated from medical school.

After medical school, he emigrated to the United States and finished his residency in Washington, DC. My mother was in nursing school at the time, and my parents met and fell in love very quickly. My mom is five feet ten inches tall and my father was only four feet ten inches tall. The height difference made them a very cute couple! When they had their photo taken together, my mother would often sit down while he stood beside her. Or he would position himself in a higher spot so that their faces were side by side in the photo. My father was very charismatic and handsome. People were really drawn to him. He was a natural storyteller, and people used to crowd around him as he told stories in an animated way.

When my parents decided to have a child, they went to many doctors to find out if there was a chance that my father's condition could be passed down to his offspring. They were told not to worry, that my dad's condition was not genetically inherited. Years before in Argentina, he had been told that his condition was called rickets, which is caused by a lack of vitamin D in childhood. Even though my father was a doctor himself, he was terrified of having surgery and didn't really follow up on his own health care or even ask that much about it. My mother became pregnant without concern. At first all was well, although I was born prematurely and weighed only three pounds, three ounces at birth. I had to be in the intensive care unit for quite some time before my parents could bring me home, but other than that, they didn't think that there would be any issues. For a time, that was true.

My parents doted on me. I was a princess to my father and mother. Both of my parents always showered me with love and attention, for which I will be forever grateful. I always felt cherished.

It was only over time that my parents learned that I have the same skeletal issues as my father. As a result, my father learned the truth of his own condition through the process of finding out how best to care for his child. And through it all, my mother cared for both of us. My father dealt with a great deal of guilt throughout his life because he felt responsible for my disability.

As a child, I viewed disability through the lens of how other people reacted to my father when they first met him and how he responded to those reactions. His strategy was basically not to take himself too seriously. My father was a psychiatrist and jokingly called himself "The Shrink." He even had a personalized license plate on his car that read SHRINK, and he loved it that people laughed every time he got out of the car. Like me, he rejected the notion of the label of *handicapped* and taught me how to disarm awkwardness through a smile or joke. He taught me not to worry so much about the stares because they were just human nature. He said that the world is like a field of blue flowers, and when a pink flower appears in the field, what do you do? You look at it!

I often think of the Smokey Robinson song "The Tears of a Clown" when I think of my father. He presented a happy and secure exterior, but I wonder if that was a mask for his true feelings.

Were there tears when no one was around? My father had a large personality, which may have been to compensate for his small stature. It's hard to know exactly how he felt because my father died many years ago. My mother was there for me through it all. She remarried and found happiness with my stepfather and is a doting granny to my son, Ricky.

Ricky also overcame many obstacles growing up with attention deficit hyperactivity disorder (ADHD). ADHD is a disorder that is marked by inattention (difficulty with maintaining focus), impulsivity (acting hastily), and being overly active. Ricky is a successful young adult today. He received special education services throughout his school years. I learned a great deal from him throughout his childhood and continue to learn from him to this day. He is resilience personified! The experience of raising a child with a disability taught me about the importance of maintaining high expectations

for children, even when we want to protect them from frustration or disappointment. Ricky is an amazing person, and I am a very proud mama. I'll share many stories from my experiences as a mother throughout this book.

Through these varied perspectives, I am able to share both the practical and the personal: practical strategies for supporting children with disabilities and their families, along with my own personal stories that illustrate the importance and reasoning behind the strategies. I will share stories of my own personal experience, my experience as a mother, and my experience as the daughter of a parent with a disability in these pages.

As we explore the issues related to supporting children with disabilities and their families, I hope you will reflect on the experiences that make up the stories from your own life and examine your own attitudes and beliefs. This quote from Marion Wright Edelman really speaks to my heart: "The sea is so wide, and my boat is so small." It does seem as though the sea is wide and that we have a long way to go to make early childhood inclusion the norm rather than the exception. My boat is small, but I also know that my boat is not the only boat. I have many partners in this work, including you. Together we make a mighty fleet on behalf of children and families.

You also bring different perspectives to this work. You may be a person with a disability, just like me. Are you the parent of a child with a disability? a sibling? a grandparent? a spouse? a partner? a friend? Are you a preK teacher? a home visitor? a caregiver of infants or toddlers? Do you work in a Head Start or Early Head Start program? Do you work as an early childhood special-education teacher in a public school? Do you work in a child-care center or take care of children in your home? Do you coach other educators or provide professional development or technical assistance? Would you like to contribute at least a little piece of your life to making the world a better place for each and every child? There is a place for all of us in this work.

Obviously, I don't know all of you. I don't know what has led you to this point in your life where you have chosen to learn more about inclusion. But I do know that you are reading this book because you would like to make a difference. The amazing thing is that we all want to be accepted. We are each unique. We are each living in a body that we did not choose. And we all want to belong. We all face challenges. We each bring something to give to this world, and we all are important partners in this beautiful concept that we call inclusion. Children and their families depend on us to get it right. They depend on us to view every child as worthy of love, happiness, and the opportunity to learn alongside their peers and achieve their greatest potential. They depend on us to know and believe in our hearts that every child can fly.

ACKNOWLEDGMENTS

Every Child Can Fly has been a labor of love involving my immediate and extended family, friends, and colleagues. I would like to thank all of the people who supported me along the way:

My dear husband, Rick, thank you for supporting me with love, words of encouragement, and endless acts of picking up the slack around the house when I was, as you say, "in the zone."

My adored (and adorable!) son, Ricky, thank you for giving me the gift of motherhood and for the greatest gift of all, the chance to be *your* mother. You are the inspiration for this book and the reason behind my passion for this work!

My mother, Eileen, and stepfather, George, thank you for patiently listening to every detail with so much love and support as I negotiated my way through the writing process.

My friend, colleague, and mentor, Karen Nemeth, who encouraged me, shared her wisdom with me, and connected me to her own professional networks. I am forever grateful!

My friends near and far, too many to name, who encouraged me, shared stories from their own experiences, and sent me photographs of their own children and classrooms to use in this book.

My colleagues current and past, also too many to name, but a special shout-out to the ECTA Inclusion Team, the North Carolina early childhood community, and friends from the OHS and OCC TA systems.

My colleagues and friends who agreed to review all or a portion of this manuscript. Your comments and suggestions were so valuable! Thank you to Camille Catlett, Judy David, Valerie Krajec, Dayana Garcia, Alissa Rausch, Catasha Williams, Megan Vinh, Debbie Cate, and Thomas McGhee. Let me return the favor someday!

My friends at the White Plains Children's Center in Cary, North Carolina, and the New School Montessori in Holly Springs, North Carolina, thank you for welcoming me into your programs and for giving me the opportunity to learn from you and to photograph the beautiful children in your classrooms.

My editor, Stephanie Roselli, for her guidance and patience as I learned about the early childhood publishing industry.

You all inspire me daily. Thank you for helping to make this book come to life and for sharing in my joyous passion for increasing inclusive early learning opportunities for young children and their families. We are a mighty fleet!

Introduction

I started out in the early childhood education field more than thirty years ago as a preschool teacher for a diverse and spirited group of four-year-olds. Actually, I really started out in the field when I worked as a nanny all through college. Yes, I was Jani the Nanny. The energy that young children bring to the world has always inspired me. Being around children makes me happy! Even as a child myself, I had always wanted to be a teacher. For a time, I was just a little bit intimidated by children who are taller than me, so teaching preschool fit the bill. Each child came to my classroom with unique strengths and abilities that unfolded before my eyes over the course of our time together. At that time, I didn't think about my classroom as being inclusive. In my mind, children were children were children were children. All different and wonderful in their own way. Reflecting back, I remember some of the children who would likely have received special education services if we had collaborated with the school system on their behalf.

I remember Danny who used to gaze up at me blankly through thick, smudged glasses. His hair was "as red as a copper penny," as they say in the South. I remember constantly cleaning those glasses for him. When his glasses got especially dirty, he would just let them slide down his nose and would peer over them at me like a freckle-faced librarian. Even after I cleaned his glasses, he would still bump into the furniture in the classroom. I remember keeping him up close to the visuals during circle time so that he could participate in our daily routine together. A vision impairment?

I remember Caleb and his strong, clinging hugs. He seemed to love fiercely but also acted impulsively with aggression toward other children. I felt concerned for their safety. His parents once asked me to join them on a visit to their family therapist to describe Caleb's behavior at school and problem solve together. A case of attention deficit disorder?

I remember Ashley with her love of dinosaurs and preference for outdoor play in the sandbox. Her skin was like porcelain, and I remember her wide-set almond-shaped eyes and flattened nose. Ashley did not speak at four years old, and I had to put my hand on her shoulder to get her attention. A case of Down syndrome?

A child with ongoing toileting issues? A child who rocked and swayed in the book area when she became overstimulated? I can think of countless examples. Of course, these diagnoses of children from thirty years ago are completely irrelevant. I would argue that it would not have mattered back then either. Would I have gained special knowledge to know the label that might have been used to describe Caleb? Absolutely not! I only share those memories because they are a reminder that an inclusive classroom is just like any other classroom. We never questioned whether or not a child belonged in our program. Everyone belonged. Everyone was welcome.

Many of you are educators in programs just like the one where I started out in my early childhood journey. That journey led me to support Head Start teachers as an education and disability services manager and later to provide support through workshops and technical assistance to Head Start programs across the country. I taught at a community college, and later I designed child-care-quality initiatives and drafted policy as an administrator within the North Carolina Division of Child Development and Early Education. Then, I supported other child-care leaders to do the same. About ten years ago, I started working at the national level, providing technical assistance for leaders through projects funded by the federal Office of Head Start and Office of Child Care within the Department of Health and Human Services, Administration for Children and Families. Now I serve as a technical assistance specialist for the Early Childhood Technical Assistance (ECTA) Center at the Frank Porter Graham Child Development Institute at the University of North Carolina at Chapel Hill. Through my work at ECTA, I provide support to state leaders working to increase the number of children served in inclusive settings. These leaders are working hard to change a system that has been very difficult to change over the years.

For children aged three to five in the United States, the special-education system places children with disabilities in segregated classrooms more often than not. Rather than placing children with disabilities in classrooms with their peers without disabilities, they are often put into classrooms where all the children have a disability.

This is not a realistic approach. As a person with a disability myself, I work alongside people with and without disabilities. I spend my free time in my community around people with and without disabilities. We are fortunate that our world is a place of diverse abilities, races, ethnicities, gender identities, sexualities, and everything else that makes us unique individuals. Our world is inclusive, and our community spaces, schools, child-care programs, Head Start centers, and all other early childhood education programs should be, too.

Unfortunately, young children with disabilities face many barriers to being included in all facets of life in their community. Rausch, Joseph, and Steed (2019) recently highlighted some of the research related to exclusion of children with disabilities from community spaces such as parks and playgrounds (Burke, 2012) to early care and education environments (Barton and Smith, 2015). The researchers point to social barriers created by the lack of accessibility in community playgrounds (Ripat and Becker, 2012) and the subtle messages that children with disabilities and their families receive that lead them to feel that they just do not belong in these community spaces where children without disabilities learn and play (Prellwitz and Skär, 2007). As you might imagine, this type of social exclusion is very harmful for children and families and can have long-term impacts on their ability to participate in learning opportunities and engage with others (Stegelin, 2018).

Numerous studies have explored the barriers to inclusion. These barriers include a lack of funding or other resources for providing individualized supports and a lack of professional-development opportunities for early childhood educators and administrators (Rausch, Joseph, and Steed, 2019; Weglarz-Ward, Santos, and Timmer, 2019). However, researchers have consistently found that the most frequently reported barrier to inclusion is the attitudes and beliefs held by educators, administrators, system leaders, and policymakers. Inclusion tends to exist in the ivory tower and not in practice because our thinking has not been challenged about what it means to be an educator for each and every child, regardless of ability. We must work together to create a system in which inclusion is the norm rather than the exception.

We know that children do not need to be "ready" before they can be included with their peers. Rather the program, whether home-based, center-based, or a family child care, should be ready for the children. Delaying inclusion until a time when you think the child is old enough, advanced enough, or anything else "enough" flies in the face of the goal and purpose of inclusion, which is to ensure children with disabilities have supported opportunities to grow, learn, and thrive alongside their peers.

SOME THOUGHTS ON TERMINOLOGY

Words matter. Language is a powerful influence on the perceptions we have of the world around us. We need to be careful with our words. As advocates for inclusion, we want all children to have a sense of belonging. We want all children to feel welcomed in our childcare programs, our family child-care homes, our Head Start and prekindergarten programs, our schools, and in our world. This starts with the words we use.

Is it really okay to label a child who is still in the process of growing and developing? This question is an ongoing struggle for me. As a result, I choose to focus on the practice of inclusion of all children, rather than any specific label. Because, like it or not, we need the labels now. Without the labels in our current system of education, the need for services and supports would be overlooked and the funding would be lost as well. I often wonder if the labels that help us to justify the supports and services for a child actually do more harm than good overall. It is true that labels do serve a purpose. In addition to their use in demonstrating a need for access to services, labels are also a communication tool among service providers, a way to specify a group of people for advocacy purposes and a way to categorize effective teaching practices. However, labels also can promote a negative self-identity, create stigmas, lead to overgeneralization, and limit expectations that a family may have for their child.

DISABILITY

What is *disability* anyway? It's basically a term that humans created to sort people into the categories of "abled" and "disabled." This assumes that the person with a disability has no ability at all, which of course is completely untrue. We all need help in some aspect of our lives. The term and concept of *disability* is entirely dreamed up by society, and when you look at the notion more closely, well, it kind of falls apart.

> *"All of us, at some time or other, need help. Whether we're giving or receiving help, each one of us has something valuable to bring to this world. That's one of the things that connects us as neighbors—in our own way, each one of us is a giver and a receiver."*
>
> **—FRED ROGERS**

There is a continuum of ability in every aspect of human existence. Do you have a disability because you are not a writer? Is my friend disabled because she can't play basketball like Michael Jordan? Of course not! There is diversity in what human beings are capable of doing. We have strengths in some areas of our lives and challenges in others—every single one of us! The term *disability* itself is used to refer to a specific inability to do something that society expects all human beings to be able to do, such as walking upright on two legs, communicating with words rather than with hand gestures, or even thinking and learning in a certain way. Ultimately, it's a concept that humans created as shorthand for people who act, behave, interact, or accomplish things in ways that are different from most other people. The thing is, doing something in a different way doesn't have to imply that it is the wrong way to do them. In most cases, the ability to act, behave, interact, or accomplish in different or unique ways is celebrated.

Disability assumes that the individual is unable to navigate the world in an acceptable way, when in fact she simply navigates the world in a different way. All disability categories are subjective! Even types of disability that we would think are straightforward turn out to be much hazier when you zoom in on them. For example, the difference between what is considered poor eyesight and what is considered blindness is a relatively arbitrary distinction. Often, the ability (or disability) is dependent on external factors. For example, my husband is unable to hear out of one ear. In a crowded restaurant, he would likely be considered deaf. In a quiet setting, one on one, his ability to hear is mostly unimpaired. Children with attention issues can often focus intently when they engage in an activity that interests them. Disability is never as fixed or obvious as some might think.

The definitions of disabilities within the medical field change continually, as science evolves over time. For example, as researcher Subini Annamma and colleagues (2013) note, in 1973 the American Association of Mental Deficiency changed the definition of *intellectual impairment* from an intelligence quotient (IQ) score of 85 to an IQ score of 70, and thereby determined that a whole group of people were suddenly "cured" from the label! Even though the term *disability* is subjective, we often use the word in a way that implies certainty.

Some writers have drawn attention to these issues around the word *disability* by using the term *dis/ability*. In writing this book, I have chosen to stay with the conventional spelling of the term, acknowledging the many limitations. This entire book, in my opinion, is its own commentary about how educators and the practice of inclusion serve as disrupters of the way that society defines *disability*. Ultimately, inclusive programs offer each child the path to navigate the world in their own unique way. We create the space, the practices, the culture, and the community so this may be.

SPECIAL

Given where we are in the evolution of terms in education systems, which words should we choose to use? Most people with disabilities, including me, prefer to use the term *disability* rather than *special needs*, because *special* implies that we have needs that are different than others. We don't have "special" needs; we have human needs. When we regard children as having special needs, it isn't a far jump to believe that they will then need to be segregated from others in "special" environments and "special" classes. Special education is a service, not a place. Children do not need a special place just because they need certain services or supports.

The language of special needs also implies that children with disabilities need "special" educators. Let me be clear here: I love and respect the special-education profession and special-education professionals. I have learned so much from these professionals who have devoted their lives to that particular field of study. And the field of early childhood education needs those who understand and can teach others to implement the supports, strategies, and evidence-based teaching practices designed specifically for children with disabilities. However, if you were to ask the progressive leaders in the special-education field today, they would tell you that the ultimate goal of special education is to help children find success in the general-education classroom as much as possible, through accommodations, services, and other necessary supports.

In this book, I will highlight strategies that are key to supporting children with disabilities in inclusive programs, but my friend, there are many more strategies out there. Special educators will teach you something new every time they set foot in your program. My concern is that the term *special educator* implies that they must have some sort of magic intellectual pixie dust to serve as an educator of children with disabilities. This is just not so.

PEOPLE- OR IDENTITY-FIRST LANGUAGE

The use of people-first language is an approach that recognizes the person before the disability and uses accurate, strengths-based language to describe qualities, characteristics, and actions in a respectful way (Snow, 2016). When we describe a child with a disability, it is recommended that we use people-first language; for example, refer to a child who has autism as a "child with autism" rather than as an "autistic child." This acknowledges the fact that autism is something the child has, but it is not who the child is. She may have autism, but she is much more than that! Autism is just one of the features about the child, and people-first language recognizes that fact.

Language is very personal, and people with disabilities and those who support them are a diverse group with diverse perspectives. In fact, some people with disabilities have chosen to embrace the labels and, rather than using people-first language, they advocate for what is called identity-first language, such as "autistic child." This perspective arises from the idea that disability is a natural part of the human condition and is nothing to be ashamed of, that "disabled people" should be proud of that identity.

I know it's confusing. My advice for which language to use when you are speaking with an adult with a disability? Ask the person what they would prefer. Individuals have different preferences. I am a strong believer in people-first language. The thought of calling a child an "autistic child" rather than a "child with autism" makes me feel uncomfortable. While I certainly agree that there is no reason to be ashamed of disability, I stand with the people-first language approach for young children. Until a child is old enough to make those decisions, I think that it is important to use people-first language to reflect the fact that children with disabilities are children first. Like all children, they have many strengths, and disability is what they have and not who they are. In fact, disability may very well be a temporary situation and not a lifelong part of their identity. In any case, our society is just not there yet in terms of letting go of the negative stereotype that exists around disability. As Erin Barton, an associate professor of special education at Vanderbilt University, notes, "Children with disabilities do not need to be repaired or fixed. Just like all children, they need support to succeed." All children are special, and all children need some form of individualization to thrive and succeed. Children with disabilities are children, first and foremost. Families, specialists, and educators can work together with combined expertise, sharing our lessons learned on behalf of the children we love.

My hope is that, as educators shift our approach and practice, the shift in language and the shift away from the use of labels will follow.

This book is intended for early childhood educators who may not have a degree in special education but who seek to understand how best to support all children in their programs, regardless of ability. My hope is that this book will demystify the early intervention (EI) and early childhood special education (ECSE) systems for my early childhood educator colleagues. We will explore the research base and the legal foundations of inclusion, as well as the ways that the laws are implemented by health and education systems. We'll also explore inclusion from the perspective of the family and offer guidance for navigating these systems from screening to service delivery. In addition, we will explore the learning environments and teaching practices that are necessary to create high-quality inclusive experiences for young children.

HOW THIS BOOK IS ORGANIZED

If you are looking for a guide that tells you all about specific conditions such as Down syndrome, cerebral palsy, or ADHD, you won't find that here (but I will include some links in appendix B, so check those out if you're curious). The good news is that you really don't need to be an expert in any specific disability to be an expert in supporting children. Every type of disability includes tremendous variations from person to person in how it presents to the world, so there would never be a way to learn everything.

We may worry that we will accidentally do something harmful to the child, and that's certainly understandable. But ultimately our job is to find out how to best meet the individual needs of a child. We do this by getting to know the child, talking with family members, and starting with an assumption of competence. We ask questions such as, "What have you noticed about how your child learns best? What has worked well at home?" As we build our understanding from observing the child and talking with the family, we find that, over time, our fear will fade.

A mother whom I met recently shared that finding out about all of the variability within her daughter's condition turned out to be one of her greatest lessons. She found that the name of the disability didn't matter all that much. She said, "When I learned that cerebral palsy is really just a term to describe a difference in muscle tone, it opened up all of the possibilities in the world for my child. Who cares that she has cerebral palsy? We just need to make sure that she gets the physical therapy that she needs to strengthen her muscles!"

In this guide we will focus on inclusion as a value to embrace in our culture of early care and education. Inclusion is a process, a collection of strategies and individualized approaches to meet the needs of each and every child. We'll start in chapter 1 with the definition of *inclusion* itself, the research base around inclusion, and how the laws and regulations in the United States are structured to promote it. In chapter 2, we'll dive into the worlds of early intervention and early childhood special education to better understand how these systems work on behalf of children and families, from referral to service delivery. Chapter 3 looks at families and how early childhood educators can support them through the EI and ECSE systems. This starts with screening, evaluation, and assessment, which I address in chapter 4. Chapters 5 through 9 provide a deeper dive into how we can support children and families to achieve their goals, provide inclusive learning environments, and use inclusive, equitable, and culturally responsive teaching practices. The final chapter addresses how to do all of this while staying healthy and strong, with a sense of balance throughout our lives. In appendix A you will find a glossary of terms, and in appendix B you will see a collection of online resources for when you want to dig deeper and learn more. Each chapter also includes highlighted resources and reflection questions to extend your learning. You will find lots of practical tips and strategies throughout these pages.

"Inclusion is not a 'place' but a culture that we create when practices are based on rights, inclusive belonging, and contribution"
(Hampshire & Mallory, 2021).

While I was writing this book, *you*, the early childhood educator, were always on my mind. Again and again, I thought to myself, "What would have been helpful to me when I was working directly with children and families?" This book represents a collection of answers to that question, and I hope you will find answers to your questions as well.

CHAPTER 1

Inclusion: What, How, and Why

History will judge us by the difference we make in the everyday lives of children.

—NELSON MANDELA, FIRST DEMOCRATICALLY ELECTED PRESIDENT OF SOUTH AFRICA

What do we mean by *inclusion*?

But first, a story. This really happened.

Early one morning last spring, I was sitting on my deck in my pj's drinking coffee when the most amazing thing happened. My deck looks out over a grassy area where birds gather. It's usually a very peaceful spot, but on this particular morning, it was a very different sort of scene. I was taking a sip of coffee when I noticed the sky seemed to get a little bit darker, as though there were a shadow over the sun.

A giant hawk with a huge wingspan and an evil look in his eye soared right by me. I gasped in shock as he flew down to a nearby tree and then BAM! He snatched a baby bird right out of its nest.

The bird's parents weren't around. It happened too fast. Nothing could be done. The hawk had his prize and curved back around to glide past me, the baby in his claws.

But that baby was really squirmy. Squiggly squirmy. And loud. That baby squirmed and squawked and must have been too much trouble, because before I could blink, the hawk dropped the baby! The baby squirmed through the air, twisting, turning, and wriggling down to the ground into the tall grass.

Was it alive?

Should I go get it?

Now let me tell you that I am not an expert in foreign languages. Certainly not the language of bird. But that baby was definitely saying, "Mama! Help! Come get me!" I know that for sure. And after a while, the mother did come around. She fluttered around the baby, and I could tell she was upset. It was as if she were thinking, "Sweetheart! How did you get yourself into this predicament? I can come and feed you, but I can't put a half-grown baby on my back and fly away!"

The baby squawked and squawked. Distressed, the poor mama bird fluttered around, and eventually she flew off. After a time, the baby went silent and stayed silent for a long time. Would you think less of me if I told you that I went back to chilling out with my coffee? (I was in my pj's after all.) Then a crazy, jerking motion rustled the grass where the baby had fallen. And suddenly, believe it or not, that little baby flew. It was a wobbly, pitiful-looking fly, but it was a fly nonetheless. I jumped up and cheered as it flew out of my view.

Isn't that resilience?

The only thing that baby had ever known was sitting in the nest, waiting for mama to come with food. That baby had never flown. And it certainly didn't know about a hawk! Imagine what was going on in that little baby bird brain after being snatched up and then falling to the cold, hard ground.

And yet that baby bird flew.

As you might imagine, I told this story to all of my friends. My early childhood educator friends immediately made the connection to children. As educators, we are the ones down there on the ground, waiting to teach the baby birds when they leave the nest. Think about the children in your program. What did they know about life outside the nest before you met them? And how did they leave the nest?

Some children leave the nest in a gentle sort of way; others leave in a traumatic way. And yet they all arrive in our early childhood programs with different skills and abilities. Some come to us with mama bird by their side. She leaves them with a peck on the cheek, and they already know how to fly. Others seem to know only how to squawk and carry on and kick and fight and roll around on the floor. They may not fly in a straight path, and they may not fly in the same way other birds fly, but all children can fly in their own way, in their own time, with our love, care, and support.

This is what inclusion means to me. Every child belongs. Every child is unique. Every child has strengths. Every child has the potential to fly.

What is your definition of inclusion? I imagine that it has grown and changed over time—and may change again as you read this book and reflect on how inclusion aligns with your own values and priorities as an educator. My understanding of and thinking about inclusion and the concept of disability in general have certainly evolved and changed over the thirty years that I have worked in the early childhood field. How does our field define inclusion? What do we really mean by that term?

INCLUSION AS DEFINED BY THE EARLY CARE AND EDUCATION FIELD

According to the Kids Count Data Center (2021), provided by the Annie E. Casey Foundation, and the most recent US Census Bureau (2020) report, there are 23.4 million children ages birth through five in the United States. Of that number, 11.4 million children are under the age of three, and 12 million are ages three through five. How many of those children have a disability? That number is a little bit trickier. We know from the federal Office of Special Education's most recent annual report to Congress (US Department of Education, 2020) that in 2018, 409,315 infants and toddlers received early intervention services and 815,010 children ages three through five received early childhood special education services. This includes services provided across the continuum of placement. In other words, this could reflect a child served in an early childhood program alongside his peers, but it also includes children who receive services in a hospital, special school, or at home. For this book, we focus on how to support children with disabilities in the same early childhood settings that they would attend if they didn't have a disability. This concept is the key element of what we view as inclusion, but the truth is that it's about a lot more than that.

In 2009, two of the leading early care and education (ECE) and early childhood special education (ECSE) membership organizations came together to present a unified vision for inclusion in early childhood. This joint position statement developed by the National Association for the Education of Young Children (NAEYC) and the Division of Early Childhood of the Council for Exceptional Children (DEC) defines inclusion in this way:

"Early childhood inclusion embodies the values, policies, and practices that support the right of every infant and young child and his or her family, regardless of ability, to participate in a broad range of activities and contexts as full members of families, communities, and society."

In addition, these two membership organizations indicated a set of outcomes, or desired results, of inclusion for children with and without disabilities and their families:

- A sense of belonging and membership
- Positive social relationships and friendships
- Development and learning to reach their full potential

The "Policy Statement on Inclusion of Children with Disabilities in Early Childhood Programs" (US Department of Health and Human Services, US Department of Education, 2015) states, "All young children with disabilities should have access to inclusive, high-quality early childhood programs, where they are provided with individualized and appropriate support in meeting high expectations." Both of these statements reflect the fact that young children with disabilities should grow and learn alongside their peers with and without disabilities. However, simply learning side-by-side with your peers is not the entire picture. The statements also refer to providing individualized supports and maintaining high expectations. The statements share the vision that inclusion in early childhood will lead to inclusion in elementary school, middle school, high school, college, and the workplace. Early childhood inclusion leads to inclusion "in all facets of society throughout the life course" (HHS and ED, 2015).

This is a definition and vision that we can all embrace! But how can we make it happen? How can we make sure inclusion is successful?

 ## DEFINING FEATURES OF INCLUSION

The NAEYC and DEC joint position statement proposes three defining features of inclusion:

- **Access:** "providing a wide range of activities and environments for every child by removing physical barriers and offering multiple ways to promote learning and development"
- **Participation:** "using a range of instructional approaches to promote engagement in play and learning activities, and a sense of belonging for every child"
- **Supports:** "broader aspects of the system such as professional development, incentives for inclusion, and opportunities for communication and collaboration among families and professionals to assure high quality inclusion"

What does this look like in an early childhood setting? Access starts with just the ability to get in the door. An inclusive child-care program implements policies that promote access, so families know it is a program open to all children. This is evident from the wheelchair ramp at the front entrance to inclusive practices in the classroom. An educator might arrange his classroom so that all children can access all learning centers. For example, Miguel benefits from having a cube chair to sit in at circle time because his upper-body strength is still developing. Laura uses a wheelchair, so her classroom has wide-open aisles, and the sand table is the perfect height to allow everyone to play. The environment and activities are planned using principles of universal design, which is a way of thinking about teaching and learning that allows flexibility for children to access and use materials or demonstrate competence. (We explore this in more depth in chapter 6.) Educators promote access by offering spaces and learning opportunities that work for all children with or without disabilities. Of course, inclusion is about more than just getting through the door. Inclusion is about ensuring that all children have a sense of belonging, membership, and being active participants in the program.

To promote participation, an educator might individualize activities to offer a variety of ways for children to join in on the fun and learning. We know that children are more alike than they are different, and we also know that children want to be as independent as possible. For example, Abby, who uses crutches to walk, holds the stop-and-go sign during Red Light, Green Light, so she can participate even though it is a running game. Ben, a child with a communication disorder, chooses the game he wants to play by pointing to a picture of the game rather than saying his choice. Carly, a child who is extra wiggly during circle time, holds a fidget toy to help her stay focused. Educators use these accommodations and modifications so all children can participate with success.

Supports are provided by the program or implemented at the system-level to ensure that the efforts of educators are successful and can be maintained. For example, a school district might invite Head Start educators to join special-education staff for a professional development workshop of mutual interest. Or a state may give extra points to inclusive programs as part of the quality rating and improvement system (QRIS) or may offer financial incentives to cover unexpected costs.

As noted in *The Preschool Inclusion Toolbox: How to Build and Lead a High-Quality Program* (Barton and Smith, 2015), the three defining features of access, participation, and supports are dependent upon factors such as strong family involvement, supported peer relationships, specialized supports, individualized teaching practices, collaborative teaming, ongoing evaluation, and staff professional development. High-quality inclusive programs start with family involvement, while always keeping the child at the center.

> *We recognize inclusive education as the process of (a) redistributing access to and participation in quality learning opportunities; (b) recognizing and valuing all child differences in learning activities, materials, and interactions; and (c) creating opportunities for non-dominant and under-represented groups to share their narratives and advance solutions for equity, with particular attention given to the interplay of multiple and intersecting social identities (e.g., ability, race, language) in learning contexts (e.g., home, school, and community settings)"* *(Morgan and Cheatham, 2021).*

Throughout this book, we will further explore these defining features and think about their practical application in your program and for your role as an early childhood educator.

FEDERAL LEGISLATION

In addition to these three defining features, we can think about the "how" of inclusion through the lens of the laws that have been put into place to protect children and families, as well as to guide our education system and society as a whole. Following are brief summaries of these laws. In chapter 2, we will discuss how these laws affect children and families, and the resources section at the end of this book includes links to information with detailed guidance for interpreting the legislation. For now, this is the view from 30,000 feet above.

INDIVIDUALS WITH DISABILITIES EDUCATION ACT (IDEA)

The Individuals with Disabilities Education Act of 1973 was reauthorized in 2004 and is the key federal law that governs how states, territories, jurisdictions, and public agencies (referred to throughout this book simply as *states*) provide services for infants, toddlers, preschoolers, and school-aged children with disabilities. IDEA supports providing early intervention services to eligible infants, toddlers, and their families and providing a free appropriate public education through special-education services to eligible children ages three through twenty-one. The federal Office of Special Education Programs (OSEP) administers funding to states to enact the legislative intentions of IDEA. States then share a portion of the funding with local agencies. Programs serving infants and toddlers, birth through age two, fall under Part C. Programs serving children ages three through five fall under Part B, Section 619.

> Where can I learn more about IDEA? A good place to start is the website developed and maintained by the US Department of Education: https://sites.ed.gov/idea/

Part C—Programs for Infants and Toddlers with Disabilities

States receive Part C grants to provide comprehensive early intervention services for children birth through age two who have disabilities or developmental delays and their families. State legislators determine which agency—such as a health, human services, or education agency—will receive and administer Part C funds. The services must be provided in the child's "natural environment," which means the environment where the child spends the majority of time, such as the child's home, child-care program, Early Head Start program, or grandparent's house.

The services a child receives are determined by the Individualized Family Service Plan (IFSP) team. The IFSP team includes the child's parent or guardian, early intervention service providers, and other team members. Infants and toddlers are eligible if they are experiencing a developmental delay and/ or have a diagnosed medical condition. There is state discretion in defining these criteria, which may include infants or toddlers who are at risk for a delay or disability. It is important that you know how your state defines eligibility, and you can find that information on your state's Part C website.

Part B, Section 619—Preschool Grants Programs

Part B, Section 619 of IDEA authorizes grants to states to provide special education and related services to children with disabilities ages three through five. Just as in Part C, there are some eligibility and service components that are left up to the states to determine, including the ability to serve two-year-old children with disabilities who will turn three during the upcoming school year. States must make a free and appropriate public education (FAPE) available to all eligible children with disabilities ages three through five. These early childhood special education and related services must be provided, to the maximum extent appropriate, in the "least restrictive environment" (LRE) based on the child's unique strengths and needs. This means that when a decision is made about where IDEA services are to be provided to the child, the first option should be the place where the child would typically be if she did not have a disability at all. For preschoolers, this would likely be in a child-care program, Head Start or public prekindergarten program, or other regular early childhood education setting.

Children are deemed eligible for early childhood special-education services through a multidisciplinary evaluation. A team of qualified professionals and the parent or guardian of the child make the determination of eligibility based on the child's educational needs. Special education and related services are then outlined in the child's Individualized Education Program (IEP).

Both Parts C and B, Section 619, require multidisciplinary teams to evaluate and develop service plans for eligible children, but there are different eligibility criteria, evaluation procedures, types of services, service settings and recipients, and systems of payment. It is important to know about the distinctions between Parts C and B, Section 619, eligibility and services, including how they are defined and carried out in your state. Early childhood educators play an important role in supporting the child as she works toward the goals outlined in the IFSP or IEP. This happens through collaboration with families, early intervention, and early childhood special education partners.

AMERICANS WITH DISABILITIES ACT (ADA)

The ADA is a civil-rights law that addresses equal opportunity and reasonable accommodations for people of all ages with disabilities. Enacted in 1990 and amended in 2008, it is the law that prohibits discrimination against people with disabilities in schools, employment, transportation services, and other public services. Head Start, public prekindergarten, child care, and other early childhood programs must comply with ADA; however, religious organizations are exempt and do not have to comply. Under ADA, programs must implement policies, practices, and procedures so that everyone, including children with disabilities, can fully participate in the programs. ADA also includes requirements intended to ensure that new public facilities are accessible for everyone and that owners of older facilities remove barriers when this can be done without undue expense.

Where can I learn more about ADA? A good place to start is the website developed and maintained by the US Department of Justice: https://www.ada.gov/index.html

In addition, programs cannot have eligibility criteria that explicitly exclude children with disabilities. For example, a child-care program cannot require that all children be toilet trained, because this may result in discrimination against children with disabilities. Programs cannot exclude children unless they pose a "direct threat" to the health or safety of others or unless their participation would require "fundamental alteration" of the program. Finally, programs cannot charge higher fees for children with disabilities or refuse a child admission because of concern about increases to insurance costs.

SECTION 504 OF THE REHABILITATION ACT OF 1973 ("SECTION 504")

Section 504 is also civil rights legislation and applies to any entity that receives federal funds through a grant, loan, or contract. In early childhood programs, this might include funding for Head Start, child-care subsidy, public prekindergarten services, and/or the federal food and nutrition program. Generally speaking, Section 504 indicates that individuals with disabilities cannot be discriminated against or excluded from participation in any program or activity receiving federal funds. In addition, accommodations may be required to ensure that individuals are not excluded. The federal statute for Section 504 is brief and very powerful:

"No otherwise qualified individual with a disability in the United States . . . shall, solely by reason of her or his disability, be excluded from the participation in, be denied the benefits of, or be subjected to discrimination under any program or activity receiving Federal financial assistance" (Pub. L. 93-112, 1973).

What does it mean to have a disability under Section 504? The criteria are much broader than the criteria for IDEA and ADA. There are three possible ways to be considered eligible under Section 504:

- An individual can have either a physical or mental impairment that substantially limits one or more major life activities;
- or has a record of such an impairment;
- or is being regarded as having such an impairment.

There is no religious exemption under Section 504 as there is within ADA. If an early childhood program is run by a religious entity and the program receives federal funds, the provisions of Section 504 still apply.

Federal programs and funding streams outside of IDEA have also reinforced the importance of inclusion through policy and practice. For example, the Head Start Act (2007) requires that at least 10 percent of children enrolled in the program must be children with disabilities. Many child-care programs receive funding through the federal Child Care and Development Block Grant (CCDBG), and this program requires that states prioritize services for children with disabilities.

Where can I learn more about Section 504? A good place to start is the website developed and maintained by the Federal Department of Education: **https://www2.ed.gov/about/offices/list/ocr/504faq.html**

We can clearly see that our federal government agencies, federally funded programs, membership organizations, and federal legislation support the inclusion of children with disabilities in early childhood programs. Why is this so important?

RESEARCH ABOUT THE BENEFITS OF INCLUSION

BENEFITS FOR CHILDREN WITH DISABILITIES

We know from a large body of research that inclusion is beneficial for every child (Rausch et al., 2019; Lawrence et al., 2016; Weiland, 2016; Justice et al., 2014; Barton and Smith, 2015; Strain and Bovey, 2011). Children with disabilities who are included in high-quality classrooms with peers have been found to make positive gains across all areas of development (Holahan and Costenbader, 2000; Odom et al., 2000; Rafferty et al., 2005). It is critical for children with disabilities to be exposed to a variety of rich experiences where they can learn in the context of play and everyday interactions alongside their peers.

Inclusive early childhood environments have been found to promote peer relationships between children with and without disabilities, and typically developing peers serve as role models for language and social interactions (Weiland, 2016). Researchers have found that children with disabilities who interact with peers with higher-level social skills often imitate these behaviors and skills in the future (Banda, Hart, and Liu-Gitz, 2010; Holahan and Costenbader, 2000). The research on the development of social and emotional skills for children with disabilities in inclusive settings is strong, and the benefits have been found to continue to the elementary school years and even beyond (Strain, 2014).

Studies, including one from researchers Annette Holahan and Virginia Costenbader (2000), find that young children with disabilities in high-quality inclusive early childhood programs make larger gains in their cognitive, communication, and social-emotional development compared to their peers in segregated settings. Children can learn effectively in inclusive settings when they are given appropriate modifications and adaptations to the curriculum and, in some cases, to the way the classroom is arranged. Remember access, participation, and supports.

"Almost thirty years of research and experience has demonstrated that the education of children with disabilities can be made more effective by having high expectations for such children and ensuring their access to the general education curriculum in the regular classroom, to the maximum extent possible"
(IDEA, 1973, 2004)

Research has also shown that inclusion benefits children with all types of disability. Some of the most impressive outcomes have come from studies by Yvonne Rafferty and colleagues (2003) and others about inclusion of children with very significant developmental needs. Children with significant needs make progress in language and literacy goals (Green, Terry, and Gallagher, 2014) as well as social and emotional development (Strain and Bovey, 2011). Keep in mind, for inclusion to be successful, it will look different for different groups of children. Some children will need more accommodations than others. For example, a child with limited mobility might need accommodations to the classroom environment, the outdoor play area, or even to the building itself. Some children who use technology-based tools to communicate will need staff who are trained and feel competent to use the tools. Inclusion is not a one-size-fits-all kind of approach.

BENEFITS FOR CHILDREN WITHOUT DISABILITIES

Studies by researchers Virginia Buysse and colleagues (1999, 2002), Alice Cross and colleagues (2004), Samuel Odom and colleagues (2001, 2004, 2006), Phillip Strain and colleagues (2011, 2015), and others show that inclusion benefits children without disabilities as well. When children learn and grow in a community where, regardless of ability, they receive supports that allow them to thrive and reach their highest potentials, they and the community benefit (Strain and Bovey, 2011). Children without disabilities who are served in an inclusive environment show greater cognitive, language, and social skills compared with a classroom of only children who are typically developing. Buysse and colleagues (1999) and Soukakou (2012) found that inclusive classrooms tend to be of higher quality, so children without disabilities benefit from that

higher level of quality, whether it is access to advanced technology, skilled educators, or other quality indicators. Researchers Laura Justice and colleagues (2014) found that children without disabilities learn from their peers with disabilities. Children learn about empathy and adaptability from every unique individual they encounter (Diamond and Huang, 2005). Through experiences of playing together, children with a diverse range of abilities develop a sense of equality and togetherness that is impossible to achieve in segregated settings. Inclusion allows children to learn about differences, while highlighting similarities at the same time. Inclusive play helps children develop an awareness, respect, and understanding of diverse abilities (Allen, 2018). In any case, young children seldom have the concerns that adults have about differences.

Buysse, Goldman, and Skinner (2002) found that children without disabilities served in inclusive settings have advanced social skills. Through experiences with children who are different than they are, the children develop more accepting attitudes and are less likely to hold on to negative stereotypes. In addition, children tend to develop a sense of pride from the experience of supporting and learning alongside their friends who may look, think, or act differently than they do.

BENEFITS FOR EARLY CHILDHOOD PROFESSIONALS

Inclusion has the potential to benefit educators and other early childhood practitioners as well as children. Jane Leatherman (2007) found that educators believe that the inclusive classroom is a great place for young children as long as there is adequate professional development and support for the educators. Mulvihill, Shearer, and Van Horn (2002) found that once educators received professional development related to serving children with disabilities, they were better able to assess children's needs and identify barriers. Educators in inclusive settings have access to early intervention practitioners, special education specialists, therapists, and other colleagues who bring fresh perspectives and innovative teaching techniques that work well for *all* children, not just the child with a disability whom the practices were designed to support. These educators also tend to hold higher expectations for children with disabilities and are more likely to design activities based on children's interests or preferences. Researchers Allen and Schwartz (2001) describe inclusion as "belonging to a community—a group of friends, a school community, or a neighborhood." Inclusion benefits everyone!

COST BENEFITS

Studies have also examined the cost of inclusion compared to educating children with disabilities in separate, "self-contained" classrooms and have found that inclusive classrooms are actually more cost effective (Strain and Bovey, 2011). For example, Samuel Odom and colleagues (2001) found that it typically is not more expensive to serve children with disabilities in regular early childhood settings. In fact, they found cost benefits across multiple settings, including public schools, community-based child care, and Head Start programs. Inclusive preschool classrooms were found to be less expensive than segregated classrooms operated by the school district. Successful programs were able to align or braid together the funding streams to share costs.

BREAKDOWNS IN IMPLEMENTATION

Educating children with and without disabilities together in the same classroom and program is the widely promoted practice found in early childhood education (ECE) and early childhood special education (ECSE) higher education programs across the country. However, students who graduate with degrees in ECE and ECSE programs are often surprised to find that many child-care programs and even school-based preschool programs do not practice inclusion. Data from the OSEP report to Congress (US Department of Education, 2020) show that fewer than half of young children ages three to five receive special education preschool services in regular early childhood programs. OSEP defines a "regular early childhood program" as one that includes a majority (at least 50 percent) of children who do not have an IEP (OSEP, 2020). This category includes programs such as Head Start, public prekindergarten, private preschool programs, and child care. In spite of the benefits of inclusion, OSEP data show that three-year-olds are the least likely group of young children to receive services in inclusive settings; instead, they are served in segregated settings (US Department of Education, 2020).

We know that inclusion is the right thing to do for children and families, yet the choice is made again and again to segregate children with disabilities, to educate them in "self contained" classrooms occupied only with other children who have a disability. Any child with a disability could spend her day and receive special-education services in a regular child-care program, Head Start program, or state prekindergarten program. Still, every day more than half of preschoolers with disabilities receive their services in segregated settings.

Head Start led the way for inclusion early on. It was the first federally funded early childhood program to feature *mainstreaming*, a term used prior to the adoption of the word *inclusion*, as a key program component. Inclusion of children with disabilities is part of the culture of Head Start, and successful educators within the program support the practice. Head Start is a regular early childhood program placement that local school districts can make available to families of preschoolers with IEPs. Yet the most common diagnosis of children with disabilities in Head Start is speech and language impairment, while children with significant impairments are frequently directed to self-contained classrooms in the school system. Many private child-care programs are reluctant to enroll children with disabilities, and when they do enroll them there is a chance of suspension or expulsion. In child-care centers, expulsion rates of children under the age of five are thirteen times higher than expulsion rates in K–12 classrooms. As noted in a 2006 study, 39 percent of child-care providers reported at least one expulsion in the past year (Gilliam and Shahar, 2006).

In the 2020 annual report to Congress (US Department of Education, 2020), OSEP stated that of the 409,315 infants and toddlers served under Part C, 89.7 percent received their early intervention services primarily in the home setting. Of the 815,010 children ages three through five years who received Part B, Section 619, services, only 40 percent attended a regular early childhood program for at least 10 hours a week and received special education services in that setting. This means that the majority of preschoolers did not have access to IDEA services in a regular early childhood program alongside their peers. States are required to report these data each year, and the trend for most states is that the number of children served in inclusive settings rather than segregated settings remains unchanged. Data from the OSEP show that the number of children with disabilities ages three through five who received special education services in inclusive settings has inched up by about 5 percent since the 1980s. This is clear evidence that necessary changes are slow and difficult to achieve.

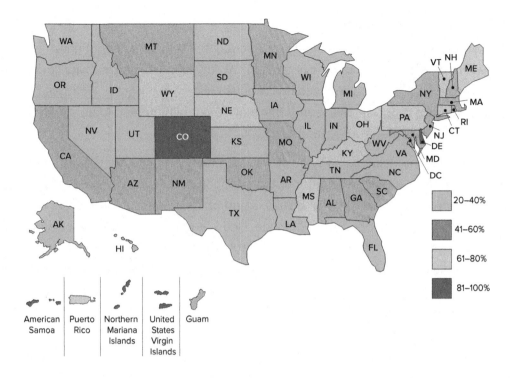

Source: https://www2.ed.gov/fund/data/report/idea/partbspap/allyears.html

This map shows where each state stands, based on the number of children ages three to five with disabilities who are placed in and receive special education services in an inclusive regular education setting. The states with the light-blue shading are the states where only 20 to 40 percent of young children receive services in an inclusive setting—and as you can see this is almost half of the country!

There have been many initiatives to foster inclusion in early childhood education. There are laws and regulations. There are policy statements and white papers. There are research studies galore.

Why is this occurring? What are the barriers to inclusion and why do they exist?

BARRIERS TO INCLUSION

Researchers have worked hard to understand the barriers to inclusion and have found a variety of factors that contribute to the problem (Rausch et al., 2019; Barton and Smith, 2015). The practice of using self-contained special education classrooms to educate young children is deeply ingrained in the minds of many school administrators. They claim that a "special" classroom will foster a sense of community, provide a distraction-free environment, or offer opportunities for specialized instruction. However, a 2011 study by Julie Causton-Theoharis and colleagues found that there is nothing "special" about special education classrooms that could not be provided in regular education settings. In addition, the researchers found that those features were not even present in the six self-contained settings that they observed and studied.

Many of the barriers boil down to issues of perception. For example, school administrators describe a concern over a lack of resources to fund inclusive settings, when research has shown that inclusion is typically less expensive than traditional approaches (Odom, Buysse, and Soukakou, 2011). Ultimately, the concern over resources is a matter of logistics rather than funding. Some states have explored alternative funding and staffing structures. For example, the *Virginia Guidelines for Early Childhood Inclusion* (Virginia Department of Education, 2018), identifies four models of inclusion: the individual teacher model, reverse inclusion, the coteaching model of collaboration, and the itinerant model of collaboration.

- **Individual Teacher Model** is set up so that one teacher with expertise in both ECSE and early childhood works with a group of children with and without IEPs. The single teacher is skilled in meeting the needs of both groups of children.

- **Reverse Inclusion** is a strategy of using an ECSE classroom (with ECSE-trained educators) and recruiting children without disabilities to attend so that children can learn together in an inclusive environment. This model requires that at least half of the children who attend are children without disabilities.

- **Coteaching Model of Collaboration** combines the expertise of an early childhood educator and an ECSE educator who share responsibilities to meet the need of all children in the classroom. The ECSE teacher may be present for all or some of the school day. In this model, both teachers equally share planning and implementing expectations in the program and helping children to attain their IEP goals.

- **Itinerant Model of Collaboration** uses an *itinerant,* or visiting, ECSE educator to provide expertise and supports for regular early childhood programs instead of using that funding to staff a self-contained classroom in a public school. To help a child or group of children make progress toward IEP goals, itinerant teachers provide direct services as well as consultation and professional development for families, teachers, directors, and support staff. This strategy is an effective way to build the capacity of early childhood educators to serve children with disabilities, and they also learn strategies that are effective for children without disabilities too. Everyone benefits!

Each of these four models can help to address barriers, but they are dependent on an educated early childhood workforce. The need for strong systems of professional development exists across all models of inclusion.

Educator professional development with a focus on supporting children with disabilities has also been cited as a barrier to inclusion (Weglarz-Ward, Santos, and Timmer, 2019). We know that educators benefit when they have the professional-development experiences necessary to feel competent and confident in their role. Professional development is needed to address an educator's lack of experience, build understanding, and provide strategies that will lead to quality inclusive environments (Barton and Smith, 2015; Yu, 2019). However, the need for professional development is often a cover for an underlying negative attitude toward inclusion (Knoche et al., 2006; Mulvihill, Shearer, and Van Horn, 2002).

In 2015, researchers Erin Barton and Barbara Smith set out to better understand the barriers to inclusion. They conducted a national survey of state and local education administrators to identify the challenges to preschool inclusion. They learned that the most frequently reported barriers to inclusion were attitudes and beliefs. The people who responded to the survey reported a number of unsubstantiated beliefs about inclusion, such as the fear that it would cause some children to "lose out," that staff weren't prepared enough, that children with disabilities needed to be "ready" for inclusion, that parents didn't want it, that it would be harmful to typically developing children in some way, that blending funding to support inclusion was illegal, and even that children with disabilities just didn't belong in general education programs. All untrue!

Ableism—prejudice against people who have disabilities—and other barriers to inclusion, such as funding constraints, lack of staff professional development, or policy issues, manifest in a variety of ways.

One sentiment that I hear from some early childhood educators is that children with disabilities have extensive needs that cannot be accommodated without specialized care. Researchers have found this as well, showing the educators' comfort level decreases as the severity of the child's disability increases (Buysse et al., 1996; Stoiber, Gettinger, and Goetz, 1998). Now, it is true that a very small percentage of children do have needs that may require intensive supports provided in a one-on-one sort of way. Take a look at this visual from OSEP.

This represents the number of students with disabilities ages three through five, organized by disability category, who were served under IDEA, Part B, in the United States and its territories during fiscal year 2018–2019. You can see that the vast majority of children served either have a speech and/or language delay, developmental delay, or autism. A very small percentage of children have more significant impairments. For such a small percentage of children, our education system can afford to

Deaf-blindness	181
Traumatic brain injury	1,158
Visual impairment	2,697
Emotional disturbance	2,882
Orthopedic impairment	5,111
Multiple disabilities	7,702
Hearing impairment	8,865
Specific learning disability	8,909
Intellectual disability	13,369
Other health impairment	26,104
Autism	92,990
Developmental delay	307,335
Speech or language impairment	337,707

Source: https://sites.ed.gov/idea/osep-fast-facts-children-3-5-20]

provide the supports they need in a regular early childhood setting, even if it does mean that they may need to receive one-on-one support for a portion of the day.

This misunderstanding results from a lack of information. Research from Avramidis, Bayliss, and Burden (2000, 2002) found that teachers' beliefs are influenced by their own personal experiences and their opportunities to spend time with other people with disabilities. In addition, teachers tend to have more favorable views of inclusion for children with lower levels of need, such as those with

speech delays, and negative views of inclusion for children with a perceived higher level of need. These perspectives are difficult to address, in part because, as this image shows, the knowledge and skills that we hold are measurable and can been "seen," like the part of the iceberg above the waterline. But attitudes and beliefs are the hidden part of the iceberg.

Our education system works to influence our knowledge and skills, but the way that we truly feel about inclusion is the primary reason that preschool children with disabilities are most likely to be served in segregated classrooms. The negative feelings early childhood professionals may have about inclusion are not rational, but all the research and public policy in the world is unlikely to affect that perspective. What will affect attitudes and beliefs?

We base the way that we feel about the world through direct experience and through stories. Human beings are social creatures. We make sense of the world through our interactions with each other and through the stories we tell each other. Storytelling and our relationships with each other provide an organizing framework for our brains that are eager to make meaning out of the information we receive.

FAMILY STORIES

The most important consideration related to inclusion is that families want and need inclusive education and care environments for their children. Cathryn Booth-LaForce and Jean Kelly (2004) found

"Programs, not children, have to be 'ready for inclusion.' In our research, we found that most successful inclusive programs view inclusion as that starting point for all children" (Schwartz, Odom, and Sandall, 1999).

that many families struggle to find quality child care that they can afford, and the lack of access is particularly difficult for families with a child who may need additional supports, services, or specialized care. Parents of children with disabilities face barriers in finding care, such as a lack of available slots, scheduling challenges, and concerns about quality (Glenn-Applegate et al., 2011). The consequences for families of not finding care may include job disruptions, greater financial strain, health challenges, and increased stress (US Census Bureau, 2019).

> *"When a family has a child with disabilities or a loved one is suddenly disabled . . . their only option is to include them. During meals, daily routines, visits with relatives, vacations, doctor's appointments, and the like. Each family decides how best to support that person . . . in whatever context should arise. Shouldn't this be the same with our schools?"*
>
> **—TIM VILLEGAS, DIRECTOR OF COMMUNICATIONS, MARYLAND COALITION FOR INCLUSIVE EDUCATION**

Families of children with disabilities are often open to sharing stories about their experiences. In 2005, Yvonne Rafferty and Kenneth Griffin surveyed teachers and parents from an inclusive early childhood program. They surveyed parents of children with disabilities and parents of children without disabilities. They found that all the parents and all the teachers had positive views about inclusion and believed that it benefits children with and without disabilities. We can imagine that the family of a child with a disability may worry that their child will not get sufficient attention or will not be treated well by others. The family of a child who is typically developing may worry, too, that their child will not get sufficient attention. They may think that the child with a disability will take all the attention. But when you think about it, these are common concerns that most parents have when they send their young children out into the world. Will my child get the attention he needs? Will he be loved? Will he be cared for?

I can relate to all of these family perspectives. As the parent of a child who had an IEP from kindergarten through twelfth grade—I can relate. As a former preschool educator who supported families and children with diverse abilities—I can relate. But perhaps the most unique perspective that I bring to this issue is described in the preface: I was a child with a disability.

Throughout my childhood, I was taken out of school for months at a time for surgeries. This photo was taken following one of those surgeries when I was about four years old. I remember feeling so vulnerable in that cast.

During the COVID-19 pandemic, we learned a lot about providing supports from a distance. Educators and service providers tried to adapt practices to a "new normal." Families had to adapt as well. We shifted strategies and tried to be flexible. Families and children worked diligently to modify schedules so that learning could happen at home. Many families and educators experienced isolation and exclusion during the pandemic. Family challenges ranged from feelings of inadequacy about homeschooling expectations to experiencing depression and loss to struggling with financial obligations. The pandemic led to extended school closures throughout the United States, requiring teachers, families, and children to teach and learn in entirely new ways. Continuity of learning and growth is critical for all children, particularly those with disabilities, and their families. What did the pandemic teach you? I learned so much about myself through that experience. I learned through my own feelings of isolation that I still have a need for inclusion, a need for friends and community.

RESOURCE SPOTLIGHT

The Council for Exceptional Children's Division of Early Childhood (DEC) developed a set of recommended practices to bridge the gap between research and practice, offering guidance to parents and professionals who work with young children who have or are at risk for developmental delays or disabilities.

There is even a version of the recommended practices that includes examples to help bring the concepts to life. The practices are organized around eight domains: leadership, assessment, environment, family, instruction, interaction, teaming and collaboration, and transition. You can access the practices at no cost on the DEC website. (See appendix B for a list of resources for this chapter.)

At the time, my friends with young children shared their concerns about the demands of homeschooling, and it reminded me of the times when I was out of school as I recovered from surgery. When I was in preschool, I had been out of school for a couple of months, which seemed like a really long time to me as a child. My teacher reached out and asked whether my mother might be able to bring me to school to celebrate Valentine's Day with the class. My mom thought it was a great idea because she knew how much I missed my friends and how much I loved Valentine's Day. I loved the candy hearts and cupcakes with pink frosting. I loved the little foldable cards sealed with a sticker or lollipop. I loved the mailboxes that we used to make. We would trade valentines with everyone in the class, and everyone decorated a mailbox for their cards. Do you remember that? I loved it all.

I remember feeling nervous about going into the classroom after what felt like such a long time. I worried about what would happen when my friends saw me in my body cast. Would they stare at me? Would they even remember me? But my mother felt that it was important for me to reconnect with my friends at school. She and my teacher assured me that it would be fine. And you know what? It was fine. It was better than fine, because not only did I have my own mailbox, but everyone had made me a valentine. While this is not really a story of the common definition of inclusion, it is a story about a time when I felt included. It is a story about membership. It is a story about belonging. It is a story about supporting a child to build friendships and connect with her peers.

Memories of times when we have felt included, either as a child or as an adult, can guide us as educators. Early childhood inclusion can be the experience that launches a child into a lifetime of feeling welcomed and included in all community settings. Throughout this book, we'll explore how to make that happen for the young children in your program. Together we can foster inclusion for all of the children, all of the families, and all of the baby birds as they learn to fly.

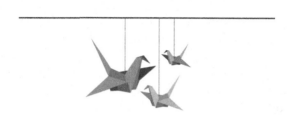

QUESTIONS FOR REFLECTION

- What does inclusion mean to you? How has your understanding of and perspective on inclusion changed over time?
- Do you remember a time when you were able to give a child the sense of belonging and membership? How can you have more moments like that one?
- What did you learn from the research on inclusion in this chapter that surprised you?
- What questions do you have about federal legislation on inclusion?

CHAPTER 2

Understanding Early Intervention and Special Education

*If we don't stand up for children,
then we don't stand for much.*

**—MARIAN WRIGHT EDELMAN,
FOUNDER AND PRESIDENT EMERITA
OF THE CHILDREN'S DEFENSE FUND**

My son, Ricky, was adopted from Ukraine. Given that I inherited my disability through genes passed down to me by my father, I was concerned about passing those genes to my own child. My husband, Rick, and I went through genetic counseling and learned that a biological child of ours would have a fifty/fifty chance of inheriting my disability. Even though in some ways it would have been amazing to have a child with some of our physical features, I remembered how guilty my father had felt about passing along the condition, even though he had not had access to the science the way we did. Would I choose to give birth to a child knowing that he or she may well need multiple surgeries? Nope, not for me. Rick agreed, and we made the decision to adopt—the very best decision of my life!

At that time, Rick and I had been married for nine years without children. When Rick was ready to move forward with the adoption, I was really, really ready, so we decided to adopt internationally. Believe it or not, at the time this was the quickest route. I researched it and found that adopting a baby from Ukraine was a quick process. In January 2000, we made the decision to adopt, and by May 2000, I was the mother of Ricky Vadim Kozlowski. Life is full of irony, however. Even though we were able to raise a child without an orthopedic impairment, we did not have a path free from obstacles. (Is any parenting path free from obstacles?) But we were still lucky, right from the beginning and still to this day. As soon as we met him, it was clear that Ricky was one in a million. What a smart, kind, and resilient little boy! He was seventeen months old when we adopted him from an orphanage in Simferopol, Ukraine.

Simferopol is in the Crimean Peninsula, which you may know about from the news as a result of the Russian occupation of the area. It is a beautiful place, right by the Black Sea and full of history, castles, and unfortunately, a great deal of alcoholism and poverty. We don't know much about Ricky's history before he joined our family, including his medical history. We just had to be open to the wonder and adventure that this little toddler brought to our lives.

What a wild adventure it was! While still in Simferopol, Ricky took his first wobbly steps from my husband's arms to mine. He was tentative and shy with us at first. It seemed that most of the children in the orphanage spent a lot of time in their cribs. It was hard to know for sure what his life was

really like because we were just popping in and out for visits while we completed the necessary paperwork. On one visit though, we came in to see one of the caregivers feeding Ricky through the bars of his crib. Did anyone ever hold him or comfort him when he was sad? I worried about this early deprivation. I remember being worried that he was only learning to walk at seventeen months, when most children take their first steps at around their first birthday. But his shyness did not last long. By the time we were back at the hotel in Kiev, he was running down the hallways, squealing with delight. We were worried that he would wake up the other guests in the hotel!

Back home in the United States, Ricky continued to grow and develop at a surprising pace. He learned words quickly and was, as they say about most toddlers, into everything. His curiosity was unrivaled! Every cupboard must be explored! He frantically grabbed any item within his reach and turned it over and over in his hands, smelled it, tasted it, eager to understand all these new discoveries in a suddenly wide-open world.

This curiosity was nonstop, and it was almost as though he couldn't stay in one place for long because there was too much to explore somewhere else. Ricky was constant motion, running from toy to toy. I couldn't engage him in pretend play activities or really anything that didn't involve lots of movement. He didn't want to be held for long and would squirm away from us so that he could get down and explore. He wanted to figure out how everything worked and loved to take things apart. Mealtimes were over in an instant because sitting in his high chair during a calm activity like eating dinner was too much for him to bear. When we would go out to eat, we immediately had to clear away the salt and pepper shakers and other condiments on the table, because Ricky would grab them and put them in his mouth.

I knew toddlers were curious, but this seemed excessive! It also verged on dangerous. He seemed to have very little fear and gravitated toward things that might hurt him. Fortunately, many of my friends are early childhood educators themselves, and they were happy to serve as sounding boards for me. They suggested that I reach out to the early intervention program and set up an evaluation. This led to an IFSP and home visits that felt like a lifeline. What a relief to have someone validate my concerns and offer suggestions! It's worth mentioning that, despite my education and relative confidence as a parent, I still needed help. Reaching out in this way can be intimidating to families and educators alike. For our family, the participation in early intervention set us up for success. We began a long road through systems of early intervention and early childhood special education that ultimately led to a successful high school graduation. We were fortunate to be able to access services for Ricky at the earliest age, when they could be the most effective. It all started with a referral. Not from a doctor or a professional but just a phone call from a mother who reached out for help. That was my first step.

In the following pages we'll explore the steps in the process of obtaining early intervention and early childhood special education services, the key components of each system, outcomes for children and families, and the transition process from program to program.

EARLY INTERVENTION AND EARLY CHILDHOOD SPECIAL EDUCATION STEP BY STEP

Early intervention (EI) and early childhood special education (ECSE) are quite similar in the steps from a referral to the development of the IFSP or IEP. Let's start with an overview of the steps and then dig in deeper to the specifics of Part C and Part B, Section 619.

STEP 1. THE REFERRAL

Children are referred to EI or ECSE in one of two ways: the system known as Child Find or by referral of a parent or teacher, doctor, or other professional. Each state is required by IDEA to identify, locate, and evaluate all children who may benefit from EI or ECSE services. When a child is identified as possibly having a disability and as needing special education, parents may be asked for permission to evaluate their child. Parents can also call the Child Find office and ask that their child be evaluated.

What Is Child Find?

Child Find refers to the policies and procedures in each state that ensure that all children with disabilities, from birth through age twenty-one, who live in the state and need EI or ECSE are identified, located, and evaluated. Child Find procedures may include:

- Public announcements through newspaper, television, radio, social media

- Meetings with private and home school representatives/organizations

- Use of websites

- Community service fairs

- Parent mentors and collaboration with other public agencies

STEP 2. EVALUATION

Evaluation is the step in the process when parents and EI or ECSE staff seek to learn whether the child has a disability that requires the provision of services. For EI, the question is whether or not the child would benefit from services to help with growth and development. For ECSE, the focus is primarily about the child's educational needs. Parental consent is needed before a child may be evaluated. Under the federal IDEA regulations, the evaluation must be completed within a specified timeframe after the parent gives consent: forty-five days for EI (Part C) and sixty days for ECSE (Part B, Section 619). However, if a state's IDEA regulations give a different timeline for completion of the evaluation, the state's timeline is applied. The evaluation must assess the child in all areas related to the child's suspected disability or delay, and the results are used to determine whether or not the child is eligible to receive services.

STEP 3. ELIGIBILITY DETERMINATION

A group of qualified professionals and the parents look at the child's evaluation results. Together, they decide if the child has a developmental delay or disability as defined by federal and state laws and regulations, *and* they determine the supports necessary to meet the needs of the child. Keep in mind that, while IDEA does provide some guidance around eligibility determination, there are many areas where individual state governments make those decisions, so it's important to know the guidelines in your own state. If the parents do not agree with the eligibility decision, they may challenge it.

For Part C, children are deemed eligible based strictly on whether they have a developmental delay or a diagnosed physical or mental condition with a high probability of its resulting in developmental delay. For Part B, Section 619, it is a little different. In addition to being determined eligible within a certain category, the team must also determine whether the child needs special education. This is an important part of the team's decision because, for example, a child might meet the criteria by having a visual impairment, but due to corrective lenses does not require special education.

STEP 4. IFSP/IEP MEETING

Once the child is found eligible, the EI or ECSE staff set up a meeting to determine the services that the child will receive. The IFSP meeting is arranged by EI staff; IEP meetings are usually arranged by professionals at the local education agency (LEA), which is usually the local elementary school. Parents are notified of the meeting, and it is scheduled at a time and place that is convenient for all participants. During the meeting, the team will identify annual IFSP/IEP outcomes/goals and consider the services needed to support those goals. The team will also discuss where the services will be provided. If the parents consent to let the child receive the services as described in the IFSP/IEP, the child can begin to receive services as soon as possible. If the parents do not agree with decisions outlined in the IFSP/IEP, they can ask for mediation or even file a complaint and request a hearing. (This process is described in more detail in chapter 3.)

STEP 5. PROVIDING SERVICES

Following the IFSP/IEP meeting, services can be provided as long as the parents give consent to the services and the plan is carried out as written. The child's parents and educators should receive a copy of the IFSP/IEP. All of the child's educators, caregivers, and other service providers should have access to the IFSP/IEP and know their responsibilities for carrying out the plan.

The plan includes the accommodations, modifications, and supports that must be provided to the child. For EI (Part C), states are required to provide services in a timely manner. How soon is *timely*? This is determined by the state, and clarification is provided on the state's early intervention website and in parent information materials. For ECSE (Part B, Section 619), local education agencies have up to ten school days to begin service delivery once the IEP is developed and signed.

STEP 6. PROGRESS MONITORING

The child's progress toward the annual goals is measured as stated in the IFSP/IEP. The child's parents are regularly informed of their child's progress and whether that progress is enough for the child to achieve the goals outlined by the end of the year. These progress reports must be given to parents at various points throughout the year.

STEP 7. IFSP/IEP REVIEW

For the IFSP, it must be reviewed by the team at least annually, with a six-month periodic review to ensure that the child is making progress toward IFSP outcomes. For the IEP, it is reviewed by the IEP team at least once a year as well, or more often if the parents or school ask for a review. If necessary, the IFSP/IEP is revised. Parents, as team members, must be invited to participate in these meetings. Parents can make suggestions for changes, can agree or disagree with the IFSP/IEP, and can agree or disagree with the placement.

If the parents do not agree with the IFSP/IEP services and/or placement, they may discuss their concerns with other members of the team and try to work out an agreement. Several options are available, including additional testing, an independent evaluation, asking for mediation, or a due-process hearing. They may also file a complaint with the state education agency.

STEP 8. CHILD REEVALUATION

At least every three years, the child must be reevaluated. The purpose of this evaluation is to find out if the child is still eligible for IDEA services and to learn about any changes to the child's service and/or educational needs. Keep in mind that the child could be evaluated sooner than three years, if the child's parent or education staff ask for a new evaluation.

STEP 9. FOR THREE-YEAR-OLD CHILDREN: TRANSITION FROM EI TO ECSE

In almost every state, at age three children with IFSPs must be determined eligible for continuing special education and related services. If eligible, an IEP must be developed in place of the IFSP before the child's third birthday for services to continue.

UNDERSTANDING PART C AND PART B, SECTION 619 OF IDEA

In chapter 1, we had a 30,000-foot view of Parts C and Part B, Section 619 of IDEA. We learned that Part C is the portion of the law that pertains to services for infants and toddlers and that Part B, Section 619 is the portion of the law that pertains to services for children ages three through five. We also learned that both Parts C and B, Section 619 require multidisciplinary teams to evaluate and develop service plans for eligible children, but that a variety of eligibility criteria, timelines, and types and locations of services are available. Let's explore the key components of both Part C and Part B, Section 619.

PART C—EARLY INTERVENTION SERVICES FOR INFANTS AND TODDLERS

The section of the IDEA statute that relates to services for infants and toddlers with disabilities is under Part C. In the 2020 annual report to Congress (US Department of Education, 2020), OSEP reported that about 3.5 percent of children nationwide, ages birth through two years, received early intervention services. The law expects the services to be provided in a coordinated way across the state and outlines specific requirements that states must meet in order to receive funding (OSEP, n.d.a.). Let's take a look at these requirements.

Rigorous Definition of *Developmental Delay*

Young children and their families are eligible for Part C services if the child is under the age of three and experiences developmental delays in one or more areas of development or has a diagnosed physical or mental condition with a high probability of resulting in developmental delay. For Part C, each state must establish the criteria for eligibility. Thus, the law requires states to define what is meant by the term *developmental delay*. States also have the option of serving infants and toddlers who are *at risk* of developmental delay. The important point to remember here is that once states determine the definitions of *developmental delay* and *at risk*, they may serve only children who meet those definitions. The at-risk category includes children with a diagnosed condition that has a high probability of leading to developmental delay, as well as children who are deemed at risk because of other factors, such as low birth weight, child abuse or neglect, nutritional deficiencies, or prenatal drug exposure (20 USC 1400, 2004). Once children who meet those definitions are identified, they must also be served upon parental consent.

State governments make the policy decisions related to eligibility determination for Part C

Basic differences come from different underlying goals:

Goal of Part C: To support families in supporting their children

Goal of Part B, Section 619: To support a child's access to the general curriculum

Where Do I Find Out about Part C Eligibility Guidelines in My State?

The Part C eligibility criteria for each state are listed on the ECTA Center's Part C eligibility page. To connect families with resources in your state, it is important that you know the specifics related to eligibility. A good place to find that information is through your state Parent Training and Information (PTI) Center. There are nearly 100 PTIs and Community Parent Resource Centers (CPRCs) in the United States and its territories. You can find your parent center online. (See appendix B for a list of resources for this chapter.)

services. For example, states determine the criteria within Part C Early Intervention programs about whether or not to consider infants or toddlers who are at risk for a delay or disability as eligible for services. As of 2021, only six states actually support children who are at risk for a delay or disability, meaning that many children who would likely benefit from services are not eligible for them and are missing out on important interventions that would strengthen their development. Including at-risk children in Part C eligibility and investing early in their growth would improve their developmental outcomes and prevent future learning and behavioral challenges. More federal funding for IDEA would likely increase the number of states that would include at-risk children in Part C eligibility.

Child Find System

The law requires states to maintain a central directory with access to information about services, resources, and experts, and to engage in public-awareness efforts so that other organizations know how to identify and refer children to the early intervention program. Part C emphasizes finding and serving children at the earliest possible age.

Did You Know?

The Children's Equity Project and the Bipartisan Policy Center recently released a report titled *Start with Equity: From the Early Years to the Early Grades* (Meek et al., 2020). The report includes a collection of data related to the inequities in our early intervention and early childhood special education systems. For example, racial disparities exist in access to early intervention services. Children of color who are eligible for services are less likely to receive them and more likely to face challenges while receiving them. This is due to a variety of factors, including insufficient outreach and a lack of culturally competent services. According to Feinberg et al., (2011), Black children are five times less likely to receive early intervention services than White children. Early educators can play a role in addressing these disparities by raising awareness about the availability of early intervention services and supporting families if challenges arise.

Evaluation and Assessment

States are also required to provide timely, comprehensive evaluations that show a child's current developmental level of functioning. In addition, Part C programs may also conduct a voluntary family assessment to determine the resources, priorities, and concerns for the family as a whole.

Individualized Family Service Plans

An Individualized Family Service Plan (IFSP) is the plan that Early Intervention providers develop with families to guide the delivery of services. IFSPs are based on an in-depth assessment of the child's needs and the needs and concerns of the family. The IFSP itself is the written agreement with the family and all providers that details all the services and supports that will be provided. Developing an IFSP uses an interagency approach by involving representatives of several agencies and other resources that can help the child and family.

Usually, a professional called the *service coordinator* is assigned to assist the child's family through the IFSP process. The IFSP clarifies the frequency of services, where the services will be provided, and who will be responsible for assisting the child and family. The IFSP includes child and family goals and outcomes and must be reviewed and revised every six months, or more frequently if conditions warrant or the family requests a review.

Research-Based Early Intervention Services

States must also have a policy that ensures that services are research based and available to all infants and toddlers with disabilities and their families, including those who may live on an American Indian reservation or those who may be experiencing homelessness. What are the services families may receive through early intervention? Examples include physical therapy, occupational therapy, speech therapy, audiology or hearing services, assistive technology, family counseling, medical services, nursing services, nutrition counseling, and service coordination.

Services in Natural Environments

A key principle of early intervention is that infants and toddlers learn best through everyday experiences and interactions with familiar people in familiar contexts. This principle is supported through the IDEA requirement that services be provided in natural environments. For infants and toddlers, a natural environment is any place the child and family live, learn, and play, such as the home, community, child-care center, or Early Head Start center. Children are served in natural environments in most cases, and other settings are only used when services cannot be achieved satisfactorily in a natural environment.

Staff Professional-Development System

States must have a comprehensive system of professional development to make sure that staff who provide early intervention services are qualified and appropriately trained to understand a child's unique needs and are capable of supporting the family.

RESOURCE SPOTLIGHT

The OSEP-funded Center for Parent Information and Resources ("Parent Center Hub") has a set of online modules called *Building the Legacy for Our Youngest Children with Disabilities* for parents and educators to help with understanding Part C. You can access the modules online. (See appendix B for a list of resources for this chapter.)

Procedural Safeguards

States must ensure that families are afforded certain legal rights related to confidentiality, prior notice and consent, due process, and access to services. All agencies that provide early intervention services must adhere to these legal safeguards that protect the rights of children and families, and they must ensure that families know their rights.

Supervision and Monitoring

State lead agencies must monitor programs to enforce the Part C obligations and report the results to the public. If there are issues, states must provide assistance to correct the issues.

State Complaint Procedures

States must have written procedures to resolve complaints and establish solutions if a family is inappropriately denied services.

State Interagency Coordinating Council

Each state must have a state interagency coordinating council (SICC) that provides guidance to the program and includes representatives from early childhood programs at the state and local levels, as well as families who receive EI services.

Data Collection

Each state must collect information about its program and must report the data to the secretary of education within the federal Office of Special Education Programs each year.

PART B, SECTION 619—EARLY CHILDHOOD SPECIAL EDUCATION SERVICES FOR CHILDREN AGES THREE THROUGH FIVE

As discussed earlier, IDEA's Part B, Section 619 provides special education and related services for children ages three through five if they have a disability and need these services. In the 2020 annual report to Congress (US Department of Education, 2020), OSEP reported that nearly 7 percent of preschool-age children received early childhood special education. IDEA funds also can be used to provide services to two-year-old children with disabilities who will turn three during the school year, if consistent with state policy. Just as with Part C, states receive funding to provide services under Section 619 if they meet certain requirements. In the following sections, we'll explore the key components of Part B, Section 619.

Free and Appropriate Public Education

One of the ways that Part B, Section 619 differs from Part C is that states are required to offer services for free. Section 619 services are provided as part of the state's education system, and the law states that every eligible child has the right to receive a free and appropriate public education (FAPE). Therefore, children with disabilities who have unique educational needs receive services at no cost to the family, if the child's IEP team determines that the services are necessary for the child to participate in the state education system.

Appropriate Identification

States are also required to have Child Find in place for Part B, Section 619. This refers to the policies and procedures that ensure all children with disabilities who need special education and related services are located, identified, and evaluated. In this case, Part B, Section 619 differs from Part C in that the parent or family member must make the referral, which further reinforces how important educator-parent relationships are for the benefit of the child. Professionals can partner with family members to support them with the referral process and advocacy skills.

As with Part C, qualified staff must administer the evaluations; the results are used along with other required information to determine eligibility. Note that it is *evaluations*—plural. No single measure or assessment serves as the sole criterion for determining eligibility.

RESOURCE SPOTLIGHT

The OSEP-funded Center for Parent Information and Resources ("Parent Center Hub") offers a set of online modules for Part B called Building the Legacy. The modules are for parents and educators to help them understanding Part B of IDEA. You can access the modules online. (See appendix B for a list of resources for this chapter.)

Disability Categories under IDEA, Part B, Section 619

IDEA lists thirteen disability categories under which individuals may be eligible for services:

- Autism
- Deaf-blindness
- Deafness
- Emotional disturbance
- Hearing impairment
- Intellectual disability
- Multiple disabilities
- Orthopedic impairment
- Other health impairment
- Specific learning disability
- Speech or language impairment
- Traumatic brain injury
- Visual impairment

Note: *Developmental delay* is also a category of disability in some states. Children who have a certain diagnosis, such as autism or a visual impairment, may also be placed into several different categories, depending on other factors.

Individualized Education Program

The individualized education program (IEP) is a written document that outlines the educational needs and services to support the individual child. A team of people, including the child's parents or guardian, regular and special-education teachers, a school-district representative, and others, meets to review the assessment information available about the child and design a program to address the child's educational needs that result from his or her disability. IEPs must be reviewed at least annually. An IEP for a preschool-aged child includes information about the child's needs, annual goals, how progress will be measured, special education and any related services, supplementary aids and services, and necessary training for school personnel.

A Note on IEP Terminology

What's the difference between *related services* and *supplementary aids and services*? Related services include speech therapy, physical therapy, occupational therapy, interpreting services, counseling, mobility services, social work services, and other similar services. Supplementary aids and services refer to the supports, such as accommodations, modifications, assistive technology, and so on, that help a child access and participate in learning activities in a regular early childhood program.

Least Restrictive Environment

During the IEP meeting, the team determines the services a child needs and where those services will be provided. The IDEA emphasizes educating children with disabilities in inclusive settings alongside children without disabilities, with any needed supports to ensure that the child is successful in that setting. One way to think about this is to consider special education as a service, not a place. Therefore, to the greatest extent possible, special education services should be provided in the setting or environment in which the child would be educated if he or she did not have a disability. Sounds like inclusion, right? In the law, this is referred to as the *least restrictive environment* (LRE) and is frequently a regular early childhood program.

For preschool-aged children, these regular early childhood settings may be a program such as a public or private preschool program, Head Start, child care, Title I program, state pre-K, or other early care and education program. To determine the LRE, the team must first consider the supplementary aids and services the child would need in a setting alongside children without disabilities. Only when the team determines that the education of a particular child with a disability cannot be achieved satisfactorily in a regular early childhood educational environment, even with the provision of supplementary aids and services, can the team consider placement in a more restrictive environment. Placement decisions should be made based on the child's individual needs, the LRE, and consideration of family preferences.

Parent Participation

States must meet regulations designed to ensure that parents are active participants in the process of developing their child's IEP and are involved in their child's education in an ongoing way. Parents are also essential stakeholders for states and local agencies as they develop and implement programs to serve children under IDEA.

Procedural Safeguards

States must develop procedural safeguards that will protect the rights of the child and family, such as the ability to participate in meetings about their child, to request an evaluation, and to receive prior written notice if changes are to occur. Parents must provide consent before their child is evaluated or receives services, and parents' rights are also protected if there is a disagreement between the school system and the family. These procedural safeguards are explained in further detail in chapter 3 (OSEP, n.d.b.).

Who's in Charge of EI or ECSE Services in My State?

Each state has an early intervention (Part C) coordinator and an early childhood special education (Part B, 619) coordinator. The coordinators can play an important role in services for young children with disabilities and their families by providing information and supporting the development of systems to promote inclusive early care and education. The ECTA center maintains an online list of the IDEA contacts in each state and territory, including names, titles, and contact information. To find the IDEA Part C contact in your state, visit **https://ectacenter.org/partc/partc. asp#contacts**

To find the IDEA Part B, 619 contact in your state, visit **https://ectacenter.org/sec619/ sec619.asp#contacts**

CHILD AND FAMILY OUTCOMES

Early intervention and early childhood special education programs have an ultimate goal of supporting young children and their families to have a successful future at home, in school, and in their communities. Programs strive to support families in their efforts to care for their children and in their own hopes, dreams, and goals for their children. One way that this happens is through the use of child and family outcomes. An *outcome* is the benefit that a child or family experiences as a result of the services or supports they receive. EI and ECSE programs develop child and family outcomes in partnership with the family and then track them not only as a method of measuring progress made by the child and family but also as a way to improve their programs and measure their own accountability. Given that data is collected on outcomes that measure individual and program progress, the process can also serve to measure the success of the whole IDEA system. When children and families achieve success with these outcomes, then the system is working!

Of course, there is never any guarantee of success, and we know that the accomplishments children and families achieve are based on a variety of factors, including the services they receive through EI or ECSE. Even in the best system, it is unlikely that all families or children will meet all of their goals, but the process itself can help families and programs understand what success will look like.

CHILD OUTCOMES

Child outcomes are assessed and measured through observation of children in their everyday routines and activities. While goals and outcomes specific to the individual child are included in every IFSP or IEP, there are also big-picture outcomes that have been established for all children who receive EI or ECSE services. Across the country, IDEA requires programs to measure three global early child outcomes to help us understand what children know and are able to do in areas that are important to their future success. States are then required to collect assessment data and report this information annually to the Office of Special Education Programs (OSEP).

The three child outcomes are:

- Children have positive social skills including positive social relationships.
- Children acquire and use knowledge and skills including language and early literacy.
- Children take appropriate action to meet their needs.

These child outcomes are referred to as *functional outcomes*. Functional outcomes are meaningful to the child in the context of everyday living. When we consider the progress a child makes on functional outcomes, we're really looking at how a child is able to carry out the important activities in everyday life. Each of these three outcomes is not just about one behavior that a child is able to know or do. Functional outcomes are a collection of behaviors across many aspects of development that a child needs to know or do to be successful in everyday life.

> *"Child and family outcomes are connected. A positive outcome experienced by the family serves to promote the child outcomes, and outcomes achieved by the child benefit the family."*
>
> **—ECTA CENTER WEBSITE**

EI and ECSE programs are required to measure each child's progress toward these three child outcomes upon program entry and exit, although many programs check progress toward the child outcomes more frequently. States use different approaches to measure child outcomes. Most use a process called the Child Outcomes Summary, which uses a seven-point scale to summarize how a child is doing in each of the three outcome areas. This process relies on a team approach. The team, including the child's parents, considers multiple sources of information about the child, such as results from an assessment tool, as well as observations from the child's parent, family member, or teacher, to determine the point rating.

Want to learn more about these functional child outcomes? The ECTA Center developed a helpful infographic that you can access here: https://ectacenter.org/~pdfs/eco/three-child-outcomes-breadth.pdf

FAMILY OUTCOMES

Parents play a critical role in EI programs in particular, because for infants and toddlers the child's family members are often the people who implement the interventions. The family is a child's first teacher, knows the child best, and is best equipped to make decisions on behalf of the child. Because Part C also includes a family component to the services, there is an expectation that states report on family outcomes. Family outcomes under IDEA, Part C are measured through the completion of an annual survey that helps programs and policymakers understand how successfully the early childhood system is supporting families as they meet their child's needs. States use surveys to collect family-outcomes data, but the questions and processes vary from state to state. States are required to report the percent of families participating in Part C who claim that EI services have helped their family to do the following:

- Know their rights
- Effectively communicate their children's needs
- Help their children develop and learn

Part B, Section 619 programs have fewer reporting requirements related to family outcomes. They are required, however, to report how schools promote parent involvement in their child's education. Of the parents of children receiving special education services, states must report the percentage who say that the school facilitated parent involvement as a means of improving services and results for their child. Of course, it stands to reason that when families are equal and active participants in the IEP process and understand their child's goals and the process by which they were developed, they will be more likely to report positive parent involvement.

▶ TRANSITIONS

Transition is a natural part of all of our lives. In this context, transition is the process of a child moving from one location, program, or environment to another. Children experience multiple transitions in the early years. It may be the transition from playing in the home setting to playing in a center-based child-care setting. It may be from group to group within a setting, such as moving from playing in the infant room to playing in the toddler room. Or it may be the transition from a preschool program to a kindergarten program. Most of these transitions are expected or are due to a decision that the family makes; however, the transition from EI to ECSE at age three is due to changes in the systems that serve the family.

The transition between systems can be disruptive for the family because it is dictated by the law rather than by the family's needs. Therefore, IDEA includes provisions intended to support families during the transitions from early intervention to early childhood special education and then to kindergarten. Programs must plan for transitions and work together to make sure that families experience the transitions in the smoothest way possible.

TRANSITION FROM EI TO ECSE

As indicated in the step-by-step section earlier in this chapter, in almost every state, children with IFSPs must be determined eligible for continuing special education and related services at age three. If the child has been evaluated and is determined to be eligible for early childhood special education, an IEP must be developed in place of the IFSP before the child's third birthday so that services can continue. Parents can participate in the evaluation process, and if the team determines that the child does not qualify for special education services, parents can learn about other community agencies that might be able to help.

The transition process typically happens three to six months prior to the child's third birthday. This can be anxiety producing for families, because the thought of their toddler entering preschool is a big deal. It also is a shift from the family focus of early intervention to early childhood special education's focus on the child as an individual. Part C programs work to support parent preparation, participation, and decision making in the process, so that they can learn about the different systems of EI and ECSE. The conversations begin well before the IEP meeting, offering families an opportunity to share their thoughts, questions, feelings, hopes, and concerns about early childhood special education. If the family speaks a language other than English, programs will need to determine how to translate materials into the home language and set up interpreter services to foster effective communication. Programs will develop a transition plan with the family that indicates the steps in the process and provides information about community programs that the family may be interested in visiting prior to making decisions about placement. Before the transition conference, school districts can provide information about services available, the evaluation process, parent rights, and how the IEP is structured.

During the transition conference, the Part C program can include staff from the local education agency (LEA) at the meeting to let them share information and answer questions about the IEP process and how special education services will be provided in the preschool program that the parents select.

Following the transition conference, the child will be re-evaluated to determine eligibility, and an IEP meeting will be arranged. Parents should remember that they can invite anyone they want to attend the IEP meeting. If the child qualifies for services, the parents are encouraged to participate in the goal-setting process for their child during the IEP meeting. With parental consent, the transfer of information can begin, and the LEA staff will have access to the IFSP, recent assessments, and any other relevant information.

After the IEP is developed, the receiving program may also help parents as they visit and meet the staff at the setting where services will occur. Children are also supported during the transition and may want to talk about the change and visit the new setting. Parents can read books with their child about attending preschool and can provide their child with opportunities to play with children who go to the new program.

TRANSITION FROM ECSE TO KINDERGARTEN

The transition from preschool to kindergarten is an important time in any child's life and can be especially daunting for families who have a child with a disability. How will she do in elementary school? Is she ready? Will other children accept my child? Will she be able to be successful in an environment with increased expectations? These are often family concerns, but

What Options Are Available for Children Who Do Not Qualify for IDEA Services?

Many times, children who received early intervention services as an infant or toddler may not qualify for early childhood special education under Part B, Section 619. In this case, the family should be referred to other community organizations that may be able to help. Another option is to ask the school if supports could be provided through a Section 504 plan. Section 504 requires programs to provide preschool children with disabilities equal access to the program, with reasonable accommodations and modifications. Although these accommodations are not considered "special education," they may be available and helpful as a secondary option. For example, a child may have attention issues that do not warrant an IEP, but the child might still benefit from preferential seating during circle time or the use of other supports to maintain focus in the prekindergarten classroom. Another example would be a child who has a special health-care need such as asthma. The child may not have any specific learning goal related to the health-care need, but it might still be helpful to have necessary accommodations written down in a plan. The family could ask to have these accommodations in writing in the form of a 504 plan, which would describe when and how the supports are to be implemented. The Office of Head Start has created a fact sheet about options for children who do not qualify for IDEA services. (See appendix B for a list of resources for this chapter.)

Supporting Families During Transitions

Whether it is the transition from EI to ECSE or from ECSE to kindergarten, transitions are an important time for families. Here are some tips for how you might support families as they prepare for a transition:

- Offer to share your knowledge about their child's strengths, abilities, interests, and challenges with the receiving program

- Consider the supports their child will need to be successful, and share the strategies with the receiving program that are working well at home or in the child's current early childhood program

- If English is not the language spoken at home, find out about available interpreter and translation resources

- Offer to help organize medical records, IFSP/IEPs, evaluation and assessment information, and other key information to share with the receiving program

- Make a list of questions and concerns the family may want to address during the transition conference or IFSP/IEP meeting

- Prepare their child by reading books about the transition, visiting the new program, and meeting the new education staff if possible

- Ensure ongoing communication by finding out how the receiving program will share information with the family about how their child is adjusting to the new setting

in reality, the school should be ready for the child rather than expecting the child to be ready for school.

Sometimes, this transition can be stressful because children respond to the shift in different ways. Some children may become withdrawn and shy, while others may exhibit behaviors that are challenging to adults. In addition to supports provided by the early childhood educators, community programs may be available to support children with mental-health needs related to transitions, learning how to manage change effectively, improving social skills, and strengthening peer relationships.

Just as in the transition from EI to ECSE, communication between programs is the key to success. If the child and family's first language is not English, make plans to support communication by translating materials into the home language and providing interpreter services. The team should include preschool and kindergarten staff, school administrators, family members, and others who come together to coordinate transition activities before the kindergarten year begins. The transition plan should describe the steps in the process and the differences between ECSE and kindergarten. If the family gives permission, it can be helpful for preschool staff to share key records with kindergarten staff and work collaboratively to design services and supports for the child in the new setting. Once education staff assignments are made, it will be important for the family to meet with the kindergarten teacher to learn about the curriculum and daily routine. The receiving school should provide opportunities for families to learn about kindergarten policies and visit the new classroom. Once the school year begins, families should be encouraged to be as involved as possible in their child's kindergarten classroom, and staff should provide ongoing communication about how the child is adjusting to the new setting.

All the components of EI and ECSE are dependent on strong family engagement. As early childhood educators, we play an important role in supporting families throughout the process. In chapter 3, we'll dig into the ways that families can have a voice in the process and how we can support them to be the best advocates for their child.

RESOURCE SPOTLIGHT

To learn more about the differences between IDEA Part C and IDEA Part B, see this resource on the eligibility and services delivery policies: **http://www.infanthearing.org/ earlyintervention/docs/aspect-idea- part-c-and-idea-part-b.pdf**

REFLECTION QUESTIONS

- What kind of relationship do you currently have with the EI or ECSE programs in your community? What are the strengths of the relationships? How might the relationships be improved?

- In your role as an early childhood educator, home visitor, program leader, or other service provider, how do you communicate with EI or ECSE programs about the services you offer to children and families?

- What information or skills would be helpful for you to learn from EI or ECSE programs? How might you set up a collaborative venture together?

CHAPTER 3

Working with Families

Before I got married, I had six theories about bringing up children; now, I have six children and no theories.

—JOHN WILMOT, SECOND EARL OF ROCHESTER, POET

Being a parent is hard work! I remember the concepts I had about motherhood before I became a mother and how much they changed when motherhood became my reality. I had a master's degree in child development. I had worked as a nanny and as a preschool teacher. I would be the Mary Poppins of Motherhood, right? Wrong. I made many mistakes. I placed many tearful calls to my own mother asking for advice and endured many moments of sitting on the front steps with a pounding headache and desire to just curl up into a ball. Why was this so hard?

When Ricky was little, I read a book by Susan Maushart called *The Mask of Motherhood: How Becoming a Mother Changes Our Lives and Why We Never Talk About It*. The premise of it is that motherhood is hard, and often it is difficult for women to be honest about the challenges they face in this new life stage. People don't want to hear about how stressed out you are or about how the lack of sleep is making you crazy or about how you struggle to keep your worst impulses at bay. Typically, people want to hear, "He is the light of my life," or "I can't imagine what life would be like without her," or "She makes my world complete." They want to hear that it's all flowers, rainbows, hearts, and little imprints of baby feet and hands. Which at times were my experiences. But not always.

In addition to ADHD, Ricky struggled with what the experts call *sensory processing disorder* or *sensory integration disorder.* Certain features of everyday life related to how we experience the world through our senses were challenging for him. He tended to overreact to sensory information related to sight, sound, and touch. For example, loud noises could turn even the most fun experience into a stressful event. Bright, overhead, fluorescent lights seemed to affect his behavior and create anxiety. A scratchy tag on his shirt collar felt unbearable to him. A fun trip to Disney World? We're going to see Winnie the Pooh! Yay! Um, not so much. In addition, Ricky was extremely impulsive and would dart into the street as soon as I opened the car door. His nonstop energy left me exhausted and filled with constant worry. My carefree days before motherhood were gone in an instant, and I mourned the loss of my former self. When I did confide to my closest friend about these feelings, she responded with, "But this is what you wanted! You went across the world to find him! And he is just so adorable." All true. And good grief, I didn't want to send him back! He was *exactly* what I wanted, and motherhood was exactly what I wanted too. I just didn't expect to feel incompetent. I didn't expect that parenting would be so difficult.

I could really relate to Maushart's book. I thought that being the mother of a child with a disability wasn't just a mask of motherhood but a hazmat suit! I struggled with many things that seemed above and beyond the typical motherhood experience. In addition, it just isn't human nature to admit to the things that make you feel inadequate. Why would a parent want to be honest about the things that aren't going well? Before Ricky was diagnosed, we were trying to understand whether the impulsive behaviors were typical or were a product of our parenting skills. Does he have a real condition that could be due to the way his brain is developing? Do we just need to improve our parenting practices in some way? I may understand child development, but I absolutely did not feel like a parenting expert. I didn't want to admit these struggles to most of my family, neighbors, and friends. In some ways, the worries I had were too frightening for me to admit even to myself. I felt alone.

I later learned that I was not the only one who feels this way. The research backs me up on this point. For example, Whittingham (2014) found that parents of children with disabilities often face unique challenges, such as an increased burden of care and greater parental stress. They also found that parents of children with disabilities are more likely to experience anxious and depressive symptoms. In our society, we often blame the parents—the mother in particular—for the child's behavior (Peer and Hillman, 2014). That fact was why it was difficult for me to be honest about my challenges as the mother of a child with ADHD.

It doesn't have to be this way for parents and families. Early childhood educators can play a huge role in supporting families by linking them with other families through a parent center or other community resource, by helping them as they navigate the early intervention and special-education systems, or just by offering a listening ear and friendship. This role we play can be especially important for families in rural areas, tribal communities, or urban areas with limited resources. In some areas of our country, community resources are just about nonexistent. In these cases in particular, parent groups and the support early childhood educators provide are critical to child and family well-being.

We know that the families we serve in early childhood are different from one another. There are single parents, grandparents, older siblings, stepparents, and related and unrelated aunties and uncles. We support families who speak languages other than English. We support foster families, families with multiple jobs, family members with a disability, families who are dual language learners, families with different cultural identities than our own, families who are experiencing homelessness, families who live on a Native American reservation, families who do not have cell phones or computers, and families who depend on cell phones and computers.

We know that children may be brought up in a variety of family structures. I believe that family members, guardians, and friends of the family serve the same important role as our traditional notion of the parent. Therefore, I have elected to use the terms interchangeably throughout these pages. Whether a parent is biological, adoptive, assigned, or chosen, the function of the role remains the same and should be respected as such.

Families are the enduring presence in the lives of children with disabilities. Families are the most important partner for early childhood educators. And from the perspective of the family, from screening to referral to coordinated planning and service provision, early childhood educators are key partners in the provision of IDEA. Families should know what their rights are, and together you can explore their role in the decision-making process and as their child's advocate.

In the following pages, we'll explore the relationship-based practices you can use as you support the families in your program, including those families who may be from a culture that is different from your own or who speak a different language from yours. We'll discuss ways that you can engage families through difficult conversations and share information about the legal rights that parents and families have through the process and even after the development of the IFSP or IEP. Through all of these stages, I have found that the most important element is the relationship that built and maintained with each family. Let's start with some concrete practices that you can use to build those relationships.

RELATIONSHIP-BASED PRACTICES

Before we dig into parent rights under IDEA, it's important to remember that any partnership with families is dependent on a strong relationship. This is especially true for partnerships with families of children with disabilities or suspected delays because they may be particularly vulnerable during the early days of learning about their child's disability. I certainly was! A healthy relationship begins as soon as you know that the child will be joining your classroom or program. What are some of the questions that you typically ask a family? To better meet the needs of the child in your program, find out key information about the child from the family's perspective. Ask questions such as the following:

- What is the most important information that we should know about your child?
- What are your child's strengths?
- What are your child's challenges?
- How does your child communicate with others?
- What language is most often used at home?
- Does your child prefer certain foods?
- Does your child have any food allergies? Are there certain foods that we should avoid serving your child?
- How comfortable is your child around other children? Does your child have siblings or other children who live at home with you?
- Does your child have a preferred object at home? Is there something from home that you could send to school that would give your child comfort?
- What are the favorite activities that your child likes to do at home?
- What makes your child happy?
- What makes your child upset?
- How does your child let you know when he needs something?
- When your child is upset, what do you do at home to provide comfort?
- How does your child comfort himself?

FAMILIES AND CULTURE

The family culture matters. In fact, it matters so much that I have devoted all of chapter nine to the importance of cultural and linguistic responsiveness. Family culture is important to consider as you design the learning environment, consider teaching practices, and provide supports to families through the EI and ECSE systems. For example, families who have immigrated to the United States may feel uneasy about sharing personal information or participating in formal EI or ECSE meetings. They may be unsure of their rights or the rights of their children. They could also be concerned about immigration enforcement or worried about their ability to communicate effectively in a language that is different from the language spoken at home. Share information with families that might ease some of their worry. For example, all students in the United States have a right to a free appropriate education, regardless of immigration status. Immigration status has no effect on eligibility for early intervention or special education services.

Potential for mistrust can arise when family members have had negative experiences with community or human-service agencies in the past. Did a family member have a negative experience with the foster-care system, the judicial system, law enforcement, or the educational system? Those experiences can lead to mistrust of supports offered by you as an early educator or by community agencies and the education system in general. Families who have endured traumatic experiences may pass those stories along through the generations, and they become part of the family culture and belief system.

We know that certain groups have been marginalized throughout our history in the United States. This historical trauma can also interfere with our ability to reach out and connect in a meaningful way with families who are part of a different cultural group than our own. This is a great opportunity to do some personal reflection. You might ask yourself, "What are my initial reactions to this child and her family?" "What do my reactions tell me about my personal beliefs and assumptions?" If we do our best to stay open-minded and approach the situation with the intent to learn and discover together with families, these challenges can be overcome.

Approach families with empathy when talking about these complex situations. When we take the time to understand the family's perspective and listen to their concerns, we build a culture of caring, kindness, and belonging. This trust will go a long way as you navigate a new path together on behalf of their child. Show families sensitivity and respect for their family values, language, and culture by:

- **learning as much as you can about the family culture** so that you can be sensitive and respectful. The Office of Head Start developed a set of "Cultural Backgrounders" about various refugee and cultural groups new to the United States. Of course, each family is unique with their own cultural practices, but finding resources like these can provide basic information to begin conversations with families as you learn how to best support them.

- **using a variety of communication strategies** to reach families. Start the relationship with the family by asking them about their preferred method for communication. Remember that not all families have access to the internet, but research by Rideout and Katz (2016) found that most families have access to a smartphone, so the free translation apps (such as Google Translate) can be helpful tools.

- **making sure that there is someone who can communicate with families in their home language,** if at all possible. Reach out to community agencies that offer free translation services or have a volunteer who can come to the program and serve as an interpreter during important meetings. When families speak a language other than English, you can share with them that EI and ECSE programs have an obligation to communicate meaningfully with the family in the home language. Programs must provide free and effective language assistance, such as translated materials or an interpreter. Families have a legal right to access school documents and meetings in their home language. That includes special education paperwork and communication. Both oral and written translations of special education information require expertise in the services and terminology. Ideally, the translation and interpretation will also take cultural factors and nuances into account and should be provided in a format that is accessible and user-friendly. After the information is translated, it's critical that families understand the terms—and the implications of those terms. You can serve an important role in this part of the process by sharing information about these considerations with families and supporting them to be strong advocates for their child.

RESOURCE SPOTLIGHT

The National Center for Pyramid Model Innovations (NCPMI) has developed a questionnaire called "My Teacher Wants to Know" that programs can use to learn about a child and ensure a smooth transition. You can access a couple of examples online. (See appendix B for a list of resources for this chapter.)

ENGAGING WITH FAMILIES FROM A DISTANCE

The COVID-19 pandemic taught us a great deal about engaging with families from a distance. We learned that doing so can be especially challenging, even under the best circumstances. However, there are certainly benefits as well. Children with some types of disabilities or children who are medically fragile may need remote educational services, regardless of whether in-person programming is available. This may also be true for families who live in rural locations where it is difficult to join an IFSP/IEP meeting in person. How can we reach out to families and provide support in a virtual world? Here are a few things to keep in mind.

- Start by finding out the family's preferred method of communication. How would they like to receive information? What is the best way to share information? They may prefer email, phone calls, texts, or online video meetings. When in doubt, offer families options to choose from.

- Remember that not all families have internet connections, or they may have limited data plans. Keep those cost considerations in mind. If possible, programs should find ways to provide the funding needed to support families with these costs. Similarly, not all families have a computer to access video lessons or video meetings. It may be easier to connect with a phone call or text. In addition, educators can drop off lessons and materials for the child, with detailed instructions for the parent, and then check back in after a time to see how the lessons worked.

- If you are able to connect with a video call, practice the technology ahead of time if possible. Some educators share videos with families as preparation. For example, families might need support with entering the virtual meeting room or classroom, muting and unmuting the microphone, or changing the background of the screen.

- To the greatest degree possible, provide families with information ahead of time. Make sure to connect with families as soon as possible if there is a schedule change.

Maintaining a strong connection with families will be helpful for many reasons, but these relationships are especially helpful when you have a concern about a child's development. At some point, there will be a child in your program who is not meeting developmental milestones, and your support will be instrumental in helping the family and child access needed services. We explore this further in chapter four, but when thinking about how to approach these discussions, preparation is key. Before the conversation, you will want to collect information, organize your thoughts, and build your knowledge about the referral process and available resources. I also recommend that you practice the conversation with a peer prior to talking with the family. Another strategy is to practice the conversation by yourself just looking in a mirror. It sounds strange, but it really will help you to feel more confident and comfortable when the time comes. Your confidence will project strength, which can help parents trust, follow your suggestions, and take action on their child's behalf.

Request a time to talk with the family, so that everyone can focus on the discussion and you won't feel rushed. This is not a conversation to have at drop-off or pickup time! Find a time that works for everyone and a place that is comfortable, quiet, and private. Assure the family that the discussion will remain confidential. Be ready with information for next steps. If you come to the meeting with the name and phone number of the community resource that you think will be most helpful, the family will be more likely to reach out for assistance.

HAVING CHALLENGING CONVERSATIONS

The National Center on Parent, Family, and Community Engagement has identified six key relationship-based practices that can help to foster trust and strengthen the bond between family member and educator:

- Describe the child's behavior exactly as observed.
- Focus on the family-child relationship.
- Value a family's passion.
- Support parental competence.
- Actively reflect on the family's perspective.
- Reflect on your own perspective.

For example, Elliott is a four-year-old boy in your Head Start program. He did not attend any other early learning program prior to joining your classroom, and you are concerned that he doesn't engage with the other children in the class. You want to talk with his mother about it, but you know that it is best to do so in a positive way. Consider these strategies when having a conversation that might be challenging.

Describe the child's behavior exactly as observed.

Difficult conversations go more smoothly when there is a foundation of positive interactions. Start with positive observations that are likely to be reassuring to the parent. These observations are different than compliments. Parents need to know that you recognize and appreciate their child's unique strengths. It's easier to face challenges together when the child's strengths have also been carefully observed together.

For the example with Elliott, you might first share with his parent that you noticed that Elliott builds elaborate structures in the block area. "Elliott frequently chooses to play in the block area, and yesterday I noticed that built a garage for the toy cars. He used lots of different sizes of blocks, and the result was very impressive!"

In chapter 4, we further explore the important skill of observing children in partnership with families. It's a skill to be honed and perfected.

Focus on the family-child relationship.

Especially as we prepare to have challenging conversations with families, we want to be extra careful to recognize and highlight that the family-child relationship is the primary one in the child's life. These conversations are challenging because families care so much! When a family has an emotional reaction to a concern, it shows the depth of their emotional connection and dedication. Recognize what the family is already doing to support their child.

"I can tell that Elliott has lots of experiences with building things. He's really creative in the block area! Does he like to build things at home? What kinds of building materials are favorites at home?"

Value a family's passion.

When we bring a concern to parents, their reaction is rooted in their powerful drive to protect their child, as well as in their passionate hopes for their child. For these first conversations about developmental concerns or behavior to be successful, we have to be patient as family members process and react to the information. Be as specific as possible when describing the concern, and share concrete examples of the behavior to illustrate your point, while acknowledging that the family will also have examples to share.

"I notice that Elliott tends to play alone in the block area. Even when other children are around, he tends to shift his body away from them so that he can play privately. Have you watched him play with other children at home or in your community?"

Support parental competence.

Always take families' perceptions about their child's development seriously. Often, they might suspect a concern before the professional does. Supporting a parent's competence means listening for their observations and concerns before you tell them about your understanding of the challenges. Such support reinforces the parent's expertise and makes it more likely that you can share your observations effectively.

"I hear what you mean about Elliott's tendency to enjoy playing by himself. He does seem happy when he is playing alone, and it's true that some children gravitate toward group play more than others. I'm wondering, though, if he does like to play with other children sometimes. Have you noticed any of those times?"

Actively reflect on the family's perspective.

When there's a developmental concern, it's critical that we actively reflect on the family's perspective. Invite parents to share their own observations of and goals for their child and the family. Be respectful at all times, and offer many opportunities for the family to ask questions. Remember, it can be difficult to learn that your child may have a developmental concern. The questions you hear may be coming from a place of fear or anxiety.

If your initial reaction is to disagree, take some time to reflect on their perspective. Parents become true partners when they share their stories with us, and that happens only if they consider us to be someone they trust. Ask the family about their preferences for interaction, because sometimes it's easier to have these conversations by email rather than face to face.

"Thanks for sharing your perspective about Elliott and playing with others. Would you mind keeping an eye on how he is with other children for the next week or so? Then we could come back together and share our observations with each other. We can meet in person to talk about it or have a conversation on the phone or by email. Does that sound okay? What is your preference for communication when we reconnect?"

Reflect on your own perspective.

It's also important to reflect on your own perspective as you talk with parents about your concerns. Your expertise, of course, is valuable. But while your role is to provide support and guidance, you aren't there to promote your own vision of how you think the family should operate, even if you think you know better than the parent about some things. If you and the parent speak a different primary language, bring someone who speaks the same language as the parent into the conversation. Clear and natural communication is vital to these conversations.

"Thanks for meeting with me again. I've thought a lot about our last conversation and spent some more time observing Elliott with his peers. Were you able to observe him as well? What are your thoughts? There are resources available to help us think this through if you are open to exploring this with a professional."

PARENT RIGHTS UNDER IDEA

To help parents and families to be their child's best advocates, we must first understand the rights that parents have under the law. The IDEA law is clear that parents are their child's first teachers and should be the ultimate decision-makers about services for their child. What are the key parent rights under IDEA? Parents have the right to the following:

- Confidentiality
- Receiving an explanation of procedural safeguards
- Use of parent's native language or preferred mode of communication
- Opportunity to review their child's records
- Participation in meetings

- An independent evaluation
- Prior written notice of meetings
- Giving or denying consent to services
- Opportunity to disagree with decisions
- Mechanisms to resolve disputes

(CPIR, 2017; ECTA, 2012)

As a parent of a child with a disability who had an IFSP and later an IEP, I can attest that the process often felt quite daunting. I received so many parent rights handbooks that I could have wallpapered my house with them by the time Ricky turned ten! We were fortunate to have many caring and encouraging educators and service providers along the way. They helped us understand our role in the process as well as our parental rights before the evaluation, during the IFSP/IEP meeting, and after the meeting when services and accommodations were provided. I give a ton of credit to the educators who supported us along the way, and ultimately led us to a successful high school graduation.

RESOURCE SPOTLIGHT

The section on having challenging conversations is adapted from *Talking with Families About Their Child's Development*. That resource and CONNECT "Module 4: Family-Professional Partnerships" are available online. (See appendix B for a list of resources for this chapter.)

Let's look at parent rights before the evaluation, during the IFSP/IEP meeting, and beyond.

BEFORE THE EVALUATION

Before any evaluation can be completed, the agency that does the evaluation must provide the parent with prior written notice and with a procedural safeguards notice. The procedural safeguards notice was shared with me through those parent rights handbooks that I mentioned. In addition, the agency must obtain parent consent. What exactly does all of this mean?

The term *prior written notice* "refers to the public agency's obligation to inform parents a reasonable time before it proposes to take specific actions or refuses to take specific actions—in this case, initiate an initial evaluation of the child" (Küpper and Rebhorn, 2007).

The *procedural safeguards notice* "refers to the comprehensive written explanation that public agencies must provide parents on specific occasions to, among other things, fully inform them of IDEA's procedural safeguards. 'Upon initial referral or parent request for evaluation' are two occasions that trigger the provision of the procedural safeguards notice" (Küpper and Rebhorn, 2007).

"*Consent* within IDEA has a very specific meaning that rises out of, and is closely tied to, its provisions regarding prior written notice. Consent, in IDEA, means *informed written* consent. The comprehensive description of a proposed or refused action, as contained in the prior written notice, is intended to inform parents fully about a specific issue. Only by building that foundation of understanding can *informed* consent be given" (Küpper and Rebhorn, 2007).

Once parents have given consent for an evaluation, you can help them think about the types of questions the team will discuss when it meets. Conversations and decisions about the appropriate settings, particularly for children transitioning from Part C to Part B services, are individualized, so there are several things to consider.

The ECTA Center offers a list of questions that you can use for personal reflection as well as group reflection with families and other partners when considering preschool settings. "Team Decisions for Preschool Special Education Services: Guiding Questions" (n.d.) is available online. (See appendix B for a list of resources for this chapter.) This is a good document to share with families to help them understand what to expect during the IFSP/IEP meeting. The document is divided into four categories: child considerations, family considerations, curricular considerations, and support considerations. For child considerations, you'll find questions on topics such as where the child is spending his time now, what abilities and strengths the child has, and what challenges he has. In the family considerations section, the guiding questions include prompts requesting information from families on what they observe and would like to see happen. Curricular considerations include questions asking about the child's ability to participate successfully and work toward

IFSP/IEP goals, with or without modifications, in the current or proposed educational program. Support considerations are just that, thinking about what supports are needed so that the child can participate in an inclusive setting.

You can review the questions with families to find out if they have any questions about the four categories, or you can offer it if they want to practice how they might respond to the questions during the IFSP/IEP meeting. If there is a particular question or consideration that the parents want to make sure to address, you can role-play with parents so that they can practice sharing their thoughts. Together, you can write down a list of items that are important to the family. Then you can help them articulate why each item is important and what their child needs to be successful as it relates to each item.

In preparation for setting goals for the child, ask the question: What are your dreams for your child? Even a goal related to fun family time can be worked into the IEP in some way. For example, a parent might want their child to go fishing with them one day. That can be a goal written in the IEP! The IEP should be meaningful and exciting for parents too.

DURING THE IFSP/IEP MEETING

Following the evaluation, the team will gather to discuss the results and determine a plan. The IDEA law is clear about parent rights during the IFSP/IEP meeting and about how to ensure parent participation. To make sure that every parent has the opportunity to participate in the meeting, each public agency must:

- notify parents early enough so that they have the opportunity to attend;
- schedule the meeting at a mutually agreed upon time and place; and
- inform parents about who will be in attendance during the meeting.

These are the required members of the team according to IDEA:

- **Parents:** Parents or guardians of the child with a disability are vital members of the team, with an expertise to contribute like no one else.
- **Special educators:** Special educators, with their knowledge of how to educate children with disabilities, are obviously a very important part of a child's IFSP/IEP team.
- **Regular educators:** If a child is participating in the regular education environment (or is going to be participating), then IDEA requires that at least one regular educator of the child be included on the IFSP/IEP team.
- **Representative of the school system:** The IFSP/IEP team must also include a representative of the school system who has the authority to commit agency resources. This person must have specific qualifications.

Diane Marie Dabkowski's article "Encouraging Active Parent Participation in IEP Team Meetings" in *Teaching Exceptional Children* offers ideas for engaging parents. You can find it online. (See appendix B for a list of resources for this chapter.)

- **Someone to interpret evaluation results:** Someone on the team must be able to interpret the child's evaluation results and discuss what they mean in terms of instruction.

- **Others with knowledge or special expertise about the child:** This could be you! Either the parent or the school system may invite others to join the team if they have knowledge or special expertise about the child. This can include other family members or even other service providers, such as Head Start or child-care educators or other staff members.

- **Child:** The child should also be included in the IFSP or IEP meeting.

(Rebhorn, n.d.)

The team will make key decisions on behalf of the child and family. During a typical IFSP/IEP meeting, each team member will take a turn in the discussion. The discussion will include talking about:

- the child's strengths;
- the parents' concerns for enhancing their child's education;
- the results of the most recent evaluation of the child; and
- the child's academic, developmental, and functional needs

(Rebhorn, n.d.)

During the meeting, the team will also discuss whether the child would benefit from additional supports or services in order to be successful, answering the following questions.

- Does the child have communication needs?
- Does the child need assistive technology services and devices?
- Does the child's behavior interfere with his learning or the learning of others?
- Does the child have a visual impairment and need instruction in, or the use of, Braille?
- Is the child deaf or hard of hearing and have language and other communication needs?
- Does the child have language needs due to being a dual language learner?

(Rebhorn, n.d.)

Depending on the answers to these questions, the supplementary aids and services can be accommodations and modifications to the curriculum, the way content is taught, or even how the child's progress will be measured. The services can also include support and training for staff who work with that child, for example, the educator in an early childhood program. The aids can include specialized equipment such as wheelchairs, computers, software, adaptive communication devices, special eating utensils, or even restroom equipment. Decisions about which supplementary aids and services are needed are made on an individual basis, but the team may use these guiding questions as a way to make those decisions:

- What activities can the child participate in without extra support?
- In what activities does the child require extra support?
- What extra supports would be required?

(ECTA Center, n.d.)

DISPUTE RESOLUTION

Once the IFSP/IEP is written, the hope is that service decisions will be mutually agreed upon by the whole team, including the parents. Unfortunately, this is not always the case, and the IDEA law is clear that parents should have a variety of options to consider when resolving disputes. Every state has its own process for dispute resolution, but there are some requirements that must be followed, depending on the option used. These options are either informal or formal in nature, and a dispute-resolution guide has been developed for both Part C and Part B. You can find the links to the dispute-resolution guides in appendix B.

INFORMAL APPROACHES TO DISPUTE RESOLUTION

In all cases where the family and school disagree, it is important for both sides to first discuss their concerns and try

What if a family denies services?

It happens. Sometimes, no matter how supportive you might be about offering services to support families, they still may choose to forgo resources and services. It's important to accept this decision and to remember that we all process information differently and at our own pace. Families will likely respond emotionally to new information about their child, and that emotional reaction can sometimes affect the way that families hear and understand the information. In this situation, early childhood educators should refrain from judgement and simply be ready to repeat the information when necessary, to answer questions, and to remind families about available resources. If you believe that by refusing services the family is placing the child at risk, then you have an obligation to share that perspective with the family and let them know how critical your concerns are to their child's development. However, the family maintains the role of decision-maker. Respect for that role will build trust, and over time, the family may be able to get additional perspective and process the information and may come back to you for support.

to compromise. Using a relationship-based approach, parents should first try the informal options before moving to the options that might feel confrontational to the agency. The first informal option is to review the child's IEP. The second is to hold a facilitated IEP meeting.

Under IDEA, the school system or other public agency determines how frequently the IFSP/IEP should be reviewed. This review must happen at least once a year, but parents have the right to request an IFSP/IEP meeting at any time. If parents are concerned about the services the child is receiving or the child's placement or any other related concern, they can work to resolve it through another meeting. At the meeting, members of the team would discuss the parents' concerns and, hopefully, come up with a solution.

This is a strategy that I used many times over the years with Ricky's IEP team. Especially when he went to elementary school, it was hard to know the best way to support him. We did a lot of trial and error. Usually, the school system was open to this strategy and agreed to meet with us more frequently. I learned through experience that respect and honesty were key to the success of the IEP team meetings.

Another informal approach to resolving disputes is IFSP or IEP meeting facilitation. This strategy is not mentioned in the law, but it is widely used by teams because it can be helpful to have an outside member of the team facilitate the discussion. An impartial facilitator can keep the team on track and address conflicts as they arise. A good facilitator ensures that everyone participates, clarifies points of agreement or disagreement, and models effective communication. Some agencies offer this service to families and cover the cost of the facilitator, but that is not required under the law.

FORMAL APPROACHES TO DISPUTE RESOLUTION

If families and the public agency still cannot reach an agreement, there are formal ways to resolve the conflict: mediation, filing a complaint, and due process.

Mediation

In mediation, parents and the IFSP or IEP team meet together along with an impartial mediator. The mediator is different from a facilitator because the mediator must be qualified and trained in effective mediation techniques. IDEA requires that agencies offer mediation, and there are specific conditions that must be followed. The process must be voluntary and can't be used to deny or delay a parent's right to a due-process hearing. The mediation process is similar to a facilitated meeting in that the team is encouraged to talk openly about the areas where they disagree and to try to reach agreement. In mediation, the meeting participants make the decisions about any changes to occur that will resolve the dispute.

Filing a Complaint

Given the fact that services are provided at the local level, the state education agency (SEA) will not know if there is a dispute unless the parents file a state complaint. In this case, the parent would write directly to the SEA and describe in a signed document how the local agency has violated the law under IDEA. Every state develops its own form that parents must use, so it will look different from state to state. In most cases, the SEA must resolve the complaint within sixty calendar days and must send out a document that includes the reasons for the final decision. This method is different from mediation. In mediation the team resolves the conflict; when parents file a state complaint, the SEA makes the decisions.

Due Process

When due process is used as a way to resolve disputes, parents and the school present evidence before an impartial, qualified person called a *hearing officer*. The hearing officer then issues the decision following a due-process hearing. A due-process hearing occurs in a formal, legal setting where both parties present their perspective through witnesses, documents, and other evidence. The process begins with parents filing a confidential complaint, and IDEA has specific guidelines for what the complaint must include. Parents may hire an attorney to help them with filing the complaint and representing them through the process. IDEA requires that parents and the local agency must first hold a meeting to try to resolve the situation without having to go to the due process hearing, but if a due-process hearing is held, the hearing officer will make the final decision, and the school must implement the decision as soon as possible (CPIR, 2019; CPIR, 2008). Due process is the final formal option for dispute resolution.

UNDERSTANDING THE FAMILY'S PERSPECTIVE

Regardless of where they are in the process, it will likely be a stressful experience for parents. It certainly was for me! Knowing that this is true, the Office of Special Education provides funding to support a network of parent centers across the country, so that families can access support regardless of where they are in the process. There are nearly one hundred parent training and information centers (PTIs) and community parent resource centers (CPRCs) in the United States and its territories. The hub for these parent centers is the Center for Parent Information and Resources (CPIR). This parent center hub is staffed by people who are not just advocates by profession but also have a personal stake in the work as a parent, sibling, spouse, and so on. Educators can find lots of information on the hub to share with families so that they can better understand their rights as active participants in their children's education.

Early childhood educators can be valuable partners to parents as they navigate through the uncertain waters. Every time Ricky started a new class, I tried as hard as possible to form a strong, positive relationship with his teacher. My strategy was simple: compliments, presents, and baked goods. Offering to volunteer as much as possible helped too. I once had the privilege of attending a keynote presentation by acclaimed researcher Walter Gilliam of the Yale Child Study Center. Dr. Gilliam is an expert in preschool suspensions and expulsions, and he said that he had never known a case where a child was expelled from school when the parent also had a good relationship with the teacher. I took that lesson to heart and attempted to do all that I could to nurture relationships with

Ricky's teachers. As you can see here in this picture from his first day of kindergarten, he went off to school with first day "please be good to my child" presents for the teachers.

When I think about those times, I can reflect on the fact that my husband and I had well-paying jobs and lots of resources. We had reliable transportation and flexible work schedules. Not all families have the same resources, money, time, flexibility, knowledge, and expertise to advocate for their child adequately. Educators can help to level the playing field by being a support to parents who may not understand the system but still want the best for their children.

I kept a journal of funny things that Ricky said and did in the early years of his life. It is one of my cherished possessions. Lord knows that I never would have remembered all of those things if I hadn't written them down at the time. However, I remember thinking that I wasn't capturing the complete picture of my parenting experience, because I recorded only the positive memories. I had been worried that Ricky would come across that book as an adult and get the impression that parenting him was super challenging for me, so I recorded only the happy times. I took lots of photos like this and wrote down all of the cute, funny, and happy stories.

I kept this journal of happy stories and tried to erase the tough memories. The funny thing is that now I find those tough memories to be most informative. Those tough memories are ones that I look back on with pride because of how far Ricky has come. He has overcome adversity in his life and thrived and shined in spite of it all. I've come a long way, too, as a mother. With the benefit of years, I'm able to see that Ricky would have read stories of my parenting challenges with understanding and care. He remembers the hard times for me as a parent because they were hard times for him as well. Ultimately, I learned that parenting is about opening ourselves to all that our children are and about embracing the fact that we have both everything and nothing to do with who they are. Friends and family often say to me that Ricky has turned out really well. But children don't exactly "turn out" as if they were a pumpkin pie that you just took out of the oven. We all evolve, grow, and change through our entire lives. This is much easier to understand in hindsight.

In my current role providing technical assistance to state Part C and Part B, Section 619 coordinators, I often get emails from concerned parents who find my contact information online. They are looking for help for their child, and the desperation they feel comes through loud and clear even in an email. These parents remind me of the urgency I felt in those early years of trying to access services for Ricky. Parents who first become aware of a suspected delay react in many different ways. They may experience this awareness as a form of grief or loss. They may struggle to process information about it or may become angry or upset or receive information about it with indignation. The beautiful poem "Welcome to Holland" by Emily Perl Kingsley is a lovely tribute to those feelings that many parents experience. You can read it online. (See appendix B for a list of resources for this chapter.)

One thing that I have learned when talking to concerned family members, as well as concerned educators and other staff, is that what family members seek, in addition to the services their child needs to succeed, is just a person who will listen empathetically.

What is *empathetic communication*? Empathy is understanding the feelings, thoughts, and actions of another by taking their perspective.

We let go of judgement or criticism when we strive to understand the situation from the parent's point of view. It is not always easy to do! Empathetic communication is a skill to be honed and practiced. It's not just about the "good listening" skills that we all try to use—making eye contact, nodding, smiling, and leaning in—but it's also about tuning in to the other person's thoughts and feelings through these efforts to take their perspective.

What does that look like in real life? For example, the time of waiting to obtain services is an especially stressful time for parents. When I was providing technical assistance for disability services coordinators in Head Start, this was a common concern that they shared. How can we support families during that awful waiting time? It seems as if the decision-making takes forever! We talked about saying things such as:

How can you communicate with empathy?

- By listening with your heart as well as your ears and eyes

- By seeking to step out of your shoes and into the shoes of others who are facing challenges and to feel what it's like

- By bringing feelings into the open—noticing, naming, responding, validating

- By communicating that you understand and care

"Thanks for all that you are doing to support your child. I can tell that you are really eager to find services, and I can hear the frustration in your voice that you aren't able to access services more quickly. If I were in your shoes, I would feel the same way. It is difficult to be in this place of waiting, but I want you to know that I care about what you are going through and will do all that I can to help. I know that there is a bright future ahead for your child."

This combination of good listening, kindness, and encouragement is a gift that we can give parents during a stressful time.

My hope is that we can be that empathetic place of support for families as they navigate this journey. We can support the parent who is embarrassed by his child's behavior and lack of self-control. We can be the safe place for the family member who has internalized a sense of blame related to his child's disability. We can provide comfort to the parent who is worried that her child's actions are viewed by others as a sign that she has poor parenting skills. I was that parent. (Yes, even a child-development expert can be embarrassed by her parenting skills!) As early childhood educators, you are likely to encounter families before their child has received a diagnosis. You may even be the first person to notice a developmental delay. What do you do in that situation? It all begins with screening, assessment, and evaluation.

QUESTIONS FOR REFLECTION

- What strategies have you used to gain a better understanding of the unique strengths, needs, routines, and preferences of the families of the children you teach or support?
- What can you do to keep the family's perspective in mind when make decisions that might impact their child?
- Which resources might you share with families in your program?
- How might you build your skills for empathetic communication with families?

CHAPTER 4

Screening, Evaluation, and Assessment

Every child is a different kind of flower, and all together make this world a beautiful garden.

—ANONYMOUS

When my son entered child care for the first time, his teacher, Miss Amy, noticed that he didn't behave the same way as the other children in her class. "He darts from one activity to another," she observed. "He doesn't stay in any center for very long, and so he doesn't seem to be connecting with the other children." She showed me Ricky's art projects and the snowman that consisted of one cotton ball glued to the page. "I guess he's a minimalist when it comes to crafts," Miss Amy said. She wondered if he might benefit from early childhood special-education services. As a parent, I wasn't quite ready to hear this information, even though we had received support from an early intervention service provider when Ricky was younger. This seemed different. *Special education* felt like a much bigger deal to me. However, I did have to acknowledge the fact that Miss Amy had seen many children pass through her classroom over the years and likely would recognize when a child's behavior appeared different from other children's. Just like Miss Amy, as an early childhood educator you have the opportunity of being able to watch many children as they grow and develop.

Early childhood educators spend time with lots of different young children, and they are often the first to notice a potential delay in development. You are also a partner with families and have the opportunity to talk with them about their child's development in an ongoing way. Miss Amy was able to do both of those things, and Ricky benefited from her keen observation and willingness to share her observations with me. She knew that when developmental concerns are caught early, children benefit.

In the following pages, we'll explore your role in the screening, evaluation, and assessment process and how to support families along the way. I'll share strategies you can use when observing children as they play, both on your own and in collaboration with families as they observe their child at home. We'll also discuss the ins and outs of the evaluation and assessment process, including best practices that EI and ECSE practitioners use to determine the most effective approaches for an individual child. It all starts with a good understanding of child development and of how to spot a developmental delay.

Believe it or not, developmental delays are common. The Centers for Disease Control and Prevention (CDC) estimates that about one in six children has a developmental disability, which could affect their health, learning, and overall success in life (Boyle et al., 2011). Children who are identified as infants or toddlers can really benefit from early intervention services. Speech therapy, physical therapy, and other services for infants and toddlers are available in every state at little or no cost to parents. Sadly, more than half of the children with delays aren't identified until they start kindergarten. This is a problem that early childhood educators can solve by recognizing the signs of a potential developmental delay or disability, talking about them with family members, and accessing resources to help with decision-making.

 ## A REVIEW OF DEVELOPMENTAL MILESTONES

But what does a developmental concern or delay look like? To understand how to identify when there might be a developmental delay, we must first understand typical child development. Every child grows and develops differently, at her own pace. Some children develop quickly in some areas and a little more slowly in others. Skills such as taking a first step, smiling for the first time, and waving bye-bye are called *developmental milestones*.

The CDC website is a great place to go for information about developmental milestones in children ages birth through five. You'll find checklists organized in four key developmental domains:

- Social-emotional
- Language and communication
- Cognitive
- Movement and Physical

Each domain is important, and each supports, and is supported by, the others. Here is a brief explanation of each domain and some of the related milestones. You can find a more expansive compilation of typical milestones in child development at CDC's Developmental Milestones website.

SOCIAL-EMOTIONAL

This domain is about how children interact with others and show emotion. Examples of milestones include:

- Smiling spontaneously, especially at people
- Cooperating with other children
- Showing affection for friends without prompting

LANGUAGE AND COMMUNICATION

This domain is about how children express their needs and share what they are thinking, as well as understand what is said to them. Examples of milestones include:

- Cooing and babbling
- Pointing to show others what they want
- Singing a song from memory, such as "Itsy Bitsy Spider"

COGNITIVE

The cognitive domain—learning, thinking, and problem solving—is about how children learn new things and solve problems. It includes how children explore their environment to figure things out, whether by looking at the world around them, putting objects in their mouths, or dropping something to watch it fall. This domain also includes "academic" skills such as counting and learning letters and numbers. Examples of milestones include:

- Reaching for a toy with one hand
- Exploring things in different ways, such as by shaking, banging, and throwing
- Building towers of at least four blocks

MOVEMENT AND PHYSICAL

This domain is about how children use their bodies. It includes many milestones parents excitedly wait for, such as:

- Crawling
- Catching a bounced ball most of the time
- Eating with a spoon

Some developmental milestones fit more than one domain. For example, playing make-believe can be a social-emotional milestone as well as a cognitive milestone. Following instructions can be a language and communication milestone as well as a cognitive milestone. Playing peekaboo can be a cognitive as well as a social-emotional milestone (CDC, n.d.).

Children reach milestones in very predictable ways. There are *typical* stages when children learn how to speak, act, move, play, and learn, but every child is different, and there are variations based on the child's culture and experiences as well as individual differences. How children develop is based on a combination of factors, such as the characteristics they are born with, the culture they live in, and their experiences within their family and in other settings. Each of these factors is important in a child's growth and development, so educators must pay attention to all aspects of a child's life to support development and learning.

I love the garden quote at the start of this chapter because it reminds me that I have many flowers in my garden, and they don't all bloom at the same time. I don't expect my tulips to flower in December, because I know it is not their nature to do so. Children are the same way. Some children may take their first steps when they are one year old, and others may take longer. Child development also occurs in spurts and lags. The NAEYC Developmentally Appropriate Practices Position Statement (NAEYC, 2020) adopts the metaphor of waves and cycles (Siegler, 1996), with the recognition that development is not as straightforward a process as we once believed! Child development happens in an overlapping fashion, and it is difficult to assess skills and behaviors within the rigid boundaries of developmental domains. Children develop in different ways and the progressions are often hard to explain. My own son would achieve several developmental milestones all at once, and then it seemed as if he suddenly put the brakes on. Sometimes it seemed like a "two steps forward, one step back" type of pattern.

Keeping all of those considerations in mind, we can still use the developmental milestone tools as a way to keep track of development and learn about when a child may be experiencing a developmental delay.

BEGINNING WITH OBSERVATION

The terms *screening*, *evaluation*, and *assessment* come from the medical field, so it can seem as though those functions would have no place in an early childhood program. But if we want to support each and every child, we should be ready to work with families so that they can access early intervention or special education services if we suspect that those services might be helpful for their child. How do we determine whether or not services might be helpful for a child? We talk with family members in an ongoing way, and we observe children, keeping in mind our understanding of typical child development. The basis for all screening, evaluation, and assessment begins with the simple act of observation.

OBSERVING IN THE EARLY CHILDHOOD EDUCATION ENVIRONMENT

Watching children as they go about their day and gathering information as we watch is a powerful tool that all educators have in their toolbox. Through observation, we gain insight into a child's growth and development; but for the insight to be meaningful, observation must be objective and factual. We should only document what we see with our own eyes or hear

RESOURCE SPOTLIGHT

The CDC has a set of resources for tracking developmental milestones. Available on the CDC's Developmental Milestones website, you can find resources and information to share with families so that they can also track their child's development.

If you are wondering what a certain milestone looks like in the real world, the CDC also has a section on its website called "Milestones in Action," where you'll find a free online library of photos and videos of developmental milestones.

Another great resource is the *Head Start Early Learning Outcomes Framework: Ages Birth to Five,* which describes what children should know and be able to do across five developmental domains. This interactive tool is available online and includes links to related resources, guides, videos, and webinars. (See appendix B for a list of resources for this chapter.)

A Word about Terminology

What is the difference between screening, evaluation, and assessment? Under IDEA Part C, *screening* is a way to determine whether a child is suspected of having a disability or developmental delay (ECTA, 2020a). *Evaluation* means the procedures used by appropriate qualified personnel to determine a child's initial and continuing eligibility for services and supports, and *assessment* is defined as "the ongoing procedures used by qualified personnel to identify the child's unique strengths and needs and the early intervention services appropriate to meet those needs . . . and includes the assessment of the child . . . and the assessment of the child's family" (American Speech-Language-Hearing Association, 2021).

Questions for Use in Observations

Questions to explore through observation include the following:

- Where does the child choose to play most of the time?

- Who are the child's preferred playmates when given a choice?

- How does the child join others in play?

- How does the child understand and respond to directions or requests from others?

- Does the child's behavior vary throughout the day, such as during different routines, activities, or transitions and with different groups of children and/or adults?

- What teaching strategies engage the child most effectively?

- Which activities are the most challenging for the child?

- Which classroom materials does the child engage with the most?

- When given a choice, what does the child choose to do?

- How does the child interact with classroom materials?

- How does the child approach a new activity?

- How does the child communicate other children?

- How does the child communicate with adults?

- How does the child move?

- How does the child interact with other children?

- How does the child handle conflict?

with our own ears. Keeping "just the facts" rather than inserting our own beliefs about the behavior is critical to maintaining objective observation. Adjectives, such as *angry, fussy, sad, happy,* or even *hyperactive,* are open to interpretation. *Sad*, for example, might look different to you than it does to me. Sticking to facts takes time and patience to practice and learn, but it truly is the key to ensuring that your observational record is objective, factual, and nonjudgmental. By remaining objective, we can guard against allowing our personal views, values, or feelings to influence what we record or capture about the child.

The way we record our observations can vary. We might take notes throughout the day and collect them for the child's portfolio for the purpose of developing lesson plans that best meet the child's needs. We might ask children to tell us about pictures they create so we can write down their stories. We might use a checklist or tool that is organized in accordance with developmental milestones. We might observe children in a structured way using a grid or a tool that ensures that our observations include behaviors across all the developmental domains. We might use journal entries, photographs, videos, notes with direct quotes from the child, or even comments shared by the child's parent or family member. Some educators use work samples as a way to record children's progress. *Work samples* are collections of children's drawings, paintings, writing samples, or photographs that represent the best examples of what a child knows and is able to do at a given point in time. Trained evaluators may also use standardized assessments in a structured way. All of these examples are forms of gathering information, and they all can be helpful to strengthen our understanding about a child's development.

When it comes to everyday observation habits, some of us are very methodical and plan what and when to observe each day, perhaps alternating learning centers or children observed. Others might prefer to observe in a spontaneous way as children participate in the daily routine. Whatever your usual style, there are times when the purpose of the observation requires a different approach. For example, you might generally observe children spontaneously and take notes throughout the day but then also plan to observe a particular child at snack time to learn more about the child's use of language or the way the child uses eating utensils. If your style is generally more structured, you still might pause to observe a spontaneous play activity in the block area.

> *"What we see changes what we know. What we know changes what we see."*
>
> **—JEAN PIAGET, PSYCHOLOGIST**

Observation notes do not need to be long and involved to be effective. Some people think that they need to write several paragraphs to adequately describe what they see and hear. But, if we keep the main purpose of our observation in mind, we will know which specific details we really need to capture so that we can remember the important points of what happened, and we can keep our notes brief.

COLLABORATIVE OBSERVATION

We should also observe children in a variety of settings and at different times of the day, which is another reason why families are important to this process. Families observe different behaviors from their child in the home or in the community than we observe in the classroom. Some educators and many early intervention service providers are able to observe and assess children and interact with families during a home visit. Still, children may not exhibit consistent behaviors. Sharing the observations that you gather with families and asking them to share observations with you can be a great way to build trusting relationships. This is often referred to as *collaborative observation*. When we engage families in a collaborative process of observing their child, we are also laying the groundwork for having more difficult conversations. Keep in mind, the process of having collaborative observations is not about giving advice or telling families all the things that we know. It's not about sitting down for a meeting or filling out a form. It is an ongoing process and is essential to building a relationship with the family.

Collaborative observation can begin with sharing simple observations. For example, you might say, "I notice that Enrique always goes to the book area first when you bring him in to school. Do you like to read together?" This kind of statement gives parents the opportunity to share what they see— whether it is similar to your observation or different. It encourages them to open up to you and may lead to sharing what they see at home or even their hopes, dreams, and concerns about their child. This can be an effective strategy if you need to address a developmental concern. You can start by sharing behavior in a descriptive way and then ask the family what they have noticed. Start the conversation with behaviors that acknowledge the child's strengths and competence. Think about it as just another way that we can express that we're in this together. Parents don't have to feel that they are alone when they notice that their child is growing and developing at a different pace than other children. We can be partners as we try to figure it all out.

Besides, most parents love to share stories from home. They love to tell others about the funny or surprising things that their child says or does. As a parent, I was no different! As I shared in previous chapters, I wrote in a journal for the first eight years of my son's life and have wonderful memories captured there. As a child development expert, it was especially fun to record these memories of things Ricky said as I watched his cognitive development take shape. The following are a few examples.

"Mommy, can I keep this frog in my room? I'll give him hugs and kisses! I'll comb his hair! And when he gets hurt, I'll put a teeny tiny Band-Aid on him!"

[While walking through the woods] "Mommy, listen! I think those birds have a whistle!"

[Picking up a shoehorn] "What is this, Mommy?"

"It's a shoehorn."

"Does it go toot toot?"

Collecting stories like these and sharing them with family members is a great way to nurture those relationships.

Often, parents notice a developmental delay in their child before the professionals do. Supporting a parent's competence means listening for the observations and concerns they share with you. It might just be an offhand comment as they hand you a field trip release form. They might ask, "Do other children know how to do that by this age?" When you engage with parents in a friendly and caring way, it reinforces the parent's expertise and makes it more likely that you will be able to share your own observations in the future. Celebrate the critical role that parents have and appreciate the unique perspective that they bring.

SHARING OBSERVATIONS WITH FAMILIES

As soon as you notice that a child is not developing at the same rate as other children in your care, it is important to talk to the family. Remember, all children are different, and we do not expect them all to develop at the same pace. But over time, if you notice a child is behind her peers socially, emotionally, or in any other way, you should speak up. Discuss healthy development with all families on a regular basis.

As early childhood educators, we have a passion for the well-being of the children in our programs. Parents have that same passion for their own child. When we bring a concern to parents, their reaction is rooted in their powerful drive to protect their child, as well as in their passionate hopes for their child. Beginning these conversations can be uncomfortable. Sharing funny stories with each other is one thing, but having a conversation about a problem is a whole other thing entirely.

I remember describing myself as a "Mama Bear." Protecting my "cub" was the most powerful impulse I have ever felt. Thinking back to those first conversations with Miss Amy, I remember thinking, "My son is perfect. How can you even question that?" I had such an emotional reaction to the information she shared. Now I understand that when a family has an emotional reaction to a concern, it shows the depth of their emotional connection and dedication to their child. Families might feel judged or feel that their children are being criticized. Families can become anxious or worried when we bring up concerns.

For conversations about developmental concerns or behavior to be successful, we have to allow time and provide understanding so that parents can process the information. Parents' perceptions about their child's development should always be taken seriously. You might have an internal reaction to what seems like a parent's "resistance," when actually they may just be struggling to understand. Your concern may not fit within the concept that they have of their own child. What if they aren't seeing the behaviors at home, so it's difficult for them to imagine their child behaving in that way at school? Rather than fighting against a parent's strong emotional response to your concerns, you can work with it to help the family get through a hard time.

It can be helpful to remember that all families want what is best for their child, but "what is best" is defined by their own perspective. Families' perspectives are shaped by their cultural history, values, beliefs, and past experiences. These include values and beliefs about people with disabilities in general, concepts about testing, and what that might mean for their child and the way that their child is viewed by family members, friends, and members of their community. The family's perspective can inform and guide the conversation when you talk with them about your concerns. If parents have their own experience with a disability, they may feel extreme anxiety and worry. They may be hesitant because of language and culture. Parents may react to concerns in a way that reflects their own negative school experiences. Some families may experience grief or loss linked to the hopes and dreams they have for their child. Parents and families with a history of trauma may have that trauma "triggered" when they feel anxiety and worry about their child. Look for common ground and create shared understanding with families. When you and the child's family have a shared concern and have decided that you want to find out more about the child's development, your next step is to begin the process of screening, evaluation, and assessment. Let's break down those steps.

SCREENING

Screening (or *developmental screening*) is a brief assessment that can be completed by a parent, educator, or trained professional to determine whether or not concerns support a referral to early intervention or special education systems. Screening does not identify or diagnose a developmental delay. It only provides a snapshot of how a child is functioning in a particular area at a point in time. Remember those vision and hearing tests that you had at the beginning of elementary school? Those were screenings.

You might have also heard the term *developmental monitoring*. This is different from developmental screening because it is done by parents and educators on an ongoing basis. For example, the observations we discussed earlier could be developmental monitoring if they are used with intention and perhaps with a checklist or some other tool. Developmental screening, on the other hand, is a formal process. The American Academy of Pediatrics (AAP) recommends that children receive a developmental screening at nine, eighteen, and twenty-four months of age. The AAP also recommends that screenings be conducted with a validated screening tool by medical professionals or other staff who have special training. Both developmental monitoring and developmental screening look for developmental milestones and are important for tracking signs of development and identifying concerns.

Usually, the screening process involves assessing a child using a small number of key indicators and, depending on the tool, a screening can be completed by the child's parent, educator, home visitor, or other trained professional. Most developmental screening tools provide a quick look at major developmental milestones across domains to show whether or not a child is on track developmentally and if a closer look by a specialist is needed. Most children who have had the recommended well-child visits with a pediatrician or primary health-care provider will also have had a series of developmental screenings. The results of a screening can help you plan how to best support the development of the children in your program.

Of course, you should obtain the family's permission before conducting any screening. Tell them all about the process and why you feel that it is necessary.

Screening Resources

- **Which screening tool should I choose?** When choosing a screening tool, you should check the reliability and validity of the instrument itself. This information is important to ensure that the screening tool is appropriate for your program. If the tool is not reliable or valid, we cannot trust that the information will give us what we need to know about the child's growth and development. This is addressed in the list of screening tools contained in *Birth to 5: Watch Me Thrive! A Compendium of Screening Measures for Young Children*, which can be found online. (See appendix B for a list of resources for this chapter.)

- **What else should I know about screening?** The CDC offers a vast collection of free materials (in English and in Spanish) online that can be used as part of your observation and screening efforts. You'll find developmental checklists, a Milestone Tracker app, growth charts, tip sheets, posters, and free online professional development opportunities. (See appendix B for a list of resources for this chapter.)

Another helpful resource about screening in early childhood is the "Early Care and Education Provider's Guide for Developmental and Behavioral Screening," which can be found online. (See appendix B for a list of resources for this chapter.)

- **What should I do if I discover something that could be related to child maltreatment or neglect?** Given that abuse and neglect can negatively affect child development and may have long-term repercussions, it is important that you reach out if you suspect this type of concern. Contact your local Child Protective Services (CPS) office or law enforcement agency for help. CPS agencies have the resources to investigate the home situation and provide needed family supports. Another resource is the Childhelp National Child Abuse Hotline (available toll-free 24 hours a day, 7 days a week at 1-800-422-4453 or online at https://www.childhelp.org). They have professional crisis counselors with a database of 55,000 emergency, social services, and support resources. All calls are anonymous.

Share resources that they can refer to for more information. Let them know that this is a normal process that children go through to make sure they are on track in their development. A great source of information about developmental screening can be found on the CDC "Learn the Signs, Act Early" website. (See appendix B for a list of resources for this chapter.) The CDC even offers a free developmental milestone tracker that educators and families can use to monitor a child's development. In addition, the federal Birth to 5: Watch Me Thrive! program offers an online training course for early childhood educators. This free course provides excellent training on child development and discussing developmental milestones with parents. Details are available online. (See appendix B for a list of resources for this chapter.)

Once you have had the first conversation, engage families every step of the way, from explaining what developmental screening is to linking them to people and services that can help. Encourage families to talk to their child's health-care provider or early intervention specialist and share the results of the screening. You can even help them come up with questions they can ask their doctor as a result of the screening. Remember that families and cultures are unique, and we don't all place the same emphasis on reaching certain developmental milestones. In addition, different child-rearing practices and cultural norms may influence how and when a child reaches a given milestone. For example, in some cultures, it is not acceptable for children to make frequent eye contact with others. Be aware of these differences, and think about your own frame of reference as you decide how to communicate the information with the family.

EVALUATION

Evaluation is how we determine eligibility for services, while assessment gives us information about the child's strengths and needs so we can provide support in an ongoing way. For the purposes of determining eligibility for IDEA services, the law specifies that evaluations must be:

- Conducted with parent consent
- Timely, comprehensive, and multidisciplinary
- Conducted with qualified personnel
- Not culturally or racially discriminatory
- In the native language of the child
- Conducted so that no single source is used to determine eligibility

This last point is really important. When determining eligibility, it is critical that information is gathered from multiple sources, using multiple methods, across multiple domains of development. For example, a local school-system evaluation team might observe a child, interview the family, review the child's records, and reference questionnaires completed by the child's parents or caregiver.

Evaluation is also most effective when it occurs in partnership with the child's family. Evaluators should respect the information that families share because they know the child best. Information obtained from families is key to understanding the child's strengths and needs and for making informed decisions.

The IDEA law specifically requires that, for early childhood special education, the child must be assessed in "all areas related to the suspected disability, including, if appropriate, health, vision, hearing, social and emotional status, general intelligence, academic performance, communicative status, and motor abilities." This is important because the evaluation must be comprehensive enough to identify all of the child's special-education needs, even if they don't seem to be related to the disability category that led to the initial referral. All areas of suspected disability must be examined, so other professionals are often involved in the evaluation. For example, the child may be evaluated by speech and language therapists, occupational therapists, physical therapists, and others. While IDEA doesn't list specific tests that should be administered, it does set forth very clearly what kinds of tests should be used, how they should be given, and by whom. Tests should be given for the purposes for which they are designed and in accordance with the instructions provided by the publishers of the test. Families should also expect that tests are administered by trained and knowledgeable evaluation staff.

In addition, the IDEA, as well as position statements from professional organizations such as NAEYC and DEC, stress that the tools used in evaluations to determine eligibility should be administered in the child's home language and should take into consideration a child's culture. Tests should not discriminate on a racial or cultural basis. NAEYC and DEC have developed specific recommendations and guidance for the evaluation of children who are dual language learners. One key point is that evaluators should avoid making assumptions about data that is gathered through the evaluation process. "Many factors—anxiety, hunger, inability to understand the language of the instructions, culturally learned hesitation in initiating conversation with adults, and so on—may influence a child's performance, creating a gap between that performance and the child's actual ability, and causing staff to draw inaccurate conclusions" (NAEYC, 2003).

This careful process can take time. If the evaluation process is expected to be lengthy, families can request to have an interim IFSP or IEP so that services can begin.

ASSESSMENT

Once the evaluation is complete and the IFSP or IEP is in place, there is still a need to assess a child's growth and development in an ongoing way. Assessment is how we gather information to determine how a child is developing across domains and over time. This information is then used to plan an individualized approach for that child. How do we do that? Through careful observation. Planned and consistent use of observation is a critical form of assessment. Educators use assessment to gather information about each child to guide planning, including how best to individualize the curriculum and teaching. This could be toward a goal of ensuring that the learning environment will meet the child's needs or that the most effective teaching practices are implemented.

Educators can use assessment to learn about children's abilities and use that information to make decisions about what to observe next. We must decide how to organize, interpret, and use the information to guide and adjust our teaching practices, and we must seek input from families as we learn and share in an ongoing way. Think of it as an ongoing system to build and enhance the child's learning: we observe children and record what we see, then we reflect on that information to make adjustments to our curriculum, lesson plans, and teaching practices. And then it all starts over again with observing children and recording what we see. I know it sounds simple when these are just words on a page. It's not quite so simple when you are trying to juggle a classroom of children with many different needs, while keeping everyone safe, happy, and motivated to learn and discover. I remember days as an educator when just getting through lunchtime felt like an accomplishment! But I learned that if I just took a deep breath, got a good night of sleep, and approached the next day with a fresh perspective, I could get back into the groove and remember how fun it is to just be with children and see the world through their eyes.

"Curriculum and assessment are closely tied. Classroom- or home-based assessment tells teachers what children are like and allows them to modify curriculum and teaching practices to best meet the children's needs. Curriculum also influences what is assessed and how: for example, a curriculum that emphasizes the development of self-regulation should be accompanied by assessments of the children's ability to regulate their attention, manage strong emotions, and work productively without a great deal of external control" (NAEYC, 2003).

Children with disabilities or suspected delays depend on us to come to our work with a fresh perspective each day, ready to use our observation skills to learn about what they are able to do and to adjust our teaching practices accordingly. We can use assessment as a way to monitor progress toward IFSP or IEP goals, as well as the global child outcomes set for all children. If information gathered through assessment shows slow or no progress toward a goal, we can use the information to decide how to change our lesson plans and activities.

Gathering information over multiple points of time will help you determine if your changes in practice have promoted positive child outcomes. When a child has an IFSP or IEP, educators may need to collect assessment information about smaller learning steps to show progress and inform teaching practices. IFSP or IEP goals usually are based on progress that will be expected over the course of six months to a year. This can seem overwhelming, so breaking the goal down into smaller steps can be really helpful. The number of steps varies, depending on the child's needs and the nature of the goal. We will further explore the process of the teaching and learning cycle and breaking down goals in upcoming chapters, but keep in mind, educators are not alone in all of this! Early intervention and early childhood special-education staff are key partners in the assessment instruction cycle. Specialists can provide valuable support when a child with a disability needs specialized teaching techniques.

TYPES OF ASSESSMENTS

The word *assessment* often carries different meanings in different disciplines, even within the early childhood field. It is wise to question our assumptions when working with other team members, because the actual definition or intent of the word may vary depending on the context of the speaker and the purpose for which the term is used. You might encounter terms such as *ongoing assessment, developmentally appropriate assessment, authentic assessment, informal assessment, formal assessment, and functional assessment.* These terms can create confusion during conversations with specialists or special education staff. Let's explore a couple of these terms that particularly relate to the assessment of children with disabilities or suspected delays: *authentic assessment* and *functional behavior assessment.*

Authentic Assessment

Authentic assessment is based on the concept that we can learn the most about children when we observe them in their everyday routines and activities, rather than in a testing situation. As you may recall, Part C of IDEA requires that children be served in natural environments, so authentic assessment fits right within that framework. Observe children in real-world situations to get a better understanding about their strengths and needs. This is in sharp contrast to the stereotypical view of assessment: a professional dressed in a white coat taking notes on a clipboard as they watch a child play with a puzzle in a sterile conference room.

An educator using authentic assessment might watch as a child plays to learn about the child's ability to problem solve. Alternatively, the educator might observe a child as she builds with blocks and then might ask her questions about what she is building to assess her communication skills. Authentic assessment can also be used with observing self-help skills, such as the ability of a child to put on her own jacket. Watching a child in a classroom environment where there are expectations of "clean up and line up" can tell an assessor a great deal about the child's ability to follow multistep directions. In all of these examples, the children don't know that they are being assessed, so the behaviors or skills they exhibit are more likely to be a clearer picture of what they are actually capable of doing.

This type of assessment does have its challenges. For example, authentic assessment is difficult to do from a distance. When a child is homebound for health or other reasons, the educator would need to rely on the family for information on skills that might not occur on a home visit. This is also true for families who live in rural or difficult-to-reach locations, where it is just not possible for a home visit to take place as frequently as necessary. The recent experience of the COVID-19 pandemic has taught us a lot about assessment from a distance. Early intervention and special-education professionals learned to support families from a distance using technology. In some cases, the family might record the child using their cell phone and then upload the videos to an online platform so that the assessor could still observe the child in her natural environment. What worked well for you as you served as an early childhood educator during the COVID-19 pandemic? What lessons did you learn? These lessons are a silver lining to a dark cloud; they have taught us how to use technology in ways that will be helpful in years to come.

Functional Assessment

Functional assessment is a form of authentic assessment. It, too, is based on the principle that we collect the most accurate information about children during their everyday routines and transitions. Functional assessment uses authentic tasks in the context of a child's everyday routines, so that the assessor doesn't have to make any assumptions about the child's behaviors. All behaviors that are measured are the behaviors that the assessor observes directly. This type of assessment is also helpful when measuring functional child outcomes that are part of the IFSP/IEP process. It measures everyday behaviors in everyday activities and how the child is doing compared to peers their same age. In a functional assessment, the focus shifts from measuring specific skills in specific situations to a more complete functional picture of the child. For example, rather than assessing whether or not a child makes eye contact, smiles, or gives hugs to others, the functional assessment would focus on how the child initiates affection with people who are important in her life.

Functional assessment is also different from the conventional model in that it is performed by families and others who are knowledgeable members in the child's life, including early childhood educators. It is typically performed by a team of people who can observe the child engaged in many different types of behaviors in many natural contexts and settings. The team would then use their understanding of typical child development to assess whether or not the child's skills and behaviors are on target for what we would expect for a child of that age. This information is gathered over time, and family members play a huge role in the process.

Family members share their observations so that, when combined with information gathered through an educator's observations, a more complete and accurate picture of the child can be obtained. But are parent observations reliable? The answer is yes! In fact, Snyder, Thompson, and Sexton (1993) found that parents and professionals were highly consistent when they completed the same instruments intended to assess child development. The researchers came to the conclusion that family observations are reliable and valid and should be considered an essential part of a comprehensive assessment process. When EI or ECSE professionals involve families in functional assessment, they learn more about the child than if they had simply asked questions or reviewed developmental profiles.

Functional assessment techniques include observing child and parent interactions, asking families to describe everyday routines and activities, making portfolios accessible to families so that they can contribute to them, and listening to family stories. One teacher even included a basket at the sign-in table so that parents and families could drop off photos or notes as they signed their child in at the beginning of the day. This kind of data is far richer than data obtained through traditional methods. As a result, functional assessment is much more effective when developing the IFSP/IEP, planning services, or measuring change.

REFLECTION QUESTIONS

- What strategies work best for you to collect information when you observe young children?
- How might you engage the families in your program in a way that would foster collaborative observations?
- Which resources do you turn to when you have questions about a suspected developmental delay?
- How might you decide which screening tool to use in your program?
- Do you currently conduct regular developmental screenings? Are there resources in your community that could help?

RESOURCE SPOTLIGHT

If you'd like to learn more about assessment practices, take a look at these resources available on the ECTA Center website.

- **Practice Improvement Tools: Practice Guides for Practitioners:** These practice guides are intended primarily for practitioners working in group settings and for sharing with other practitioners in community programs. The practice guides are formatted for print as well as for viewing on mobile devices. There are even practice guides related to assessment practices, free to download.

- **Practice Improvement Tools: Performance Checklists:** These performance checklists are intended for educators to increase their understanding and use of the DEC recommended practices and for self-evaluation of their use of the practices. There are even checklists related to assessment practices, free to download. The practice guides and performance checklists are available in English and Spanish. (See appendix B for a list of resources for this chapter.)

CHAPTER 5

Working on IFSP or IEP Goals

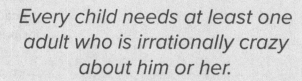

Every child needs at least one adult who is irrationally crazy about him or her.

**—URIE BRONFENBRENNER,
RESEARCHER IN HUMAN DEVELOPMENT
AND PSYCHOLOGY**

Now that you have some understanding of IDEA and the screening, evaluation, and assessment process, the next step is thinking about how to support IFSP or IEP goals in the early childhood environment. You might be thinking, "How can I do this on my own?" "Which practices should I use to help the child make progress?" "How do I fit this into an already busy day?" You can make it work for children and families by using two connected strategies: a transdisciplinary team approach and embedded learning opportunities. The good news is that you don't have to do this alone. You have a whole team of folks who care about the child right along with you, and this team can work together to support the child and family. This approach is known as the transdisciplinary team approach.

TRANSDISCIPLINARY TEAM APPROACH

The transdisciplinary team approach starts with putting families in the center of decision-making about which strategies to use to support children in reaching their goals. Families are part of the team, making decisions alongside EI or ECSE representatives, therapists, specialists, and early childhood educators. The transdisciplinary team approach is modelled in this same way. Team members share a common perspective regarding child development and supporting young children with disabilities or delays, and each member of the team brings his own expertise. Typically, one member of the team serves as the lead interventionist, who works most directly with the child and is most likely to provide activities specific to the child's needs and identified goals. This team member also receives coaching and guidance from other team members as needed. The team works together to build the capacity of parents, early childhood educators, and others in using everyday learning opportunities to encourage the development of the child's skills. The team plans the strategies to use by considering evidence-based practices, the unique needs of the child and family, and the priorities of the family.

As we explored in chapter 2, early childhood educators have an important role in the IFSP/IEP process. This role changes a bit when it is time to deliver services and work toward goals, but the perspective that the early educator brings to the team remains important. In Head Start programs, a disability-services coordinator helps to coordinate services and can serve as a liaison between the early intervention program or school district and the educator in the early childhood environment. In child-care settings, the center director may provide some of this coordination. Sometimes a consulting teacher or therapist from the EI or ECSE program works with the early childhood educator to help design specialized instruction, problem solve, and review child-progress information. Other times, the EI or ECSE program provides an itinerant (or visiting) teacher or therapist who regularly comes to the early childhood program to provide specialized instruction or therapy for a child or group of children as they make progress toward IEP goals. Itinerant teachers not only are available to provide direct services, but they also can provide consultation and professional development for families, teachers, directors, and support staff. This is a way to build your capacity to serve children with disabilities, and you may also learn strategies that are effective for children without disabilities. Early childhood educators find that itinerant EI or ECSE teachers are valuable members of the classroom. They can help you as you learn about new strategies and plan for ways to support the child in between visits.

> *"Alone we can do so little; together we can do so much."*
>
> **—HELEN KELLER**

Not all teams are created equal, and it is important to build in collaborative structures for the transdisciplinary team approach to be successful. Dunst and colleagues (2001a) reported that a successful team results in positive outcomes for children and families, but such success is dependent on several key components that also align with the DEC Recommended Practices domain regarding teaming and collaboration (2014).

What makes a team successful?

- The team includes individuals from multiple disciplines.
- Teams meet on a regular basis.
- The team has a clear and common purpose.
- One team member serves as the lead for the family.
- Family members are an integral part of the team.
- The team works together by combining knowledge, skills, and resources.
- Services are individualized for families in a respectful and culturally sensitive way.
- All members share responsibility for implementation of the IFSP or IEP.
- All members evaluate outcomes and make changes to the plan as necessary.

Fialka et al. (2021) emphasize the importance of relationships in providing care for children in inclusive programs: "Collaboration is the cornerstone to effective inclusive programs . . . . Forming partnerships between professionals and parents with children of special needs is like learning a new dance . . . . The real dance of partnership occurs when all listen to each other's music, try out each other's dance steps, and work toward a new dance that involves the contributions of partners." Shared responsibility is so important because, when team members use this approach, it is possible for the child to make progress on IFSP or IEP goals throughout the day, every day, regardless of the setting. The child is at home? Working toward goals! The child is in the Head Start program? Working toward goals! The child is in speech therapy? Working toward goals! Everyone is on the same page and is helping the child work toward his goals. This approach changes the intensity of the intervention equation.

And from the child's perspective, it is much less confusing because all of the adults in his life are consistent with how they provide support.

The following chart highlights how this strategy can result in much more time to practice for the child. It provides a breakdown of the amount of support two children receive over the course of a week, comparing pull-out therapy with support provided throughout the classroom routine. You can see that Michael receives one hour of pull-out therapy; Miguel receives three times that amount in his classroom setting, where educators prompt him to use his receptive-language skills to communicate during transitions and learning experiences even though he is not yet verbal.

| | MICHAEL | | MIGUEL | |
Day	Activity	Minutes	Activity	Minutes
Monday			• Points to his selection of breakfast items when asked, "Cereal or yogurt?" • Nods when his teacher ask if he is all done, wants more, of if he is enjoying his meal • Practices signing *more* when he wants more to eat at meal times • Makes finger and hand motions to fingerplays and songs at school	5 mins. 10 mins. 15 mins. 10 mins.
Tuesday	Points to picture cards and reads books with therapist	30 mins.	• Raises his arms when caregiver asks, "Can we change your diaper now?" • Brings his coat over when Mom says, "Let's go outside to check the mail." • Points to several animals when Dad makes their sounds during a bedtime story • Makes finger and hand motions to fingerplays and songs at school	5 mins. 5 mins. 15 mins. 10 mins.
Wednesday			• Makes finger and hand motions to fingerplays and songs at school • Points to his body parts when named during diaper change • Signs *more* during afternoon snack time • Raises his arms when caregiver asks, "Can we change your diaper now?"	10 mins. 10 mins. 5 mins. 5 mins.
Thursday	Points to picture cards and reads books with therapist	30 mins.	• Makes finger and hand motions to fingerplays and songs at school • Points to his choice when asked which T-shirt he prefers to wear: dinosaur or tractor • Points to the mouse on each page of *If You Give a Mouse a Cookie* during afternoon play time with his teacher • Raises his arms when caregiver asks, "Can we change your diaper now?"	10 mins. 5 mins. 15 mins. 5 mins.
Friday			• Practices signing *more* when he wants more to eat at meal times • Walks to his cubby when it is time to collect his things and leave with Mom, selects his coat and hands it to Mom • Raises his arms when caregiver asks, "Can we change your diaper now?" • Makes finger and hand motions to fingerplays and songs at school	15 mins. 5 mins. 10 mins. 10 mins.
Total time		1 hr.		3 hrs.

This "math" works for teaching social skills and expectations as well. Educators can use everyday routines to help children practice the skills they need to be able to communicate with others, manage their emotions, get along well with others, and engage in the learning environment in ways that will lead to success.

This is an elementary school example, but it still applies to early childhood. When Ricky was in third grade and the academic portion of school was really starting to heat up, I found that the pull-out services he was receiving were causing our family some grief. Homework time was a nightmare. Ricky would claim that he hadn't learned the concept because his teacher had taught that lesson when he was pulled out of the classroom for special services. As a parent, I was worried about how much of the regular curriculum he was missing during these pull-out sessions. Then think about it from his point of view. Every child wants to fit in to some degree, and Ricky definitely hated being singled out when his teacher called him to go off into the separate group for IEP services. Children in preschool also need to experience the full range of the curriculum, and they should benefit from additional supports without feeling that they're being singled out.

We sometimes hear about families who feel the need to advocate for an extra session of one-on-one specialized services for their child. This may very well be needed, but another option could be for a specialist to work with the child's classroom teacher, home visitor, or parent to embed activities throughout the routine of the day. This doesn't mean every minute of the day, but you can see from the previous example that the child could potentially have many more opportunities to practice and master skills to reach milestones and desired outcomes with an embedded approach. An additional benefit is that the child then may more easily generalize the skills when they are learned and practiced during regular, everyday activities.

Let's explore this further. If we consider that an advantage to this approach is that the child is able to generalize skills from one setting to another, what might that look like in real life? Let's use the speech-therapy example. Sam is working on the use of rhyming words such as *hat* and *cat*. He would certainly practice that skill during speech therapy, but with the transdisciplinary approach, he is also practicing at home and in child care as well. Sam points to his furry friend and says, "Cat!" and his mother says, "Yes! Cat! What rhymes with *cat*, Sam?" The next day, Sam walks into his preschool classroom and his teacher is wearing a silly hat. Sam points and says, "Hat!" His teacher says, "Yes! Hat! What rhymes with *hat*, Sam?" Now, Sam is thinking about words that rhyme across all the settings and with all the people who are important in his life. He has lots of opportunities to practice new skills.

This approach is also empowering for the family because family members are an essential part of the team. They have the most knowledge about the child, are the constant in the child's life, and will be the decision-makers when choices about services are presented. The specialist empowers the parent and other members of the team by providing information about the child's condition and practical strategies to facilitate the child's development.

Early intervention and special education specialists benefit from this approach as well because they are able to serve in more of a consulting role to support and provide resources to early childhood educators and families. Specialists can use their time to:

- provide services to a child within the program or classroom;
- share information about a particular disability with the family or early childhood educator;
- provide information about typical child development;
- give suggestions for activities to embed learning into the daily routine, activities, or transitions;
- demonstrate therapeutic techniques;
- observe children and provide feedback;
- suggest available resources or related services in the community; and
- answer questions and provide written information and resources.

Efforts to coordinate service delivery in this way will likely vary depending on the needs of the family, but this approach has shown that working together is better. Teams have found that, through this coordination, they have been able to discover new and better ways for meeting the needs of the child and family. Once roles are determined, it works best to put any specific agreements into writing, so that the specialist, family, and early education provider understand the expectations. The team may also decide to review agreements on a regular basis to make sure that all partners are on the same page. I can personally attest that a team approach really works! As a parent, it felt extremely supportive to have several people whom I could connect with if I had questions about my son's progress toward his IEP goals.

EMBEDDED LEARNING OPPORTUNITIES: WHAT, WHEN, AND HOW

Having a team is amazing from the family perspective. But for an early educator, the approach can seem daunting. How can we find time to work on IFSP or IEP goals when our days are filled with activities, routines, and transitions? Let's dig deeper into the what, when, and how of embedded learning opportunities.

Embedded learning opportunities provide a way to address IFSP or IEP goals during naturally occurring classroom routines, activities, and transitions, such as free-play time, circle time, learning centers, outdoor play, or even meal and snack time. This happens through short teaching episodes that can be used in many different ways for a variety of purposes, including supports for children who may need more structured and frequent opportunities to practice a skill. These short teaching episodes are an important component to what Haring and colleagues (1978) refer to as the *learning cycle*.

"Children are the living messages we send to a time we will not see."

—NEIL POSTMAN, AUTHOR AND EDUCATOR

The learning cycle is "a sequential process for both learning and instruction. It places focus on a series of steps that encourage a more thorough understanding and a deeper application of content. The learning cycle gives teachers a process for instruction while giving students a formula for learning. The learning cycle has four stages: acquisition, fluency, maintenance, and generalization." (Haring et al., 1978)

- **Acquisition** is the stage of the learning cycle when the child has begun to learn how to complete a target skill correctly but is not yet accurate or fluent in the skill. The goal in this phase is to improve accuracy.
- **Fluency** is the stage when child is able to complete the target skill accurately but works slowly. The goal of this phase is to increase the child's speed of responding.
- **Maintenance** describes the stage when the child is accurate and fluent in using the target skill but does not typically use it in different situations or settings.
- **Generalization** is the stage when the child is accurate and fluent in using the skill. However, the child is not yet able to modify or adapt the skill to fit novel task demands or situations. Here the goal is for the child to be able to identify elements of previously learned skills that they can adapt to the new demands or situation.

(Haring et al., 1978; ECTA, 2020c)

Children move to the generalization stage of the learning cycle most efficiently when educators and families use embedded instruction. Rakap and Parlak-Rakap (2011) found that embedded instruction is an effective practice for teaching a range of skills, including social interaction and communication skills, to children with disabilities in inclusive preschool programs. Additionally, they found that children who learned skills during embedded learning opportunities were able to demonstrate those skills in settings outside the classroom, while engaging in different activities with different people. And they were able to keep up those skills over time! Snyder and colleagues (2015) found that embedded instruction is beneficial in supporting children's learning because it:

- requires minimal changes to existing routines;
- maximizes motivation by following children's interests;
- highlights functional skills; and
- enhances generalization by targeting skills used in natural contexts with a variety of people and materials.

The researchers found that embedded learning opportunities benefits families too.

- Family routines may be considered in the plan.
- Learning objectives are reinforced throughout the day.

- Families are empowered as partners.
- Targeting skills used in natural contexts with a variety of people and materials and in a variety of settings enhances generalization.

The approach of embedded learning opportunities just makes practical sense. If children learn in natural environments and through activities, routines, and transitions, then we should take the learning opportunities to those settings. How can we build learning opportunities around activities, routines, and transitions? It starts with tapping into children's interests and preferences so that they are engaged and more likely to be successful. How do we find out what children are interested in? We observe them and notice the activities that they tend to gravitate toward. We also can ask families. Dunst, Herter, and Shields (2000) suggest these questions as a way to find out about children's interests and preferences from the people who know them best:

- What are your child's favorite things?
- What makes your child laugh?
- What makes your child feel good?
- What gets and keeps your child's attention?
- What gets your child to try new things?

When you find out the answers to these questions and carefully observe the child yourself, you'll be able to create what Dunst and colleagues call an interest profile. This is valuable information! In fact, Odom and colleagues (2000) found that children participating in their own interests and activities are significantly more engaged than when they are participating in adult-directed activities. Embedded learning opportunities capitalize on that engagement. So, how do you make it happen in real life? Educators who successfully use embedded learning opportunities make sure to:

- focus on priority skills—behaviors we want to create, change, or enhance;
- teach skills within context;
- teach within and across activities, routines, and transitions;
- use authentic activities and materials to support learning;
- use ongoing assessment to monitor child progress and partner with families to add to their understanding about a child's development and interests; and
- share strategies with families so they can support their child's development at home.

One way to think about this is to break the process down into steps, considering the what, when, and how of the teaching process.

- **What do we teach?** functional, meaningful, and measurable learning goals
- **When do we teach?** during planned and unplanned learning activities, routines, and transitions

- **How do we teach?** through experiences that promote engagement, learning, and mastery
- **How do we monitor progress?** by evaluating outcomes

WHAT WE TEACH

Determining the "what" of this cycle can be easy to identify if the child already has functional, meaningful, and measurable learning goals from the IFSP or IEP. These goals inform what we teach, but we may need to break down a particular goal into smaller steps. Also called "learning targets," these goals are the behaviors that we want to create, change, or enhance. For example, a mother may share that mealtimes are especially challenging now that her infant is transitioning to solid foods. Mom is hoping that her baby will explore new tastes and textures. Another example is the child who is struggling with transitions, and the parent and educator are hoping to implement strategies that will support the child as he moves from one activity to the next. This feedback, in addition to goals and objectives in an IFSP/IEP, inform the learning target. We can then plan for opportunities to work on those learning targets within everyday activities and naturally occurring routines.

We can use the SMART approach when thinking about learning targets for children.

SMART goals were first introduced as an approach to goal-setting in business by Doran, Miller, and Cunningham (1981) in *Management Review* magazine. You might have used this approach for setting goals for yourself. SMART stands for:

- **Specific:** target a specific area for improvement
- **Measurable:** quantify or at least suggest an indicator of progress
- **Achievable:** choose a target that the child will be able to achieve
- **Relevant:** work on a target that is relevant to the child's life
- **Time-bound:** specify when the result(s) can be achieved

Learning targets should be just as "smart" as any New Year's resolution! For example, I will ride my stationary bike for thirty minutes three times per week from now until March. This will strengthen my stamina so I'll be ready to go bike-riding with my children when we go on our spring break vacation.

- **Specific:** Ride the bike.
- **Measurable:** 30 minutes 3 times per week
- **Achievable:** 30 minutes isn't that long, right?
- **Relevant:** I'll be ready to join my kids in a fun activity.
- **Time-bound:** will last from January to March

But what if you have a learning target that seems too big? One strategy is to think about the first step of the behavior that would be within the child's zone of proximal development. Do you remember Vygotsky from your Introduction to Child Development courses? Vygotsky (1978) taught us about the *zone of proximal development*, which is the concept of providing just enough help and support for the child to be successful in taking that first step. Gradually the child develops the ability to do a task without help, but it all starts with a first achievable step toward the skill. Learning targets can be broken down in a number of ways:

RESOURCE SPOTLIGHT

Check out a video called "Break It Down: Turning Goals into Everyday Teaching Opportunities" from the Head Start fifteen-minute in-service suite, available online. (See appendix B for a list of resources for this chapter.)

- **Start with smaller amounts**: For example, if the goal is for Kaitlin to participate in circle time each day, we might start with the goal of five minutes of participation, and then increase the amount of time as she becomes more comfortable with the expectations of the activity. If a goal for Michael is to learn ten new words, you might start with learning two new words and build from there.

- **Provide help**: For example, if Joaquin is learning to pour milk into his cereal, we might start by putting our hands over his hands while he pours. Over time, we can provide less help until, eventually, he learns how to pour all by himself.

- **Take it step by step**: For example, if River is working on developing relationships with peers, we might break down the steps of asking another friend to play. It starts by gently tapping a friend on the shoulder and asking, "Would you like to play?" From that first step, River can build his skills by then learning how to suggest play activities, share toys with friends, and so on.

- **Use a logical order or sequence:** For example, if Jody is learning the complicated skill of riding a tricycle, we can break down that larger skill into the underlying sequence of skills. She would start by getting on the tricycle, then putting her feet on the pedals and hands on the handles. Next, she would push down on the right pedal and then the left, and so on.

WHEN WE TEACH

The "when" of the teaching and learning cycle occurs during planned learning activities, routines, and transitions. For children in early childhood environments, these are the regular routines of the day, such as mealtime, circle time, center time, outdoor play, and even diapering time for infants and toddlers. The educator and family can plan the schedule knowing that the child has an interest and need for exposure to that experience. At home, these routines are everyday family routines, such as mealtime, bath time, and playtime with siblings or neighborhood peers. For example, if a goal for seven-month-old Clara is that she will roll from her back to her tummy, then we need to plan learning experiences that promote that behavior. We need to plan time when she can be on the floor to use and strengthen her core muscles. The adults in Clara's life may need to prompt her to roll over with verbal encouragement or by placing a favorite toy nearby that she can access if she rolls over to get it. The floor time would take place in the early childhood environment during regular playtime and could also occur during a therapy session when the therapist comes to visit. Her family members would also plan time and find a safe space to regularly encourage floor time for Clara at home.

An advantage of this approach is that we are able to teach skills within the context of everyday life. We can remain present with children and be in the moment while still taking advantage of an opportunity within the natural course of the day to reinforce a learning goal. For example, if Matthew has a goal to use one or two words expressively, we can make time during periods of play to model and reinforce common phrases such as, "That's mine," or "More please," or "I did it!" We can use these phrases during mealtimes, diaper changing, and dressing to reinforce them.

This type of learning feels more authentic and can be based on the child's preferences and interests. The other advantage of this approach is that we can be strategic about the time of day that children will be most receptive to learning new skills. Zelda might be more likely to engage with her physical therapist if the session is scheduled for after nap time when she is well rested. The therapy might be most effective in a quiet part of the room with one-on-one interactions. Another child might want to practice during free play or with the company of peers. We can support families to identify their child's interests, scheduling considerations and typical activities and then use team planning time to decide how to embed those learning opportunities into the routines, activities, and transitions.

HOW WE TEACH

The "how" of the teaching and learning cycle refers to the strategies or teaching practices we use to support the child's progress toward goals. We seek to learn the strategies that will work for the individual child by talking with families, exploring evidence-based practices, and, in some cases, through trial and error. We try out learning experiences that promote engagement, learning, and mastery based on where children are developmentally, what their interests are, and what they are doing during the course of the day through hands-on exploration and practice. We follow the child's lead and work together with families to reinforce skill development in the same way across the home and group settings. We also make sure our practices are culturally and linguistically responsive. Do we know key phrases in the home languages to support children? What other information do we need to gather so that we can ensure we are responsive to a child's culture and language? How can we align our practices with strategies the family uses at home and vice versa?

A first step in embedding interventions is to think about how the interventions can fit into the child and family routine. A useful tool for organizing embedded learning opportunities is the activity planning matrix.

The following is an example of a planning matrix for a child named Tamiya. The left column lists the activities that make up the child's everyday routine. The middle column lists the specific adaptation, modification, and/or teaching strategy to support Tamiya. The column on the right indicates the person who will be responsible for ensuring the adaptations or modifications take place. In this example, when Tamiya arrives at school, her teacher will greet her and give her a choice of two activities to start the day.

The activity matrix can be a helpful way to organize teaching and learning opportunities. You can find blank forms online for free on the Head Start Center on Inclusion site. (See appendix B for a list of resources for this chapter.) Educators and families can use this tool as a visual reminder to take advantage of all the potential learning opportunities that occur each day. All children benefit from this type of approach, but it can be especially useful for children who need extra support or practice.

RESOURCE SPOTLIGHT

Head Start has developed a series of fifteen-minute in-service suites related to the topic of embedded learning opportunities. One of the suites, "Activity Matrix: Organizing Learning Throughout the Day," can be helpful for learning more about the use of the activity matrix. You can find it online. (See appendix B for a list of resources for this chapter.)

Routines and Activities	Adaptation, Modification, and/or Teaching Strategy for Tamiya's Transitions	Adult Responsible
Arrival	• Greet Tamiya on arrival. • Show Tamiya visual cues to choose between two play choices. • Support Tamiya's choice by physically joining her in her play until she is settled.	Teacher
Morning meal		
Morning play time		
Lunch		
Diapering/toileting		
Afternoon play time		
Afternoon snack		
Pickup		

Embedded Learning

1. Identify behaviors and skills the child needs to learn in order to participate in everyday classroom activities.

2. Observe the child in different activities to determine which behavior would be useful and important for promoting the child's engagement and independence in the activities.

3. Select a target behavior that builds on the child's current capabilities.

4. Examine the home and program schedule to identify those activities and routines that would provide opportunities for the child to use the target behavior.

5. Select times of the day and activities or routines during which the behavior likely would occur as a natural part of participation. Embed learning opportunities across different activities and routines that are of interest to the child.

6. Arrange the environment in ways that ensure the child's engagement in the selected activities and cue the child to the target behavior.

7. Provide the child assistance to ensure success when doing the target behavior.

8. Provide the child enough time and only as much support as needed to do the target behavior. Decrease the amount of assistance as the child learns the target behavior.

9. Respond positively to the child's use of the target behavior.

10. Provide the child multiple opportunities to use the target behavior in different activities throughout the day.

(ECTA, 2020b)

How do we know if we are heading in the right direction? When will we know if we are successful? How can we monitor progress? The activity planning matrix can be a helpful tool for these questions as well, and you could add another column to the table to record how well the child was able to accomplish the task. Some educators even include a numerical scale (1–5, for example) to assign a rating to how well the child was able to accomplish the skill. Over time, it can be helpful to see the increase in the ratings as the child builds skills and develops more and more competence.

Now that we have a basic structure in place for teaming, collaboration, and embedding interventions, we can explore ways that parents and educators can use the learning environment and inclusive teaching practices to support children as they work toward educational and developmental goals. We will do that in chapter 6.

REFLECTION QUESTIONS

- What can I do to embed effective, evidence-based teaching practices into the everyday routine?

- What are some strategies I could use to incorporate time for social engagement into the routine?

- How might I change my practice to make it more likely that all children are supported in working toward their goals?

CHAPTER 6

Inclusive Learning Environments

We make it our job to create, with reverence and gratitude, a space that is worthy of a miracle.

—ANITA RUI OLDS, FOUNDER OF THE CHILD CARE DESIGN INSTITUTE

Young children are truly miraculous. Like Anita Olds, we should design their environments with reverence and gratitude. This perspective also can help us think about learning environments with appreciation for children's strengths and interests that will provide opportunities for growth and learning. This kind of reflection is an important practice for early educators to consider for all children, including children with disabilities, who will likely benefit from an individualized approach to the design of the learning environment. This was certainly the case for my own son, who approached learning differently from the other children in his class.

Ricky was diagnosed with ADHD very early on. I have been to more IEP meetings than I can count. The ADHD affected his learning in many ways. For example, in preschool, you might walk in the classroom to find all the children sitting in circle time, while Ricky was underneath a desk examining the hardware. From the start, he was always super-inquisitive, "into things," as they say, his curiosity on overdrive. At home, I kept him close by me to make sure he didn't get into danger, and he always wanted to help me with daily chores. I tried to put him to work in every way that I could think of.

I'll never forget the time, right after we came home from Ukraine, that my friends from work sent me a toy for Ricky. The toy was a plastic tower with a ball that you could drop into the top, and the ball would spin 'round and 'round until it got to the bottom. This seemed like the perfect toy for my little scientist! I put it together and showed Ricky how it worked. "See, Ricky! You drop in the ball here, and then you can watch it go around and around to the bottom!" He dropped the ball in one time, watched it go around and around, and then took the whole thing apart. Why couldn't he just play with it the way that you were supposed to? The package on the front showed two children playing with the tower and delighting in the way that the ball rolled around and around to the bottom. Why was my child different? Why didn't he follow the rules? Looking back, the whole thing seems really silly, and the toy must have been boring to him. But at the time, I just wanted him to be okay. I worried that by not following the "rules" of the toy, it would lead to a lifetime of waving away the rules. My sweet early childhood friends said, "Don't worry about it, Jani! Let him play with it however he wants to!" Sure, that would be okay at home, I thought, but what about at school? Would the preschool learning environment accommodate this lack of structure that he seems to favor?

Preschool was a challenge in many ways. His teachers complained that he was wandering off during group activities. He mostly played alone and didn't engage in pretend play. When the class activities became a bit rowdy, he became *too* rowdy. In kindergarten, the challenges were heightened because the expectations increased. When Ricky was engaged in active play at school, it was all good. But sitting at a desk all day? Not so much. He didn't see the point in doing something that wasn't interesting. Exploring critters in the dirt on the playground? Interesting. Sitting at a desk and coloring? Not interesting. To do well in school, the ability to concentrate and focus is essential. For Ricky, the school environment was just not that interesting, and his ability to concentrate on the uninteresting stuff was pretty much nonexistent. Later, we learned that he had fine motor delays as well that affected his ability to hold a pencil or even a crayon. No wonder coloring wasn't very fun! Do you tend to gravitate toward things that are difficult? Most of us do not. My son was no exception.

On one of his first days in kindergarten, I took him into class and was planning to volunteer for a while that day. The teacher showed me that she had put Ricky's desk far away from the other children because he was very "distractible," and she felt that he distracted the others. There was my sweet child, off in the corner by himself. *This is not inclusion*, I thought. To make matters worse, the teacher had given the children a worksheet to do. Mind you, they couldn't read, and she didn't explain it, but there they were with worksheets and pencils. Ricky looked at the paper and looked at the pencil, wrote a few scribbles, and then looked up at me with the most worried face and asked, "Mommy, is this right?" It was awful. No child should experience that level of uncertainty about his own competence in kindergarten. I believe that those early years were the most challenging of all for Ricky. He decided early on that he didn't like school.

In later years, when I read over the stories in my journal and remembered the wise comments he made as a small boy or how keenly he noticed and responded to the world around him, I felt so sad. Before Ricky entered school, he was engaged with the world, learning, laughing, and growing. Then he went to school. They took my smart, inquisitive child and made him sit in a chair for hours on end. He was faced with all kinds of things that he couldn't do well—again and again and again. Fortunately, my son is resilient and succeeded in spite of the challenges. We switched schools and connected with caring and knowledgeable educators, and the situation did improve. School was never easy for Ricky, but he worked hard and his persistence paid off. Once he graduated from high school, Ricky was able to concentrate on learning about the things that interest him. He still likes to take things apart, but now he gets paid to do so! A few years ago, he graduated from a program at a community college where he learned how to fix giant diesel engines like those found in farm and construction equipment. Ricky works as a mechanic, and he loves his job.

As early childhood educators, we often have opportunities to think differently about education. Children with disabilities or suspected delays need us to do just that. They need us to design their learning environments in ways that consider the child's perspective, with activities that are individualized for the diverse learning styles that young children bring to the program. In the following pages, we'll explore strategies for how you can create learning environments that are accessible and engaging for all learners. We'll discuss how to use concepts such as universal design to make decisions in your program, how to intentionally think about learning spaces, and how to incorporate assistive technology and other strategies to accommodate for various learning styles. All of this is possible! And it begins with those three defining features of inclusion: access, participation, and support.

ACCESS, PARTICIPATION, AND SUPPORT REVISITED

The three defining features of inclusion—access, participation, and support—can guide us as we create individualized learning experiences. Access is all about providing a wide range of activities and environments for every child by removing physical barriers and offering multiple ways to promote learning and development. This could be realized through the use of principles of universal design for learning (UDL) (CAST, 2008).

ACCESS

Developed by the Center for Applied Special Technology (CAST), UDL is based on the understanding that children learn in different ways. Therefore, educators should use multiple methods for imparting information, multiple ways of asking children to share and demonstrate what they are learning, and multiple ways of engaging children. Children have choices for activities so that learning is based on their interests. Rather than a single approach that will accommodate everyone, UDL is all about providing multiple ways to learn to meet the needs of diverse learners. UDL is a framework that can help educators think differently about expectations for how children learn, engage with the environment, and show competence. There will always be children who need individual accommodations and supports. Using a UDL framework creates an environment that is ready for every child. It is about ensuring that each and every child is able to access the entire learning environment.

PARTICIPATION

Participation is achieved by using a range of instructional approaches to promote engagement in play and learning activities and a sense of belonging for every child. This suggests active teaching strategies so that children have lots of opportunities throughout the day to work toward individual goals as outlined in their IFSPs or IEPs.

Key Questions in Universal Design for Learning

- **Multiple means of engagement:** How do you provide options for children to be engaged and motivated to learn?

- **Multiple means of representation:** How do you present information so all children can perceive and understand it?

- **Multiple means of expression:** How do you provide opportunities for all children to show what they have learned?

SUPPORT

Supports are essential to high-quality inclusion. Providing children with access to the general learning environment is important, and ensuring that they are actively and meaningfully participating in high-quality learning opportunities is key, but those two features are not enough. Supports for educators, such as professional development, opportunities for collaborative teaming and mentoring, and access to resources and supplies, set up the overall climate for an educator to be successful. Without these supports, high-quality inclusion is not possible. Let's zoom in and explore the finer points of an inclusive learning environment.

DEFINING AN INCLUSIVE LEARNING ENVIRONMENT

Individualization depends on engaging and accessible environments and age-appropriate equipment, materials, supplies, and physical spaces. Waxman, Alford, and Brown (2013) define *individualization* as the idea that each child learns differently, so we need to personalize instruction and learning environments to match the experiences and interests of the child. Learning also takes

The ECTA Early Care and Education Environments Indicators of High-Quality Inclusion detail the key elements necessary for implementing high-quality inclusive practices in early childhood settings. They are designed to assist educators in providing effective supports and services to young children with disabilities and are intended to enhance high-quality inclusive practices implemented by early care and education staff. You can access the early care and education environments indicators online. You'll also find indicators for other parts of the system, including state, community, and program-level indicators.

The Inclusive Classroom Profile is another tool that can be used to assess the learning environment and educator practices with a lens focused on supporting the developmental needs of children with disabilities in early childhood settings. (See appendix B for a list of resources for this chapter.)

place within the context of the relationships we have with others. Developmentally appropriate schedules, lesson plans, and other experiences that staff and families can alter to make necessary accommodations to support all children, especially those with disabilities or suspected delays, are crucial.

The environment is really more than just the physical space. We can think about it in three different ways:

- **Physical environment:** space, equipment, and materials
- **Social environment:** interactions with peers, siblings, adults, and family
- **Temporal environment:** adjusting the sequence and length of routines, experiences, and activities

The physical environment is what we usually think of when we are talking about the learning environment. We must also include the social environment and the temporal environment. We don't always think about the environment in this way, but when we consider how we can make our programs accessible for each and every child, this perspective is key. Individualized programming really depends on an engaging and accessible environment on all three levels.

PHYSICAL ENVIRONMENT

The physical environment can create excitement about learning; it can also offer a peaceful place for reflection and contemplation. Ultimately, the physical environment should be a place where children not only feel safe but also feel comfortable expressing themselves. It should be a place where children can be creative and can take risks and challenge themselves as they learn and grow. The environment should communicate to children that they are important and that their thoughts, interests, and ideas matter to those around them. Young children need different types of spaces to promote physical, social, emotional, cognitive, and language development. Every area in the learning environment should be designed to offer activities and materials that prompt children to explore, experiment, and interact in different ways. The environment itself can be a powerful communicator. It can communicate safety, but it also can communicate the expectations for the early childhood environment or home.

Think about an early childhood environment or a home that you recently visited, or think about your own home or classroom. What does that physical space communicate to you? Now think about this from a child's perspective. For example, you may have pictured an environment with labeled cubbies right at the entrance to the classroom. From a child's perspective, this may communicate that there is a space for her here, a space for her personal things. Maybe you pictured a wide-open classroom or a long hallway that might communicate to a child that running is okay. The layout of the environment alone can communicate to children and can even influence children's behavior. The environment can be set up to help keep children safe, clarify routines and expectations, and promote feelings of ownership and belonging: This space belongs to all of us.

I remember visiting a program years ago where the toddler room felt sterile and bare to me. Where was the life? the fun? the energy? The educators showed me that the electrical outlets had covers on them and pointed out the handwashing practices shown on a poster above the sink. All good, but the space just didn't feel like a cozy place where you would want to hang out or a fun place to play. I couldn't imagine that parents would want to linger there with their child or that the toddlers themselves were very engaged in the space. Fortunately, it didn't take much more than some child-made artwork, family photos, and plants, along with soft cushions and snuggly blankets in a cozy corner, to make the space much more inviting. The teacher really got into the transformation and taught me a few

things as well. One cool thing that she did was to spray the scent of lavender along the doorframe every morning, because it was a calming scent to her and she wanted the children in her class to associate that calming scent with the classroom. Now, I know that's not a strategy for everyone and certainly not if we have children who are sensitive to scents, but it was something that really helped to define the environment and make it a cozy and welcoming place. This teacher knew that the physical environment should engage all of our senses—not just what we see, but also what we smell, hear, and touch.

SAFETY

Consider safety first. Educators should be able see what is happening in all areas of the classroom. Set up traffic patterns to discourage running, and define boundaries using furniture, rugs, or similar items. It is also crucial that children have the opportunity to take risks and challenge themselves. Children need these opportunities so that they can discover their own strengths and abilities and can practice new skills. Adults who give children these opportunities find that it is rare to see children taking risks beyond what they are ready for or what they are capable of doing (Almon, 2013). Often, we find that children with disabilities are coddled or overprotected, and that gets in the way of their ability to become independent and develop confidence in their abilities.

For example, Benji has cerebral palsy, and his father worries that he will get hurt while playing on the playground. However, he learned from the physical therapist that Benji needs opportunities to use his muscles so he will know his own physical limitations.

Now, Benji's dad stands back and watches him play rather than rushing in to help or holding his hand while he goes down the slide. He tries to stay out of view sometimes so that Benji will rely on his own judgement rather than always looking to him for reassurance. His dad also holds back and no longer says, "Be careful!" when Benji tries something new. Benji goes down the slide by himself and is much more confident while playing outside. Each child is unique, so it may take some time to find that right balance of "just right" amount of support.

Thinking about the physical space is especially important if you have children with mobility issues in your class. Are there clear paths between activity areas? Are rugs secured so that wheelchairs, crutches, or even little feet don't get caught on the edges? Children with visual impairments might benefit from having a tactile path they can touch as they move from one area to another. This may be made up of furniture, such as a shelving unit or bookcase, that is positioned in a way that helps children navigate. Or you could provide different floor coverings that mark the borders of the different areas in the classroom. This provides children with a degree of independence as well as safety. The photo on the previous page shows a school hallway that has been turned into a tactile pathway to explore!

LEARNING SPACES

Appeal to different kinds of learners by offering classroom areas that speak to variety and capitalize on the developmental needs, preferences, and interests of the children in the group. In each learning space, provide enough information about what to do there and how to play. Mark off each classroom area with bright tape or a textured rug underneath to indicate the boundaries of the area. This adaptation helps to communicate expectations and may be helpful as an enhanced cue for children with visual impairments.

Quiet spaces allow children to self-regulate and pull back from the environment if they need to refocus or regroup. They also offer children "breathing room" away from others, a chance to engage with books or magazines, or a chance to talk quietly with friends. Make sure to space quiet areas apart from noisy areas as much as possible.

SENSORY INPUT

Try using natural light and lamps instead of harsh overhead lights. My son and children in my own preschool classroom had sensory issues that made the harsh lighting in a typical classroom overstimulating. If you have a child with sensory issues in your classroom, visit the areas of the room at the child's level to help you to become more aware of the surroundings. Sit on the floor in an area of the classroom during the day, and ask

yourself, "How does it feel in my body to be here? Is it loud? too bright? too crowded?" This practice of considering the child's perspective can go a long way toward improving your practice.

MATERIALS

Take some time to assess the physical environment to determine how you might modify it to meet the needs of the current group of children in the classroom. Does it feel cozy and homelike? Are the cultures of the children in the classroom represented? Do you provide items for the different developmental levels of the children in the group? Are there duplicates of favorite items? Are there enough but not too many? Are items labelled so children know where they belong when it's clean-up time? Do you provide relevant books and writing materials in every area? Are there items that match children's interests?

MOVEMENT

Circle-time activities provide important opportunities for children to learn to listen to others, express themselves, and be respectful of physical space. However, these activities can be stressful for some children, because sitting still and focusing on the words of others are complicated skills that three- to five-year-old children are just learning. Keep circle time brief, no longer than fifteen minutes. Allow children who are fidgety to use fidget toys to help them focus, or they can try sitting on a wiggle seat or wobble cushion so that their bodies can move a bit while their minds work to focus. Carpet

squares are inexpensive and can help children to stay within their own boundary during group time activities.

Appeal to the sense of sound through music activities where children can sing, hum, make up silly words to a song, clap their hands, or play a musical instrument. Children may want to engage their bodies with music by swaying, dancing alone or with friends, or just by clapping their hands. Find ways that children of every ability can engage with the music in their own way.

Open spaces encourage music, movement, and freedom of expression. This can be in the classroom or home, but it also can be outdoor space. The music and movement area should be large enough for children to move around freely. You might want to include props that encourage different types of movement, like a parachute or large plastic hoops.

KEY CONSIDERATIONS FOR ADAPTING THE PHYSICAL ENVIRONMENT

Children with disabilities may or may not need modifications to the physical environment or adaptations of materials. We should always start with the assumption that all children are competent in every way, regardless of whether a child has an IFSP or IEP. Some children do need small changes to the curriculum or minor supports to get the most out of certain activities. A barrier might be a simple issue—stored materials may be hard to reach for some children—or more personalized—a child might have difficulty using the materials or following directions. In these cases, it is helpful to explore ways to increase the child's access to materials and increase participation in learning activities. The following four strategies are ones that you can think about when you design the physical environment using UDL principles to meet the needs of every child:

- Provide optimal positioning.
- Modify the response.
- Stabilize materials.
- Offer larger or brighter materials.

> *"All children are born with the disposition to make sense of their experiences."*
>
> **—LILIAN KATZ, EARLY CHILDHOOD RESEARCHER AND EDUCATOR**

Provide Optimal Positioning

Think about the child who uses a walker to walk. Can she reach all the materials in the classroom? Can she maneuver effectively between the centers? What about at home? What is the best position for a child to be able to participate in circle time? This photo shows a child using a supportive chair at circle time. Clearly, that teacher took the time to consider his perspective and found a way for him to be included as part of the group. Teachers might also want to offer several supportive chairs like this one so that his peers could use them as well, and the child won't feel singled out. There's no reason that the accommodation has to be for that one child. It can also be useful to consider a child's preferences. For example, if a child prefers to lie down during an activity, selecting an accommodation that allows her to participate while in that position may be just what you need to increase participation.

We can also think about the position of materials as a way to promote access and engagement. As you know, I am a very petite lady, so optimal position is an easy principle for me to understand. I have a step stool in pretty much every room of my house. Thinking about my own experience helped me to consider the environment from a child's perspective and our desire to promote their independence. Consider how you place materials so children can access them without having to ask for help.

Modify the Response

Is there only one right way to do things? Of course not! You can individualize the environment by being open to a variety of ways to do things and to use materials. For example, when tying shoes is too difficult, there's Velcro. If you have a child in your class who is nonverbal but is able to move

her fingers, perhaps she could use a switch device to press a button to communicate with you. She might also benefit from using visuals such as a Picture Exchange Communication System (PECS), which is a strategy that is used widely in K–12 special education. PECS is a set of pictures that represent items or actions used frequently during the course of an everyday routine. A child can point to the pictures as a way of communicating with peers or adults. The use of visuals is a great way to modify response.

We can individualize the environment by being open to the fact that there is a variety of ways to accomplish tasks and use materials. Some children with sensory issues might not like fingerpainting, for example. The feeling of the paint on their fingers is just too icky. In that case, painting with a cup, a dowel with a

sponge attached, a small toy car, or a cotton ball might increase their comfort level. We can change our perspective and realize that there is not just one way to do something.

There are also many ways to show knowledge of how to do something, an idea that uses the UDL approach and the component of multiple means of expression. When we want a child to communicate something to us, we can be open to all types of communication: sign language, pictures, electronic communication devices, gesturing, nodding, and so on. This is also referred to as *augmentative and alternative communication.* Think about all of the ways children can respond during story time. Some children may respond by using spoken words, but others may be able to respond by pointing to pictures or simply participate by helping to hold the book or turn the pages. Use technology at story time so that children can help to turn the pages of a book using the arrow keys on a computer or other electronic device. These bright round buttons can be programmed to make a particular sound that the child can use as a way to respond during play or mealtimes.

We can think about this strategy as not only modifying the response of the child but also as modifying our own response and expectations. For example, if a child has difficulty with large-group activities, you could find a special place or quiet activity as a temporary measure while the child becomes more and more comfortable with the group. For a child who needs to eat more frequently than the typical meal or snack schedule, you could provide an additional snack. Our own ability to be open to possibilities and to modify our own response is another key to successful inclusion.

Stabilize Materials

Some children with disabilities may not have good motor control, so making sure classroom materials are stable can increase participation as well. How can we ensure that puzzle pieces are stable and don't move all around or fall off of the table as the child tries to put the puzzle together? We can use rubber padding under the pieces or we can put the pieces on a tray. An art project can be clipped to a slant board for easier access on a tabletop. A book might be placed on a bookstand or a toy might be clamped down so that it doesn't move around too much. Toys can be adapted with hand splints or straps so that a child with limited mobility is able to grasp them. An educator might attach Velcro to the backs of pictures of the daily schedule so that children can manipulate them and place them on the wall schedule as

they learn about the daily routine. Using Velcro can be helpful during mealtimes as well; for example, a child might need a bowl with a stabilizer underneath so that she can eat independently without the bowl sliding around.

It is important to remember to reduce or eliminate the use of an adaptation as the child becomes more independent. For example, you may place nonslip shelf liner on the table to support Juan as he works to stack a tower of blocks, but as the weeks go by, you notice that he is stacking blocks on all types of surfaces and no longer needs the support of the shelf liner. Juan used the adaptation when

ECTA offers a free, online Assistive Technology Checklist (in both English and Spanish) that you can use to assess your program. The checklist includes procedures for identifying and using assistive technology (AT), how to identify a child's need for AT, how to select the appropriate AT to address that need, and how to use the AT to promote participation in learning activities.

The PACER Simon Technology Center (STC) helps children and adults with a variety of disabilities to use assistive technology to enhance learning, work, and independence.

AbleNet provides assistive technology, curriculum, and services to help individuals who have disabilities lead productive and fulfilling lives.

Cadan Assistive Technologies provides assistive-technology devices, alternative-input devices, switches, amplified phones, augmentative devices, large-key and large-print keyboards, Braille displays, and software. (See appendix B for a list of resources for this chapter.)

he needed it, but now he no longer needs it. Hooray for Juan!

Offer Larger or Brighter Materials

Some children might benefit from using materials that are larger and easier to grasp. That's why we have those chubby crayons for toddlers, because very young children don't yet have the fine motor skills to use the small skinny crayons. Older children whose motor skills that aren't quite developed might really benefit from those chubbier crayons. My son had fine motor delays, and we tried all sorts of pencils, pens, and crayons until we found the ones that worked for his specific needs. Children with visual impairments may benefit from using brighter colored materials. A zipper pull on a child's jacket could be altered so that it is larger and easier to grab. Spoons and forks could be modified with larger handles or made wider by taping foam padding around them, so that they are easier to grab and will allow a child to eat independently. Playing cards can be glued to pieces of foam or cardboard so that they are easier to handle. This strategy also may be useful when you think about how to use the child's interests to motivate her to participate in an activity. For example, a child who enjoys lights may be more motivated to use an assistive communication device that lights up when she presses a button to communicate.

Another way of thinking about the supports you provide is to consider them as assistive technology. *Assistive technology* is defined as "any item, piece of equipment, or product system, whether acquired commercially off the shelf, modified, or customized, that is used to increase, maintain, or improve functional capabilities." (Sandall et al., 2005)

The use of assistive technology tools and other strategies can help children gain access to, and function more independently within, classroom activities and routines. These tools can be as high tech as a voice output device for communication or as simple as the use of Velcro to fasten sneakers. Assistive technology can be used for communication, play, art activities, mealtime—the possibilities are endless!

Here are some other examples of environmental adaptations grouped by areas within the classroom.

➤ Sand and Water Play

Sand play, either outside in a sandbox or inside in a sand or water table, provides children opportunities to measure, pour, and sift, dig with a shovel, make roads for toy vehicles, build a sandcastle, or just enjoy the feeling of sand against the skin. Sensory play with sand, water, or other materials provides children with a chance to explore textures and surfaces, such as slippery beads in water, scratchy dry sand, or soapy bubbles. Accessibility tips:

Make sure children are able to access the sand and water tables. Children with limited mobility may need a chair of appropriate height to reach the full area of the table. Sometimes wheelchairs are able to maneuver up to the table, but you may need to adjust the height of the table if possible. Make sure all adaptations to the table are stable.

Offer a variety of materials to use in the sand and water table, including cups and spoons of different sizes, materials that are bright in color, and materials that can be easily grasped.

Encourage participation by including items of interest in the sand table. I remember when I was teaching in the classroom and a little girl named Ginny joined my group. At first, she was very hesitant to engage with her peers, but I learned from her father that Ginny was interested in dinosaurs, so we turned the sand table into an archaeological dig site. We added small shovels, rakes, fine-mesh sifters, paintbrushes, and plastic dinosaurs and made sure that the young scientists also had access to clipboards and markers for recording field notes.

Include materials that target different developmental needs from simple to complex pouring, sifting, and squeezing skills. Children can practice pouring with pitchers filled with sand or other dry materials. They can wring water from sponges and cloths.

If you do not have a sand and water table, it's an easy play item to create just by using large bins or buckets instead, or placing materials on a cookie sheet or plastic placemat. Lots of materials can be used to engage the senses. Try shaving cream, bath foam, lotion, playdough, silly putty, or even toy slime. Make goop by mixing cornstarch and water for a very interesting texture. Place a smaller bin for two children to use together on a tray or table for wheelchair accessibility.

Expand the play by introducing other toys. For example, toy cars added to the shaving cream can become a car wash!

If a child is squeamish about touching strange textures, put beads, uncooked rice, or dried beans in the bins. You can hide toys in the material for the child to find or place a variety of textures together. Fill bins with swatches of fabric, a variety of wooden beads, or puzzle pieces to touch, talk about different textures, or match by color, size, or texture.

➤ Art and Creative Expression

Art areas offer a chance for children to express themselves and can be set up to promote independence as well. Children may want to paint at an easel if sitting still at a table feels too confining. Allow children to explore creative expression with lots of different types of materials, from markers to crayons to pencils to chalk to watercolor paints. Variety in materials will offer multiple ways of engaging and will increase participation as a result. Accessibility tips: Offer a variety of access points for art activities. Children may prefer to paint at a table, using an easel, or on a wheelchair tray. Adapt handles to make them easier to grasp for children with motor delays. Lengthen, shorten, or widen paintbrush handles, paint rollers, and so on with foam pieces. Attach a handle to a child's hand using a Velcro strap, or attach a handle to a glove with Velcro on the palm. Tying markers or brushes to a table or easel will allow children who have difficulty getting down to the floor to be more independent in picking up dropped materials. Tape paper to the table if more stability is needed. On an easel, use tape or paper clips or binder clips to hold the paper to the surface.

Offer many different kinds of painting materials to increase interest and allow for ease of use. For example, children can paint with sponges that are easy for children with motor issues to grasp but are also usable for any child. Modifications that support a child with a delay or disability often end up as a preferred choice for all the children in the group. Children can spread paint using raw potatoes, small toy cars, squeeze bottles, or drinking straws. Nora has sensory issues and doesn't like to fingerpaint. Her mother found that she is comfortable painting when she doesn't have to get her fingers messy. In the photo below (left), Nora is painting

with a green pepper that her mom had on hand. If touching fingerpaint makes a child feel squeamish, another option is to put a small amount of paint into a plastic bag for the child to touch, hold, press, and squeeze. If messy and wet materials are stressful, start out by playing with dry textures to promote engagement—or use squeeze bottles filled with puffy paint or glue.

Attach a switch to a spin-art project so that two children can play. One child can squirt the paint onto the spin-art machine, and another can turn on the switch that makes it turn. Together they create a teamwork masterpiece! Line a shallow bucket with art paper, and place a marble dipped in paint in the bucket. Tip the bucket to make the marble "paint" the paper.

> *"Play is the work of childhood."*
>
> **–JEAN PIAGET, PSYCHOLOGIST**

Use large-sized or fingertip crayons for children who have difficulty holding on to small crayons. Markers make thick lines and need less pressure than crayons. They may be a good adaptation for children who may not see thin crayon lines or who cannot press hard enough with crayons.

I am always amazed by the innovation that educators use when thinking about creative expression for young children. For example, one educator created an art station based entirely on glue. The children collected all sorts of materials and created a class project by gluing the objects to a large board. The results are quite impressive! Every child had a chance to take part in the activity, either by contributing materials or by gluing the objects to the board. Creativity galore!

➤ Pretend Play

Pretend play areas with dress-up and make-believe activities allow children to develop positive identities. They can imagine themselves in the real world taking on specific roles and responsibilities, such as playing a clerk in a grocery store or a doctor in a hospital. The materials also allow children to interact with one another and engage in conversations and negotiate roles and activities. Accessibility tips: Have clothing available that uses a variety of fasteners, some easy, others more difficult. Include dolls with disabilities, dolls with different skin tones, and dolls that represent different cultures as part of the family of dolls available.

Include equipment related to disabilities in the dress-up area, such as glasses, canes, leg braces, hearing aids, or wheelchairs. The equipment can be pretend or made from old or outgrown equipment. Make sure the equipment is safe for children to use.

Use visuals to provide children with ideas for activities that they could do together in the pretend-play area. For example, if the area is set up like a kitchen, you could include a colorful poster in the area with step-by-step photo instructions for making a cake. The pretend play area is super versatile, and you can change out the materials to adapt to the interests of the children in your group. For example, if you have a child who is new to the group and may be feeling shy, you can help her feel welcome by including materials that are of special interest to her. For example, one classroom has a table that has been laminated with graphics to serve as a quick reminder of the pretend-play options related to eating, such as a restaurant, the dinner table at home, or mealtime at Grandma's house. Lots of options to consider!

➤ Book Area

All children benefit from having a place for quiet time and reading. Children with sensory issues might especially enjoy a cozy book area when they are feeling overstimulated. Make the area extra appealing by displaying the books in an attractive way and by offering soft cushions where children can curl up and read together or just look at the pictures. Accessibility tips: Offer story recordings for all children to enjoy, including children with visual impairments. Use an audio player with large buttons or adapt it to a large switch. Color code or use textures to identify "play" and "stop" buttons.

Make book pages easier to turn by modifying the pages with a paper clip for easy grasping. Or you can attach a small piece of foam to each page so there is more room to slip in a finger and turn pages. Offer board books or books with squishy foam pages.

Include books that appeal to children at all levels along the developmental continuum. Include a variety of books about children with disabilities and books that reflect the lived experiences of the children in the group. For example, you may want to include books that use sign language to communicate the story if your group is using sign language to communicate with a child or parent in the class who is hearing impaired.

Include social stories in the book area by making homemade books that relate to typical classroom or family routines and activities. *Social stories* (also called "scripted stories") help children understand social interactions, situations, expectations, social cues, the script of unfamiliar activities, and/or social rules. They are brief descriptive stories that provide information regarding a social situation (Broek, et al., 1994). Use pictures, objects, or pieces of material that relate to the child's life. Children with speech delays can share information about their family or home life by pointing to the objects.

Social stories can also help with reinforcing classroom rules and reminding children about daily transitions, schedules, and routines. Use pictures and/or words depending on the skills and abilities of the child. You can find sample social stories online that you can download and print. (See appendix B for a list of resources for this chapter.)

Homemade books can be a great way to add sensory materials to the book area, as well. Make a squishy book with scrapbook materials by filling plastic ziplock bags with hair gel and the "content" of your choice. You can include laminated photos, foam letters and numbers, small soft objects, pieces of fabric, and more. Make sure that each bag is sealed well, and then place it in a plastic protector sleeve before adding each page to a three-ring binder.

➤ Blocks, Table Toys, and Manipulatives

Table toys and blocks are a staple of every early childhood program. We use these materials to teach children about numbers, science, geometry, and the natural world. Accessibility tips: Make sure there

is a way for each child to be on the same level as the other children. If a child needs assistance in sitting on the floor to play with blocks, have adaptive equipment available. For example, use a beanbag chair that can be molded to the child's needs. Have all children build with blocks on a table, if no floor seating is available.

Provide laminated cards with visuals that communicate ideas of block projects that children can build together. You can find an example of visuals for the block area online. (See appendix B for a list of resources for this chapter.)

Attach Velcro to blocks to help them stay together easily. Use a variety of blocks to match the developmental and physical needs of the children in the group; experiment with different types of blocks to find out which kind works best. Some blocks are easier to stack, some are easier to grab, some are light, some are heavy, some make noise, some fasten together using snaps or magnets, some are squishy, and so on. Make your own blocks by wrapping shoeboxes with butcher paper and inviting children to decorate them. This educator put play figures of people and animals in the block area so children are naturally inclined to build the settings where they might find them.

Most electric or battery-operated table toys can be modified to turn on or off using a switch. Partner with an occupational therapist to learn more about the options for the children in your group.

Stabilize table toys so they won't move around too much. Use Velcro, double-sided tape, or a clamp to hold a toy or puzzle to the table. Another option is to place the toy in a shallow tray on the table to help keep all the pieces together and define that play area. If children have difficulty holding small toys, help them to grasp the toys better by building up handles with sponge hair curlers or pieces of foam or by attaching the toy handle to the child's hand using a Velcro strap. Some puzzles already come with knobs or handles for infants and toddlers, but you can also adapt more advanced puzzles for older children by attaching inexpensive knobs from the hardware store.

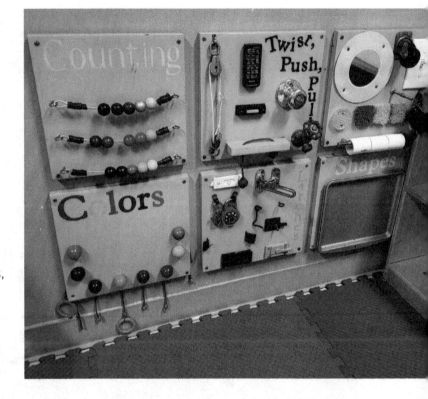

Consider the way that "real-life" items are in fact, puzzles to young children. As adults, we are experts at turning a doorknob, but children are just learning these skills. How might we use these items for play and learning opportunities? This example shows a board that was created using lots of items with buttons to press, knobs and dials to turn, and latches to unlatch—all with everyday items! Activities that are relevant to the child's everyday life will be much more engaging and will serve a variety of purposes.

➤ Outdoor Play Areas

While we have been focusing on the indoor physical environment here, it is just as important to consider accessibility and engagement in outdoor spaces in programs and homes. Outdoor spaces promote physical activity and provide an ideal setting for all sorts of activities. Early childhood educators find that, just by going outside, young children are more physically active and expend more energy. That is a huge stress reliever—for children and adults! Accessibility tips: Consider activities that children of all abilities can enjoy. For example, children can spend time gathering objects they find such as stones, leaves, and pine cones. A peer buddy can help if a child has a visual impairment or limited mobility. Provide shaded areas by using trellises, shade sails, or trees in the outdoor play space. If a child has limited mobility, bring a blanket and toys outside for a safe outdoor playspace.

Paint playground markings such as tricycle "roads" that can foster pretend play outdoors. Use this strategy as a way to highlight children's preferences. For example, the tricycle path can become a railway to encourage participation for a child who loves trains.

Swings are an excellent outlet, especially for children with sensory concerns. Swinging provides a certain kind of feedback that is very calming for some children. Children with sensory concerns also benefit from what specialists call *heavy work*. Heavy work routines are thought to provide a calming effect on the nervous system. The outdoor play area is perfect for this type of stress relief! Heavy work includes any activity that uses the whole body and provides resistance, such as carrying heavy objects or large boxes, pushing a scooter or shopping cart around, or pulling a friend in a wagon.

The outdoor environment can be a place for all sorts of activities, not just those that encourage physical activities. Bring a box of books outdoors! Paint or draw outside! Maybe the play figures that are usually indoors might have fun in the sandbox! Outdoor spaces can truly be an extension of the classroom. This is true in all kinds of weather, just as long as the right clothing is available!

Adapting the physical environment is ultimately all about being creative and responding to the needs of the child. Recognize that it may take a few attempts to find what works. Use the least intrusive adaptation, and pay attention to what interests the child to encourage engagement. When you find success with one adaptation in a particular setting, you might consider whether that same adaptation might work in a different setting. For example, if using the big spoon is working well at mealtime, then maybe a big crayon might work for coloring. Use your creativity to figure it out.

Adapting the physical environment is kind of like being a detective, thinking about the world through the child's eyes and accommodating not only based on the child's needs but also based on the child's preferences, thoughts, and feelings. How are the environment and learning activities perceived by the child? As adults, we are responsible to nurture and care for the children in our lives. In making decisions, we sometimes forget that children have their own unique perspectives on the world too.

The physical environment begins with thinking about how to create a space that communicates all of the feelings and expectations that you want children to understand. This doesn't stop with the space and materials—the social environment is a powerful communicator as well.

RESOURCE **SPOTLIGHT**

The ECTA has developed a collection of checklists that focus on adapting the environment for children with disabilities. The environmental adaptations checklist includes information about how to determine the type of environmental adaptation (physical, social, temporal, and so on) needed to promote participation in learning activities. You'll also find checklists related to child physical activity, natural environments, and environmental arrangements.

The checklists and related practice guides are available in English and Spanish. (See appendix B for a list of resources for this chapter.)

SOCIAL ENVIRONMENT

The social environment is all about the relationships we have with one another. Positive social relationships between the educator and child, the educator and parent, or the child and other children can develop through the energy that the educator brings to the environment. Relationships help us feel safe and valued, special, happy, and loved.

Families are more likely to engage with their children's teachers and share information about their child when they have an ongoing relationship with us. Children benefit from those close relationships, and they also benefit from the close and trusting relationships that the adults in their lives have with each other. Building this trust begins with what I call a culture of caring, kindness, and belonging.

When I was working as the education and disability services coordinator for a multisite Head Start program in Michigan, I encountered many different types of classrooms. As soon as I walked through a classroom door, I could tell whether or not I was entering a caring space. There was just the feel of it—the electricity in the air. There were classrooms that made my shoulders immediately relax. They felt warm, happy, and calming. I remember one of the classrooms had a wall that was painted with a giant mural of a tree. The leaves of the tree were made with green construction paper, and each child had her own leaf that was decorated with family photos. This teacher really valued connection, and the relationships with families in her class were especially important. She explained that the tree was a "family tree," because she wanted the children to feel as if they were in a happy home when they came to school. This educator knew that young children engage in positive interactions with adults in a variety of situations, including the everyday routines at home and at school. She knew that when children develop trusting relationships, they're more willing to explore the world.

Think about this from a child's perspective. Children are vulnerable in that they depend on the adults in their lives in order to survive. First and foremost, children want to know that they are in a place of safety. Children can't explore and learn or experience joy and wonder until they feel safe and secure. What does it take to provide that safe space? Children feel safe when their needs are met consistently. They feel safe when adults encourage their efforts when they try something new. They feel safe when adults greet them with a smile and are genuinely happy to see them each day. They feel safe when adults look them in the eyes and consider their thoughts and feelings. They feel safe when they know what to expect from the day. They feel safe when they are nurtured, cuddled, and treated with patience and care. When you build a unique relationship with each child and family, learn about the way they communicate, and understand their interests, preferences and needs, you help a child feel safe and secure.

The second step in building the social environment is to create a culture of kindness. This means behaving kindly toward each and every child and family, even the child who bit another child yesterday, or the child who knocked down a block tower, or the child who smeared grape jelly under the table rather than using a napkin. All children and families deserve kindness. Kindness starts with learning to see the best in all the children and families we serve. Sometimes this can be difficult because human beings have evolved with a trait that psychologists Rozin and Royzman (2001) call the *negativity bias*. At one time, this bias was necessary for survival. If our ancient ancestors were walking down a path and saw something that looked like a snake, they would be more likely to survive if they assumed the worst and jumped back. Natural selection favored those ancient

ancestors, so we, their descendants, have to make an effort to focus on the positive. Acts of kindness can retrain our brains, because kindness is something that can actually be felt in the body. Being connected to and aware of how our body feels during positive experiences is an important part of moving our brain's bias from negative to positive.

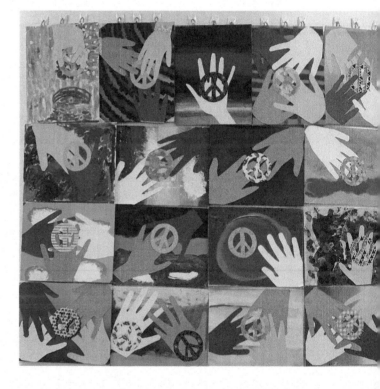

The third step in creating a supportive social environment is providing intentional opportunities for relationships to happen between children, which builds a culture of belonging or membership. How can we do this? We can set up situations that naturally reinforce relationships throughout the daily schedule and routine. We can use classroom activities to promote peer interaction. When children have opportunities to explore alongside other children, they learn how to get along and work together, improve

language and communication skills, and solve problems. For example, I remember watching a video about a little girl named Pearl who loved to play with an automated gears game. The game is played by setting up the gears on a board in a way that you think will cause the gears to interlock together and spin around. It's fun to set up the gears and then even more fun to turn the game on and watch them spin. Pearl loved this game, but due to cerebral palsy, she didn't have the motor control to set up the gears. The educator saw this as an opportunity and connected a switch to the game so that other children could sit with Pearl and set up the gears, and then Pearl was able to use the switch to turn the game on and off. Think about all of the learning that was taking place there! It became about more than understanding gears. The game turned into an opportunity to foster friendships between children. Close friendships between children create the feeling that we are all part of a bigger team. We all belong here, and we're all in this together.

When babies come into the world, they learn to trust through their relationships with adults. Those adults become the safe place for the infant. As children grow older, adults continue to serve as a safe place, but when you foster friendships among children, those peer relationships can become another safe place for the child. We know this as adults, too. Think about the times when you have had a friend in the workplace. It makes work fun! With a bit of creativity, we can make that happen for children as well. These practices are so important that I have dedicated a chapter in this book (chapter 8) specifically to supporting social and emotional development, and friendship skills in particular, through inclusive teaching practices.

TEMPORAL ENVIRONMENT

The last type of environment that we are going to explore is the temporal environment, which refers to the sequence and length of routines and activities. How can we use the daily schedule to promote a positive learning environment? How do routines make children feel? What is the "just right" length of time for a given routine or activity? How does a daily schedule in a center-based environment differ from that of family child-care program or in the home? How can a home visitor support a daily schedule in a family's home?

Young children thrive in an environment built around predictable routines. Adults are the same way, really. We generally like to know what is coming next in our daily lives. As adults, we have a certain sense of control over our schedules and routines because we keep calendars of our events, we wear wristwatches, or we check our temporal lives on our cell phones. Young children don't have the advantage of those tools, and as a result, the world can seem like an uncertain, scary place without predictable routines. Children thrive when the temporal environment is marked by clarity, consistency, and predictability. They want to understand what the expectations are, have consistent rules and routines, and be able to have a sense of what is coming next.

A predictable routine at school starts with the communication that we have with families at morning drop-off and afternoon pick-up. How do you greet children and families at morning drop-off? Did you know research supports using an intentional morning greeting routine to start the day? Cook and colleagues (2018) found that positive greetings at the classroom door can affect children's ability to focus during the day, can reduce disruptions, and can build positive relationships. What an easy intervention! When children are greeted by an adult who is happy to see them, it just starts their day off in an upbeat way. This is especially important for children who may be experiencing difficult situations at home. The positive goodbye at the end of the day is critical as well and gives us an opportunity to talk with families, building connection and trust.

DAILY SCHEDULES

When children see adults communicating and planning together, it gives them a sense of trust and safety. Posting and following a daily schedule also helps children feel safe and in control and helps them develop independence as they use the schedule to prepare for what's ahead. When children know what to expect of the day, it helps them to transition from one activity to the next more easily. Schedules create a sense of safety and predictability.

In a classroom setting we often use pictures to show children the daily schedule, so they will know what to expect and which activity is coming next. This strategy can give children a sense of control over their environment and promotes independence and self-confidence. Children can look to the schedule on their own to find out what is coming up. The daily schedule should be visible throughout the day: include a photo or graphic for each daily activity, posted at the children's eye level, and have some way to show the passage of time. For example, you or the children can remove or flip over the cards for events once they have occurred, or you can provide some sort of marker to indicate the current activity in the schedule. This photo is an example of a daily schedule that the teacher created, so the children can manipulate the activities of the day and better understand which activities come first and which come later. A pointer graphic attaches with Velcro so it can be moved from activity to activity throughout the day.

Successful educators teach children the schedule at the start of the year and after returning from vacations or other breaks. This includes teaching children about potential schedule changes. For example, if a special guest is coming during center playtime to share some music activities with the entire class, we need to make sure to let children know about this ahead of time. No surprises equals a predictable environment and happy children!

For some children, just having the daily schedule and visuals posted or talking about it one time might be all they need. But other children may need extra support. They might need extra time to think about the schedule, to interact with the materials.

I visited a classroom where the teacher had the different routines in the schedule on laminated cards hanging on a clothesline in a corner of the classroom. When circle time ended, the children could move the circle time card from the left side of the line to the right side. By the end of the day, all the cards had been moved from the left to the right. At the beginning of the year, the teacher had been intentional about showing the children how the activities of the day were moving along, and the children could take turns moving an activity card from the left side to the right side. Most children got the hang of it and lost interest in the clothesline schedule after a few weeks. However, one child really struggled with the sense of time, and the teacher noticed that she tended to engage with the clothesline activity for much longer. It was a way for the child to understand what was coming next in the daily schedule, and that helped her have a sense of safety and control over the day-to-day transitions.

ROUTINES WITHIN ROUTINES WITHIN ROUTINES (ROUTINES³)

The daily schedule gives children a sense of the main events of the day, but they do need more. This is especially true at the beginning of the year or when children are new to the program and everything is unfamiliar. We also know that the day's routine is made up of more than just the daily schedule of circle time, snack, free-choice play, and so on. There are routines within each routine. For example, your classroom might have a circle time at the beginning of the day, but you likely have a routine within circle time as well. You might begin with a greeting song and then share a story from home. Next, you look at the calendar together, and then you talk about the weather. After that, there is a lesson about friendships, and then you read a story together.

To take it even further, there is a routine within each activity that occurs during circle time, such as the steps we take during the daily calendar review. This concept is what is known as Routines to the Third Power (Routines³) (Strain and Bovey, 2011). We have routines (events such as circle time) around routines (activities such as the daily calendar review) around routines (steps within the daily calendar review, such as clapping the syllables as you say the month aloud or singing the days of the week). Regardless of the details, the most important thing about the routine is that each activity happens in the same order every single day. There is a rhythm and a pace to circle time that children can expect. They know what is coming next and are ready to engage with that activity as a result. You might even notice a reduction in the circle-time wiggles. Think about the way you feel when listening to a favorite story that a family member has told a million times. You know what is coming next, and that is part of why you are on the edge of your seat. You think, "Oh, I love this part!" Children can feel the same way about a circle-time routine and the routines within it. If you add playful elements, the routine can also build community. We all know that the silly part of our routine is coming, so get ready to giggle together! This part of the temporal environment is critically important for young children and can be a helpful teaching tool for children with attention needs as well. Routines help children answer these key questions:

- What am I doing now?
- How do I know I'm making progress?
- How do I know when I'm finished?
- What comes next?

In chapter 5, we explored embedded learning opportunities and how they can foster growth toward IFSP/IEP goals. You can use the Routines[3] concept as you plan for embedding instruction. Take a look at your daily schedule and the various routines nested inside. Where are the opportunities to embed IFSP/IEP goals into these planned, consistent, and predictable routines? Finding those opportunities for teaching and learning will offer children chances to practice the skills they are developing throughout the day.

LENGTH OF DAILY ACTIVITIES

Another aspect of the temporal environment that can be modified to increase engagement is the length of time children spend in a given activity. Let's think about the circle time example. You may find that even after implementing predictable routines in circle time, adjusting seating arrangements, focusing on children's preferences, and giving children a "job" to do (such as holding the storybook or turning the pages), certain children are still pretty wiggly. This might just be an indication that your circle time is lasting too long. As educators, we often come to this work with a notion of "what it looks like to be an early childhood teacher" and the tradition of the teacher leading circle time fits that image. The trick is to find a recipe for circle time that works for the particular group of children in your program, and sometimes that recipe is to keep circle time relatively brief. Circle for toddlers should be *very* brief. Make sure you persist in presenting circle time activities only if the majority of children are engaged. Consider offering circle time without the expectation that all children will participate for the entire time. If you work with a coteacher, another option is to divide the group into two smaller groups. Half of the group can engage in a longer circle time, while the other half spends some additional time in a free choice activity.

TRANSITIONS DURING THE DAY

Often, the times of transition from one activity to the next can be the most difficult for young children. Think about it from their perspective: "I'm in the middle of pretending to be shopping in the grocery

From a Distance: Supporting Routines when Learning at Home

Educators can offer suggestions for families who are supporting their child at home. Consider the following strategies.

- Start with simple routines that have just three or four steps. Think about the task as having a beginning, middle, and end. For example, a morning getting-dressed routine might include the steps of brushing teeth, washing face, combing hair. Families can take a photo of their child doing these three steps and use the photos to make a poster that can they tape to the bathroom mirror. An evening routine might be as simple as bath, book, and...bed! Morning and evening routines are easy for families to address, and doing these routines with consistency can be a great starting point.

- Families might involve their child in planning the day: "Do you want to play with blocks or watch a show while I work?" or "Do you want to take a walk before or after my phone call?" Providing choices when possible gives children a sense of some control in their environment.

- Engaging siblings within routines is really important. Siblings can be effective teachers, especially when peers are not available.

- Connect families with other families through weekly Zoom meetings. Families can share strategies about the routines that work for them and can provide support for one another.

- Keep in mind that many families have changing or flexible work schedules, which make it difficult to implement a consistent routine. Help children adapt to those daily or weekly changes by creating visual cues for the schedule and caregiver for that day or week.

store with my friend Lois, and suddenly I'm told that I have to put away my apron and clean up. The nerve!" Educators can smooth transitions between activities by using some intentional practices.

One strategy is to develop transition routines. Transition routines can help children to prepare for the change by making it predictable, giving them fair warning, and in some cases, offering opportunities for leadership. First, the educator must come up with a routine and teach the routine to the class at a time when children are focused. Teaching routines with puppets, role-play, or a story can be especially helpful. The routine might start with the educator giving the whole class a five-minute warning that the transition is coming up. Then she might have a routine such as a simple transition song ("Clean-up time! Clean-up time! Everybody knows that it's clean-up time!") or game to engage the whole class during the transition. Nonverbal cues work well too. You can use a whispery voice, put your fingers to your lips, or raise a finger in the air to signal quiet. During the transition, the educator gives descriptive feedback to the children who are on task: "That's great! I see Tamara picking up her blocks and putting them away!"

Individual children might benefit from additional support, such as an individualized transition warning or a special job during the transition: "Felipe is our clean-up helper today." It might be helpful for some children to have access to a simple timer or hourglass, so they have a visual for how much time is left in a given activity. Make sure that the cues for routines are sensitive to the needs of the children in your program. For example, if you have a child with a hearing impairment in your class, using a clapping sequence to signal clean-up time would not work for that child. Instead, you could flick the lights on and off so that she could benefit from the cue, and the other children in the class would benefit as well.

Allow time for children with mobility issues during transitions. They may or may not move slowly. If needed, allow for a head start as they transition from one activity to the next. This can be as simple as providing the child with a transition cue five minutes before the rest of the group.

Children have different responses to the beginning and ending of activities and even to the beginning and ending of their time in the program. Routines to say hello at the start of the program and routines to say goodbye when it is time to end can help children make those important transitions more smoothly.

CLEAR EXPECTATIONS

When children enjoy the same advantage that adults have in knowing what is coming up through the course of the day, the results can be huge. When we couple that advantage with teaching children the expectations for each point in the schedule, we really have the secret sauce! Children appreciate rules because they feel pride when they are able to meet the expectations that adults have set for them. For example, children feel pride when they come into the classroom at the beginning of the day and know where to hang up their

RESOURCE **SPOTLIGHT**

The National Center on Pyramid Model Innovations (NCPMI) has a huge library of visual supports, including transition cards to help children manage transitions appropriately. You can download the cards, print them, and laminate them to use in the classroom. (See appendix B for a list of resources for this chapter.)

The NCPMI has developed a resource that educators can use to help children learn, practice, and integrate classroom expectations. You can access the activity and related visuals online. (See appendix B for a list of resources for this chapter.)

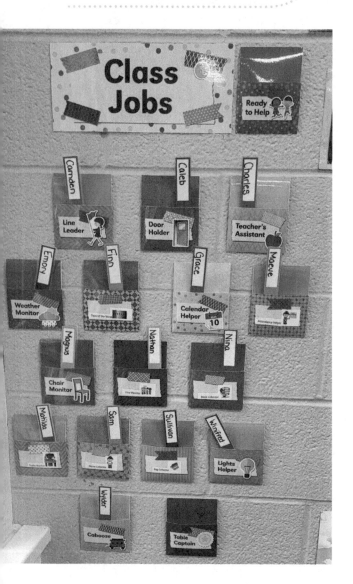

jacket, where their cubby is so they can put their backpack away, and which activities are available to them at the start of the day. You may even have a system for delegating classroom jobs, such as line leader, floor sweeper, or door holder, like the system this classroom teacher developed (below). For example, Jordan knows what to do, so he can begin his day by hanging up his jacket, putting away his backpack, choosing a classroom job for the day, and then finding a cozy spot in the book area for some reading time—all on his own.

When setting expectations with children, it's wise to focus on what they can and should do rather than using words like *don't*. You might say, "Let's use gentle hands," instead of saying, "Don't hit." NCPMI has a sample set of preschool classroom rules that are based on three key expectations:

1. Be Respectful.
2. Be Safe.
3. Be a Friend.

You can find a printable poster online that includes these rules along with the meaning behind the rules. (See appendix B for a list of resources for this chapter.) For example, "Be respectful," means that we have gentle hands, take turns, and use quiet voices and listening ears. NCPMI also recommends that programs have no more than five rules, so as not to overwhelm children. Rules should be posted at children's eye level, with visual representations for each rule.

Understanding consistent rules and expectations promotes independence and self-control in young children. When those rules are consistent over time, across settings, and between educator and family, children learn about boundaries and how to meet expectations. When children do meet expectations, make sure to provide frequent, positive descriptive feedback. You know the saying, "Catch 'em being good!" When children get that feedback, it is reinforcement that will lead to meeting expectations in the future. The positive verbal feedback or praise can be paired with other kinds of feedback such as a hug or high-five for maximum impact. How much positive feedback is necessary to make a difference in this way? The Pyramid Model and the ECTA Inclusion Indicators suggest a ratio of a minimum of five positive statements, such as telling children how awesome they are and catching children being good, to every one negative statement (ECTA, 2019).

Daily communication with families creates a sense of partnership, collaboration, and trust. This is also an example of where we find the intersection between the learning environment and teaching practices. Creating an inclusive learning environment is just the first step. Inclusive teaching practices are necessary to truly make inclusion work for each and every child.

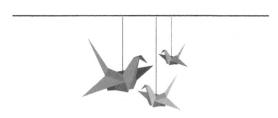

REFLECTION QUESTIONS

- How do you create environments that are welcoming to all children and their families?
- How can you foster an inclusive learning environment across all three environments: physical, social, and temporal?
- What can you do to include families as part of the community within a classroom learning environment?
- How do you reflect individual children's strengths and interests through daily routines, materials for exploration, and learning experiences?
- How will you know when children are comfortable in the learning environment and have mastered all of the steps in the daily schedule and routines?

CHAPTER 7

Inclusive Teaching Practices

How you are is as important
as what you do.

—JEREE PAWL, INFANT-PARENT
MENTAL HEALTH EXPERT

When Ricky was in the orphanage in Ukraine, his caregivers did all they could to keep the children healthy. If one child became ill, the illness could easily spread to all the children, so caregivers were careful to keep children from sharing toys with one another. They tried to prevent children from putting toys in their mouths as well. This served an important purpose for the caregivers in the orphanage, but infants and toddlers learn about the world through all of their senses. Putting things in their mouths is a favorite way that babies use to learn about an object. Because Ricky was prevented from doing that for the first seventeen months of his life, when we adopted him and allowed him to explore (clean) objects in this way, he went to town! He made up for lost time. Everything from books to the collar on his jacket went into his mouth. This was fine at home, but once he went to preschool? Not so fine.

Preschool centers in the United States also want to prevent the spread of illness. Educators spray down tables with bleach and water after meals or playtime. They clean toys if a child happens to put them in their mouth. This is understandable and a good health and safety practice. But when Ricky started preschool, the toy mouthing was "over the top" according to his teacher. When I picked him up from school one day, she took me over to a sink filled with toys and soapy water and was exasperated to tell me, "These are the toys that Ricky has put in his mouth just since noon." She was frustrated, and I was mortified. "I promise that I'll have a talk with him," I said. He was three at the time, but we would have a conversation about it. Right.

I sobbed my embarrassment to my friend who also happened to be an early childhood intervention specialist. "Why don't you find something that he could have with him all the time to put in his mouth?" she offered. Great idea! We went shopping that night and bought some large, nontoxic plastic beads and strung up a beaded necklace. It was fun!

"Now, Ricky," I said, "whenever you want to put something in your mouth, just put this necklace in your mouth instead." He loved the necklace and wore it proudly as he went to school. Yay for us! Problem solved!

When I picked him up from school that day, I was excited to hear how the necklace strategy had worked. But Ricky wasn't wearing the necklace. When I asked his teacher about it, she said, "Oh that thing? It was nasty." She handed me a plastic bag with the necklace inside, and I wanted to crawl under her desk with shame.

Ultimately, we figured out a solution by having Ricky wear a bandana around his neck. It was absorbent, and so it worked better than the plastic bead necklace. I have to say that getting to that place of compromise was heartbreaking for me as a parent. Where was her compassion? Didn't she understand that he was just a little kid who needed some sense of security? Even though it was upsetting at the time, I can appreciate how it must have felt from her viewpoint. When I was a preschool teacher, many days felt like a struggle. I remembered working in the classroom, putting in lots of time and creative energy to find a solution for a child, only to be met with indifference from the parent. Finding the "just right" approach takes time and patience from both the educator and family.

Children ages five and under learn by doing and by actively engaging with the world. They need time to practice what they

Practices are what professionals do with, and for, children and their families to support optimal development in young children and family capacity to support their children. *Evidence-based practices* . . . have been evaluated and proven to achieve positive outcomes for children and families. Practitioners can achieve positive outcomes for children and families by implementing evidence-based practices with fidelity. State and local systems must provide supports, including policies, guidance, professional development, and coaching to help practitioners implement practices (ECTA, 2021, emphasis added).

are learning, to ask questions, to investigate, and to use what they are learning in their everyday activities. High-quality inclusive programs are not just about the physical, social, and temporal environments. A huge factor in supporting children's progress are the practices used to provide positive learning experiences and to build relationships through positive interactions. How do successful educators do it? What are highly inclusive, evidence-based teaching practices?

In the following pages, we'll discuss many different teaching practices that have been found to be successful in meeting the needs of all children, including those with disabilities or suspected delays. We'll explore the steps in the planning process, how to scaffold children's learning, and how to use prompts, visual supports, and other forms of curriculum modifications. The exciting part of all of this is that the practices you find to be successful with a certain child will also work for others in your program. That is a true gift of inclusion.

A common way to approach systems of intervention is by using a tiered system of service delivery. Multitiered systems of support (MTSS) are a necessary framework for inclusion because they allow for the range of individualized approaches to universal supports for all children, regardless of ability (Carr et al., 2002). The three tiers represent options for service delivery and are marked by varying levels of intensity. Even though the strategies differ from tier to tier, all are important for successful service delivery.

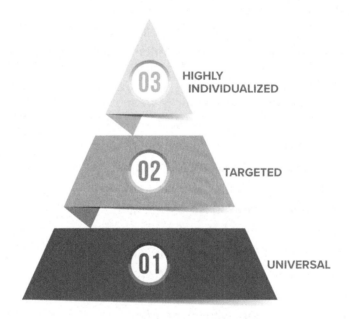

- The bottom tier is the universal level of services. All children receive high-quality early childhood education with rich learning environments and a skilled, well-qualified workforce. The notion is that most children will be successful with that high level of quality programming at the universal tier.

- The second tier is for a more targeted approach. Some children may need additional supports and intentional teaching practices focused on their specific needs. Small-group supports and specialized strategies fall within the second tier.

- The third tier includes the highly individualized practices that a very small subset of children will need. This tier includes one-to-one supports and goal setting that happens through the IFSP/IEP process. The first two tiers provide a strong foundation necessary for the intensive strategies to be successful within the third tier.

This tier structure is found in many different frameworks of practice, including the Pyramid Model for Social-Emotional Learning, Response to Intervention, Positive Behavior and Supports, and others.

PLANNING FOR HIGHLY INDIVIDUALIZED TEACHING PRACTICES

Successful early childhood educators use a wide range of evidence-based practices across all three tiers of support, and they frequently check in to make sure that the practices are effective. Begin with the end in mind. What do I want the child to know or be able to do? How will the child show that the knowledge or skills have been achieved? These questions lead to the ultimate question that focuses on planning learning experiences and activities: What kind of activities, skills, materials, and resources will lead the child to success?

Using these three questions when designing activities leads to every child receiving the most individualized approach needed to be successful. We explored individualized instruction in chapter 6, and we discussed the learning cycle in chapter 5. This approach can be expanded for use with groups of children—a method called *differentiating instruction*. Differentiation is an approach we can use to modify our curriculum and teaching practices for the benefit of all children in the program. It acknowledges that children are diverse learners, and we can accommodate that reality through different teaching strategies, using a variety of learning activities, monitoring individual needs, and reaching toward optimal learning outcomes (Suprayogi and Valcke, 2016). The concept is

What We Mean by MTSS and RTI

A multitiered systems of support (MTSS) and response to intervention (RTI) are frameworks for integrating instruction, evidence-based interventions, and assessments to meet the academic and behavior needs of all students. The essential components of MTSS are screening, progress monitoring, a multilevel prevention system, and data-based decision making (National Center on Response to Intervention, 2010). RTI is a type of MTSS that focuses on providing varying levels of assistance to students based on their needs. The four key features of the RTI model for early childhood education are multitiered systems of practices, high-quality curriculum, ongoing assessment and progress monitoring, and collaborative problem solving (Barton and Smith, 2015).

that educators are intentional about addressing the particular needs of groups of children in their program by using varied approaches to curriculum, instruction, and assessment. This approach begins with knowing the children in your program and acknowledging what they already know and are able to do. It also is based on the notion that all children have different learning needs, strengths, styles, interests, and preferences. As described above, some children will be successful only with practices at the universal or targeted tier levels, while others benefit from a much more individualized approach. For example, one child may be able to follow when the teacher demonstrates how to properly hold scissors to cut paper. Another child may need hand-over-hand support for the same activity. How do you determine which strategy to use with each child? Let's break it down step by step.

STEP ONE: WHAT DO I KNOW ABOUT THIS CHILD?

We've explored gathering data through observation and ongoing assessment, and we can use these data about the child as our first step in the planning process. Collect information, including information from an IFSP or IEP, personal observations, and information shared by the child's family and/or EI or ECSE professionals, and use the information to design the best approach to integrate into the routine. What are the child's interests? What are his strengths and skills? How does the child interact one-on-one? What does he spend a lot of time doing? What makes him smile or laugh? Which activities does the child work hard to accomplish? How does he interact in a group? Observe the child to identify interests, including the materials, toys, activities, and people that are interesting to him. When you pay attention to what a child does and says, you can usually find out what motivates that child to learn. This is true for all children but even more so for children with disabilities because they may not behave in the same way as their peers. Get to know each child, and as you watch, listen, and engage throughout the day, you will uncover the information you need to plan the best approach.

STEP TWO: WHAT WILL WORK FOR THIS CHILD?

Identifying the right teaching practice is dependent on the child's capabilities and interests. Start there and provide activities and materials that are a good fit for the child, and offer opportunities to make choices and engage in the activities and play with the materials. Give him time to explore the materials or to interact with other children. Watch and wait to see how the child uses or tries to use materials or interacts with others in the activity you planned. Children are full of surprises! You might expect a toddler to stack blocks, and then he surprises you by banging two blocks together to make a noise. A four-year-old might use those same blocks to create a village for pretend play.

The actual teaching practices you select can come from many different sources. You might find useful strategies in the DEC Recommended Practices document. Alternatively, you might discover valuable strategies in a specialized curriculum or in a research-based approach from a journal article. Over time, you will build your own collection of tried-and-true strategies that have worked well for other children who had similar needs. Successful educators choose from this wide range of practices based on the IFSP or IEP goals, as well as the strengths, needs, and preferences of the child and family. Using the selected practices, you will then plan how, when, and where to support each child throughout the daily routines and experiences to make progress toward their next steps.

STEP THREE: HOW CAN I SUPPORT THIS CHILD?

Scaffolding Children's Learning

The key term for this step in the process is *scaffolding*, which is a method of teaching in which children move to more independence as their skills develop. The concept comes from Vygotsky's zone of proximal development, in which adults provide just the right amount of help so that the child can be successful, without taking over and doing the task for the child. Think about the scaffolding set up by builders during construction. The supports are there while all of the sawing and hammering happens, but once the building is in good shape, the scaffolding is removed. The building couldn't have been built with such strength or risen to such heights if the scaffolding had not been present during the building process.

The educator first learns what the child is able to accomplish on his own, what he cannot accomplish on his own, and how he might be able to accomplish the new skill with some assistance. Scaffolding happens when educators provide supports, such as prompts, specific questions, or reminders, that can help children follow instructions and learn. Some ways to scaffold learning include the following:

- **Grouping children in ways that will foster learning:** You may group children with similar ability levels to expand learning, or you may group children with differing ability levels to encourage peer learning.

- **Providing opportunities to move to a higher skill level:** This involves offering increasingly complex tasks or removing accommodations when the child is ready.

- **Communicating expectations in a way that children can understand:** You can do this through

RESOURCE **SPOTLIGHT**

Instructional practices truly are a cornerstone of early intervention and early childhood special education. Educators, home visitors, specialists, family members, and other caregivers can use these practices to maximize learning and improve outcomes for young children who have or are at risk for developmental delays or disabilities. The "Practice Improvement Tools" resource, based on the DEC Recommended Practices, offers checklists and practice guides for families and educators in English and Spanish. (See appendix B for a list of resources for this chapter.)

simple language, role-playing, use of supports, or repetition to explain concepts, rules, or tasks. In the following photo, you'll see the strategy of using a ribbon to provide children guidance who are learning about how to walk in a line back to the classroom.

- **Using a variety of visual supports geared to children's different learning needs:** Photographs with captions, posters, calendars, and to-do lists are all ways that children may be able to understand home or classroom expectations.

- **Using scripted stories or social stories:** The educator or parent writes down a story that describes a situation that the child may encounter and the behaviors the child should use in that situation. Scripted stories can be illustrated with photographs of the child or with graphics found online. Broek et al. (1994) advise that we can use these simple stories as tools to prepare a child for a new situation, for addressing challenging behavior, or for teaching new skills. (See appendix B for a list of resources for this chapter.) Scripted stories can be particularly useful when teaching social-emotional skills, which we discuss in more detail in chapter 8.

- **Using a variety of reinforcements:** These may include signals, such as visual cues, songs, or other reinforcements. How often you use them will vary depending on the needs of the individual child.

- **Communicating with children in ways that will expand learning:** You might do this through commenting about things that interest the child so that he is more likely to respond to or repeat your comment, asking questions that require more than a yes or no answer, and expanding on something that a child says to build vocabulary. For example, Tony says, "Truck," and you say, "Yes, you have a green dump truck."

- **Setting up situations to capture the child's attention and encourage conversation:** For example, you can do something that is outside the typical routine, such as holding a book upside down to read to the child, so the child says, "No! This way!" and then shows you how to read a book the right way. Another example is a strategy called "Snack Talks," which are visual supports intended to encourage conversations during mealtimes. The educator presents a Snack Talk card to the children at the table, and the group uses it as a topic of conversation. The cards might include topics such as favorite songs, toys, books, or food. (See appendix B for a list of Snack Talks tips.)

- **Allowing for partial participation:** You can involve a child in an activity even if he cannot perform every step. Identify what parts of that activity the child can do, and then figure out the adaptations needed for the other parts of the activity. For example, Miguelito may not be able to put his coat on all the way, but he can put one arm in the first sleeve if an adult or peer helps with the other arm. Eventually, he will be able to do it all himself without help.

- **Providing opportunities for challenge:** This approach might involve placing preferred objects in such a way that the child must work on the skill to obtain the object. For example, for a child who is working on motor skills, the educator might create a reinforcement for opening a container by placing a favorite toy inside. One educator created a game for a child working on grasping skills. The child uses the tongs to place the pompoms into the glass. It's a fun way to practice the skills.

- **Creating opportunities for choice:** Children use cognitive and communication skills when responding to options. For example, you might let them take turns when choosing the book to read in circle time. Or, you might offer two different types of fruit during snack time so that a child learns the words for the items and has the chance to use the new words. Providing choices is also a way to give children a sense of control while still making progress toward an activity.

- **Modeling a task from beginning to end:** By hearing your explanation step by step, and by watching your actions, children learn to think through a task and to understand what needs to happen first, next, and so on. When it is the child's turn to try, the educator or peer can coach him along the way to reinforce learning.

- **Allowing many opportunities for repetition and practice:** All children use repetition and practice to learn about the world, and your time and patience will allow this to happen so that children can be successful.

Using Prompts and Visuals

In addition to scaffolding, prompts and visual supports can be very effective in early childhood programs, both in the classroom and as a strategy for home visitors to share with families. The Barton Lab (n.d.) at Vanderbilt University defines *prompts* as "instructions, gestures, demonstrations, touches, or other things we can do to increase the likelihood that children will respond how we want them to. Prompting helps children complete tasks that might otherwise be too difficult or contain multiple or complex steps. Supporting children using prompts (and providing positive descriptive feedback) helps them learn to complete tasks independently." Some examples of prompts include the following.

➤ Words and/or Actions

You use these all the time! For example, an educator might tap Angel on the shoulder to let her know it's time to clean up and go outside; that is using a physical prompt. She might also say, "Outside time!" which is a verbal prompt, and might point to the door, which is a gestural prompt. Then, she might playfully march over to the door and line up—an effort to model the desired behavior and another type of prompt.

➤ Response Prompting

Response prompting, made popular by Wolery, Ault, and Doyle (1992), is used to describe the process of using prompts to support learning in a specific way: ordered from most to least or least to most. A most-to-least strategy is used to support children as they learn a complex task. The adults first provide a lot of help and then gradually reduce the support as the child learns the skill. Least-to-most prompting is used when a child already knows how to do something but must be supported to generalize the skill in new situations. For example, the child may be skilled at taking turns with an adult while playing peekaboo but is still learning how to take turns when rolling a ball back and forth. The teacher starts out by providing the least amount of help necessary for the child to successfully take turns but adds in additional support as needed for the child to be successful.

➤ Visual Supports

Visual supports are a type of prompt that includes concrete things, such as pictures, symbols, or objects, which give the child information about an activity or routine as well as expectations for behavior. Visual supports are one of the most common practices used to help young children with disabilities learn new skills (Steinbrenner et al., 2020). They can be used to teach routines, increase communication skills, build independence, and minimize behavior challenges. For example, many educators use labels to identify the materials in the classroom so that children know where to put toys away when it is clean-up time. Labels give the child an understanding of expectations. When text is added to a picture on a label, the visual support also fosters language and literacy goals.

Visual directions or a step-by-step visual show organized directions for how to accomplish an activity. These can be for self-care skills, such as a morning routine, or used as a way to learn play skills. For example, in one classroom I visited, the educator had a visual in the pretend-play area that provided directions for using a pretend washer for washing doll clothes. She included photos of a child telling the doll that it was time to wash clothes, removing the doll clothes from the doll, putting the clothes in a cardboard box decorated to look like a washing machine, shaking the washing machine to get the clothes all clean, and taking the clothes out and hanging them on a clothesline. This activity taught children important pretend-play skills while also teaching them how to follow step-by-step instructions during a playful and nonthreatening time.

Visual behavior cues can help show a student what behaviors are expected in certain situations, activities, or environments. Some examples may be a picture of when it's okay to use a loud voice and when it's time to use a quiet voice, or a poster with images that describe the expectations in the classroom. Another example is posting a stop sign on a door, so children know that they should not go out of the door by themselves.

Visual communication cues help to remind a child to communicate in a particular way. For example, an educator might have a poster that reminds children to ask before going to the bathroom or a card that has the description of the words to use when asking. Visuals can also be used to represent choices that children make in the daily routine. These are sometimes called "choice boards" or "menu boards." For example, educators often ask children to choose the learning center that they want to play in during free-choice activity time. The educator might have a choice board with pictures of each activity, so that a child can point to the activity he would like to select.

A type of choice board that helps with the sequence of events is a first-then board, which is a visual display of something the child prefers that will happen after completing a task that is less preferred. In this classroom, the educator has a first-then board with multiple options for the events.

For example, the educator might use it to teach children the sequence of "first we must clean up, then we can go outside." This approach is helpful when teaching children to follow directions and learn new skills. It motivates children and gives them a sense of when they will be able to engage in their preferred activity. This strategy lays the language foundation children need to eventually be able to follow multi-step directions.

Keep in mind that often the best interventions are invisible. Especially for preschool-aged children, drawing attention to differences through the support you provide may decrease the likelihood that the child will participate in the activity. It's okay for other children to enjoy the activity, too! For example, if you are trying out a wiggle seat with Andre so that he will be able to focus during circle time, you might want to have several wiggle seats available for other children to use as well. This will take away the stigma that Andre might feel if he were the only one using the special seat.

➤ Other Sensory Supports

In addition to visual cues or prompts, consider ways to appeal to the other senses by using *sensory supports* when providing feedback. For example, you might use physical touch as a prompt or use textures or braille to label materials and play centers. Auditory cues might include using a bell ringing to indicate the start or end of an activity, a drumbeat to indicate a transition, or a song to say goodbye. Examples of olfactory cues are the fragrance of popcorn popping to let children know that it is time to clean up for snack time or the scent of lavender or other essential oils for relaxation time. These notions remind us of the principles of universal design that we explored in chapter 6 and can be useful when thinking about potential supports as well.

STEP FOUR: HOW DO I KNOW IF WE ARE MAKING PROGRESS?

Once a plan is in place, the educator, family, and team will work together to implement the practices and gather data along the way. The team monitors progress toward the achievement of goals by recording observations and sharing lessons learned with the other members of the team. When does the child lose interest in an activity or classroom material? This is often an opportunity to shift your practice to other activities or materials to match the child's attention. It could be a sign that the child does not yet feel capable with the activity you have chosen, or it could be a sign that he has lost interest due to boredom. Together, the team can reflect on what works and what does not work, to be as effective as possible. This information will also help to direct the team toward next steps for the child. Especially in the beginning, it's important for the team to meet frequently to review progress and to make planning adjustments and to try different practices or adjust the frequency or intensity of the intervention. In all likelihood, children need support only temporarily, so savvy teachers know that fading their support is critical to children's independence. Effective teachers know how to individualize support to offer just the right amount of help.

ADAPTATIONS, ACCOMMODATIONS, AND MODIFICATIONS

Adaptations, accommodations, and modifications are all types of support given to young children with disabilities or suspected delays. The terms are often used interchangeably, but there is a distinction between their meaning and use, especially for school-age children. For preschool children, the differences are more subtle, because children under five are working on a wide variety of developmental skills in many areas. Ultimately, it doesn't really matter what terminology you use. As long as you are carefully planning the activities and supports that the child needs to participate and to make progress toward their IEP goals, you are on the right track!

A Note on Terminology

- **Adaptations:** an overall term for any assistance required by a child with a disability to be successful or to experience the same opportunities as typically developing peers

- **Accommodations:** adaptations that help a child access or participate in the curriculum or activities without changing the curriculum or activity itself

- **Modifications:** adaptations that make changes to the curriculum or activity so that a child with a disability can participate and be successful

CURRICULUM MODIFICATIONS

You know that feeling of being completely engaged in an activity? Your focus is strong, you feel deep concentration, or you are in a state of absorption or deep fascination with what you are doing. That is what we want for children, because that type of engagement means that learning is taking place! Researcher Mihaly Csikszentmihalyi (1990) called this state of engagement *flow*. Just like adults, children benefit from entering a state of flow, and this level of engagement is where learning is most likely to happen. While accommodations change how children access and learn the same material as their peers, curriculum modifications change what children expected to learn. When a child is not participating, or not participating fully, in the curriculum and is unlikely to enter into a state of flow, we may find that a curriculum modification is helpful.

What do we mean by the word *curriculum* with young children? According to NAEYC,

> *The curriculum consists of the plans for the learning experiences through which children acquire knowledge, skills, abilities, and understanding. Implementing a curriculum always yields outcomes of some kind—but which outcomes those are and how a program achieves them are critical. In developmentally appropriate practice, the curriculum helps young children achieve goals that are meaningful because they are culturally and linguistically responsive and developmentally and educationally significant. The curriculum does this through learning experiences that reflect what is known about young children in general and about each child in particular (NAEYC, 2020).*

A curriculum modification is a relatively small change. It should not take a great deal of time or resources to plan and implement. Still, the change can have a big impact for an individual child. There are thousands of possible modifications. Where do you start? In *Building Blocks for Teaching Preschoolers with Special Needs*, Susan Sandall and colleagues (2019) identify eight categories of curriculum modifications:

- Environmental support
- Materials adaptation
- Activity simplification
- Child preferences

- Special equipment
- Adult support
- Peer support
- Invisible support

You'll find that there is some overlap to the categories, but it can be helpful to have them available to give you ideas when you are thinking about the best approach to use for an individual child.

Environmental Support

In chapter 6, we explored many ways to foster inclusion through the physical, social, and temporal environment. This, too, is a way to modify the curriculum to promote participation, engagement, and learning.

- Denny used to enjoy the sensory table but no longer wants to play. He has some fine motor delays, and the sensory table had become a great way to exercise those muscles. To keep him engaged, his teacher added some new toys to the table, and he now has to dig through sand to find them. His engagement with the sand table was reignited as a result!

- Margaret loves to play with puzzles, but she becomes frustrated when pieces fall off the table and she isn't able to reach them. Her teacher places the puzzle pieces on a tray to make it less likely that they will fall off the table out of her reach.

- Amber is learning to keep her body still during circle time. It helps her to focus when she can sit on a carpet square that signals the boundary for her personal space during the activity. Her mother also sewed the head of a toothbrush into the pocket of her favorite hoodie so she can run her fingers across the brush noiselessly to calm her fidgety fingers.

Materials Adaptation

Another strategy that we touch on in chapter 6 is the practice of modifying materials so that a child can participate in as meaningful a way as possible.

- Patrick is working on using a cup for drinking, which is difficult because he is not yet able to fully control the movement of muscles in his arms and hands. He uses a modified cup so that he can drink without spilling. He also has a special bowl with suction cups on the bottom for stabilization.

- Emma likes to draw, but due to motor delays, she sometimes has difficulty grasping the markers. Her teacher wrapped pieces of foam and tape around some markers as a way to make them "chunkier" and easier to grasp. Emma also loves to play with puzzles that have been modified with knobs, so they are easier to manipulate.

Activity Simplification

Savvy educators can also modify the curriculum by breaking a complicated task into smaller parts or reducing the number of steps or parts. Remember the section in chapter 5 about breaking down IFSP or IEP goals into smaller steps? This curriculum modification has a practical application.

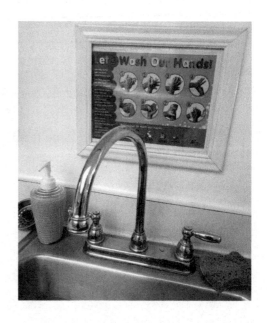

- Valora turns away when a large number of puzzle pieces are put in front of her, but she stays engaged when the puzzle pieces are given to her one at a time.

- Joey is learning the steps to wash his hands. He uses a process chart that breaks down the handwashing process into steps that he can follow.

Child Preferences

A very effective way to modify the curriculum is by identifying and integrating the child's preferences. In step one of your planning for highly individualized teaching practices, you identify a child's interests. Through this process you learn what motivates the child to remain engaged in an activity. Consider the following examples of how to use child preferences as a curriculum modification.

- Sammy loves trains. At home, his parents have decorated his room with trains and even bought him a bedspread with trains on it because he loves them so much! Transitions are difficult for Sammy, but he was able to be successful when his teacher suggested that he chug like a choo choo train when he moves from one activity to the next.

- Janice loves music. When she becomes disengaged while playing in the water table, her teacher sparks her interest in the activity by singing a song while they play together.

- Peter is anxious when going to new places or trying new things. His father knows that Peter loves books and really loves it when his father reads to him. Together they go to a new park and bring along a picnic blanket and Peter's favorite books to read.

- Josie is learning to identify and name common objects, but she doesn't seem very interested in most of the objects in the classroom. Josie is a natural "foodie," and she loves mealtime! Her teacher uses this preference and teaches Josie to name and identify fruits and vegetables.

Families are an important partner in identifying children's preferences. The following are some questions that you might ask families to find out about their child's interests and preferences:

- What is a typical day like in your family?
- What does your child like to do in the morning? afternoon? evening?
- What is your child's favorite thing to do on the weekend?
- Which routines or activities does your child not like to do? What makes this routine or activity difficult or uncomfortable for your child?
- If you could dream up a perfect family vacation, where would it be and what would you do?
- What is your child's favorite toy? Does your child have a particular attachment to an object at home?
- What is your child's favorite food? Are there certain foods to avoid?
- What holds your child's attention the most?
- What makes your child happy? When do you see your child smile or laugh?
- How does your child calm himself?

Special Equipment

Another way to modify the curriculum to build participation and engagement is through the use of adaptive devices or special equipment.

- Katie uses a walker to assist with her mobility. This makes it possible for Katie to move around the classroom and participate in all of the learning centers. Her peers know that when Katie is using the walker, they need to slow down and can help her by opening the door when they go outside.

- Mariano is not yet able to speak, so he uses picture cards and an electronic speaking device to communicate his choices.

- Thomas uses a wheelchair but also has an adaptive chair at the lunch table that he can use to access the table more easily. He uses a cube chair when he wants to play with classroom materials that are close to the ground.

- Sherice has limited eyesight, and she wears protective glasses most of the time. It's helpful to her that there is a listening center in her classroom. She loves to listen to books using headphones.

Adult Support

Engagement and participation can be strengthened for some children with support from an adult. This can happen simply by having an adult with the child to share in the activity, or it can include more intentional encouragement or help.

- Carlos uses sign language to communicate. His teacher has learned some signs that she uses to communicate with him and to explain directions to an activity that she also shares verbally with the class.

- Janelle watches her teacher as he models play strategies in the dramatic-play area. Through this adult support, Janelle is learning how to play cooperatively on her own, even after her teacher is no longer there to play alongside her.

"What a child can do in cooperation today, he can do alone tomorrow."

—LEV VYGOTSKY

- An adult holds a Styrofoam sphere tightly, while a child hammers in pegs. Eventually, she will be able to hold the sphere and use the hammer at the same time.

Peer Support

In addition to building friendships, peer support can serve as a way to increase participation in a learning activity. Not only can peers provide support through praise and encouragement, but they can also model play strategies or demonstrate other activities that their friend is learning. This happens naturally in an inclusive program as peers watch each other throughout the day and as they do classroom chores, eat, play, and learn. Sometimes the child with a disability is being helped, and other times the child with a disability is the helper.

- Mary, LeeAnn, and Destiny work together on a project. It starts when Mary makes a simple mark on the paper. LeeAnn adds to it by drawing a shape, and Destiny finishes the project by cutting a shape out from a page of construction paper and gluing it on the masterpiece.
- Judy is not eager to run through the sprinkler but is happy to do so when Luke takes her hand and they run through together. When she makes it through, Judy is all smiles as Verla and Kwanita cheer her on.
- Hanson's class is learning about appropriate peer social skills through large-group activities such as role-playing and small-group activities that promote interactions. He teaches children play skills and sets up the classroom so that there are lots of opportunities for social interaction. For example, every child has a peer buddy, and they work together during transitions and clean-up time.

Invisible Support

Perhaps the best curriculum modification of all is the one that is invisible. In this approach, educators purposefully arrange naturally occurring events within activities to increase participation. If you were an outside observer, you might not even know that a modification was in place.

- Marco has come to understand the routine within the classroom routines. He knows that after snack the class goes to another room for active play. To do that, Marco knows that he first stands on his square by the door. Next, the class leader for the day opens the door, and then the class walks to the other room. Marco is learning about following directions, roles and expectations, and sequences of events through this routine within the routine.
- During a game of Stop and Go in the classroom, children take turns with different roles. Xavier has limited mobility, and he likes to be the one to hold up the red stop sign when it's time to stop and the green go sign when it's time to go.
- Deandra is working on learning the names of colors. This happens at lunchtime when her teacher asks her to match the red plate with the red cup.

INCLUSIVE TEACHING PRACTICES FROM A DISTANCE

As discussed throughout this book, there are many instances when educators will need to provide services from a distance as they support children with disabilities and their families. This is not always a negative! Some benefits of remote instruction include:

- increased opportunity for hands-on learning at home;

- a chance to connect and build closer relationships with families;

- opportunities to teach families new skills that might result in less stress and increased feelings of competence in their approach to their child in the home; and

- the ability to create a nurturing, comforting environment for the child that may foster growth and development.

What can you do to capitalize on these advantages and still remain true to the activities that are necessary to support progress toward IFSP/IEP goals? Here are some teaching practices to consider in remote instruction.

- Consider the physical learning environment in the home setting. Talk with families about how to make the learning environment a comfortable, engaging place for the child. Children with disabilities may or may not need modifications or adaptations of materials. Explore that together with families so that your teaching practices will be more successful.

- Start with a plan, but be flexible. Regardless of the setting, supporting young children requires intentional thought and planning to achieve success. Keep in mind that plans are not set in stone when it comes to the busy lives of families. Give family members grace if they were not able to stick to the plan, and then try again the following week.

- Send home learning bags so that everyone has equal access to the materials. Include any needed curriculum modifications or adaptations to materials. For example, you

We Carry Kevan

Kevan Chandler is a charismatic, empathetic, smart, and funny young man who took a trip across Europe in 2016. This may not sound that amazing, but Kevan has a rare neuromuscular disease called spinal muscular atrophy, and he uses a wheelchair for mobility. Throughout the European trip, Kevan's friends carried him on their backs in a backpack that they designed especially for him. It's an incredible story, and Kevan continues to be an advocate for thinking about accessibility as a cooperative effort. (See appendix B for a list of resources for this chapter.)

The ECTA Center offers a series of videos and facilitator guides that shares the experiences of educators and families from across the country during the COVID-19 pandemic, illustrating how the fields of early education and early childhood special education successfully supported preschoolers and their families through the use of technology. The video series was developed for ECTA by Larry Edelman and is called *Preschool During the Pandemic: Early Childhood Education in Extraordinary Times*. A team that I worked with at ECTA created the facilitator guides, which include prompts to consider, reflection questions, group activities, and additional resources. (See appendix B for a list of resources for this chapter.)

may need to send home an array of fidget toys to help with focus and attention, or paintbrushes that have been modified with foam rollers, so they are easier to grasp. Any modification that you would typically make in the classroom should also be made to the materials in the learning bags that you send home to families.

- Curriculum modifications can work on video calls as well. For example, if you have a number of children in your classroom who are interested in small toy cars, then bring some cars to your videoconference calls to really get them engaged.

- Balance activities that depend on technology with active and movement-based activities. This way, children have a balance of time spent sitting and listening as well as time playing outside or sorting with manipulatives. It is recommended that preschool-aged children be engaged in adult-directed activities for no more than twenty minutes at a time.

- Upload videos of yourself to an online platform. It could be a video of yourself explaining a lesson to families or a video of you singing a silly song for the child to watch. Either way, uploading the video will allow the family to access the content at a convenient time.

- When providing suggestions for learning activities, offer a couple of suggestions per week. Keep it simple so families do not feel overwhelmed or guilty that they aren't doing more to support their child. Consider what motivated the child during in-person service delivery, and find virtual options.

- Encourage families to plan fun activities for their child, things that they can look forward to, such as watching a video together or going on a scavenger hunt or calling a friend or family member. If families are interested, send links to videos and online resources related to the child's IFSP or IEP goals.

- If families have a strong support system, you might suggest that a relative or family friend help the child with activities that are on the child's IFSP/IEP. This will give that parent a break. You also might find that the child puts in extra effort for a friend or family member.

- Read a book together online with just a small group. Friends and family members can be involved by taking turns with reading. You read a page, then mom reads a page, then grandma reads a page, and so forth.

- Children with disabilities may experience feelings of social isolation from their peers, so plans for social engagement are important. Set up a short video call with several children to share stories, read a book together, or play a game together. Keep the calls brief so that children stay engaged. Infants and toddlers can benefit from a video conference too! We all love watching a baby or toddler on a video call, and these virtual playdates can encourage social connections for the entire family.

- For other peer-related activities, talk with families ahead of time to find out what you can do to make sure that you've considered factors related to access, participation, and supports for the child so they can participate alongside their peers successfully. When children are able to connect, especially with each other, whether in person or by video call, take time to celebrate those attempts. Making friends isn't always easy!

- Partner with families to create the visual supports they may need. This might include a picture schedule of the home routine or certain transitions that might benefit from a "first-then" schedule. For example: "First you will do your exercises for physical therapy, then you can play on the tablet." Or, "First get dressed, then we can have breakfast together."

- Families may also want to use the strategy of teaching their child how to use a timer. This gives children a sense of control and predictability because the timer lets them know how much time is left before an activity ends.

- Remember to build in brain breaks! We all need to rest our brains after a period of attention and learning, and this can be achieved by doing something purely pleasurable, or for many children, something physically active. Children (and adults) need brain breaks at regular intervals. Generally, a break of five to twenty minutes is all it takes to recharge mental energy.

As you build your toolbox of teaching practices, you may find that strategies to support social and emotional learning are the ones that you use most frequently. Chapter 8 takes a closer look at social and emotional learning in inclusive settings and how you can foster relationship skills to last a lifetime.

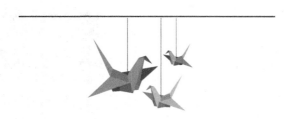

REFLECTION QUESTIONS

- What can you do to adapt your teaching practices to support highly individualized learning opportunities?
- What are you still wondering about when you consider scaffolding children's learning and using prompts and visuals?
- How will you build in time to plan for necessary curriculum modifications?

CHAPTER 8

Inclusive Practices to Foster Social-Emotional Development

We all have different gifts, so we all have different ways of saying to the world who we are.

—FRED ROGERS, CREATOR OF
MISTER ROGERS' NEIGHBORHOOD

Ask any early childhood educator about the most difficult part of the job, and nine times out of ten she will say it is dealing with children with "challenging behaviors." In my experience, this is the most frequently requested content for professional-development opportunities in early childhood. We want strategies to support children with behaviors that are challenging for adults. Of course, not every child with a disability exhibits these types of behaviors, and not every child with a disability has a delay in the social-emotional domain of development. But every child, with or without a disability, is in the process of learning important social and emotional skills necessary to form positive relationships with others and to regulate their emotions. So, if we want to create a high-quality, inclusive learning environment for each and every child, we do need to pay close attention to the social-emotional developmental domain.

This is a critical issue for all children. Challenging behavior and related difficulties with social and emotional skills can interfere with children's ability to do well in school and later on in life (Fantuzzo et al., 2007). In addition, children with challenging behavior are more likely to be rejected by peers and tend to receive less positive feedback from adults (Hemmeter, Ostrosky, and Fox, 2006). We owe it to all the children in our programs to pay attention to these issues and to teach them the social and emotional skills they will need to be successful.

In this chapter, we'll explore the form and function of behavior in young children to better understand why challenging behaviors occur in the first place. Then we'll dive into strategies that can help you as an educator, including ways to assess behaviors, develop a behavior-support plan, promote emotional literacy and emotional regulation, and help children develop new skills for making friends and solving problems.

What Do We Mean by Healthy Social-Emotional Development?

According to Zeanah and Zeanah (2001) and Zeanah and colleagues (2005), healthy social-emotional development, also described as infant and early childhood mental health, refers to the developing capacity of children ages birth through five years of age to:

- form close and secure adult and peer relationships;

- experience, regulate, and express emotions in socially and culturally appropriate ways;

- explore the environment; and

- learn all in the context of family, community, and culture.

Relationships are at the heart of what we do as early childhood educators. Through warm, nurturing, and stable relationships with children and families, we are able to teach children valuable social and emotional skills that are key to inclusion. How do we do that? It begins with understanding *why* children exhibit challenging behaviors. What do we even mean by the term?

Smith and Fox (2003) define *challenging behavior* as "any repeated pattern of behavior . . . that interferes with or is at risk of interfering with the child's optimal learning or engagement in pro-social interactions with peers and adults." Children who are described as having challenging behaviors are often those who hit, scratch, bite, kick, pull hair, raise their voices, or even throw things. In addition, challenging behaviors can be acting withdrawn, refusing to eat or speak, or attempting to harm themselves.

As a technical assistance (TA) provider for Head Start programs, the issue of challenging behaviors came up frequently in my work with educators. Most children are deemed eligible for Head Start programs based on low family income, and research has found that while 10–21 percent of *all* preschool children regularly exhibit challenging behaviors, 30 percent of children who are experiencing poverty exhibit these behaviors (Voorhees et al., 2013). So, it can be a common concern.

Consider this: The behavior that other people find challenging may very well be adaptive for the child. That is, when the child is at home or in their own community, the behaviors work well for the child. For example, the child may have found that crying and rolling around on the floor is the only way she can get the attention she needs. Is the child experiencing trauma or other difficult conditions at home that might be contributing to the behaviors? In chapter three, we explored the family context and the way that challenges can arise for us internally when the family culture is different from our own. This is an opportunity for our own professional growth and self-reflection. How can you help each child build resilience?

On the other hand, during my time providing TA in Head Start classrooms, I was often struck by the differences in what we consider to be "challenging." Our concepts about acceptable and unacceptable behavior are influenced by our own upbringing, culture, values, and beliefs. For example, Wang and Elena are coteachers in a classroom of four-year-olds, and they both see that Marcia is jumping up and down in line when it's time to go outside. To Wang, Marcia's behavior is challenging, and he feels that she is getting way too rowdy. To Elena, that same behavior is seen as spirited, and she is happy to see that Marcia is excited about going outdoors.

When educators ask for my opinion about challenging behaviors, I typically ask them to think about the behavior from the child's perspective. A child who throws a chair across the room is not a happy child. This is a child who is having challenging feelings and thoughts. This is a child who is frustrated or stressed or angry or scared. She feels out of control inside her own body, and the behavior she uses to express that out-of-control feeling is really a cry for help. I always say that the more extreme the behavior, the more desperate the cry for help. The child is not *giving* you a hard time, she is *having* a hard time. Young children do not yet have the ability to express themselves verbally, so often the communication happens through their behaviors. If we approach challenging behaviors with curiosity and try to understand the "why" behind the behavior, we can respond in a more empathetic way and take advantage of a teachable moment.

> *"All grown-ups were once children . . . but only few of them remember it."*
>
> **—ANTOINE DE SAINT-EXUPÉRY, THE LITTLE PRINCE**

BEHAVIOR HAS MEANING

As adults, we have learned over time to use words to communicate with others. Children, on the other hand, are just learning to use language to communicate, so in the absence of language, they must use their behaviors to communicate. Children let us know their wants and needs through their behavior long before they have words to express their feelings. They give us cues to help us understand what they want us to know. Infants might smile, cry, turn away, or arch their backs. Toddlers are beginning to communicate with words, but they also use facial expressions, crying, squeals, giggles, or running away. Preschoolers say words and sentences but also smile, scream, cry, kick, hit, laugh—and the list goes on.

Children will use certain behaviors until they learn new ways to communicate what they want and need. The behaviors they use depends on lots of things: their developmental stage, relationships with others, culture, and individual differences, including temperament and health issues. All behaviors have meaning, and for children with disabilities who may have special communication needs, it's important as educators that we work to figure out what the behaviors are intended to communicate.

Each behavior has a form and a function. The *form* is the actual behavior that the child uses to communicate; the *function* is the reason or purpose the child is using that behavior. For example, an infant will cry (a form of behavior) when he is trying to communicate, "I'm hungry!" (the function of the behavior). A toddler will bite her friend (form) when she is trying to communicate, "I want the toy you have" (function). A preschooler will hit his friend (form) when he is trying to communicate, "I don't want to stop playing and clean up" (function).

Sometimes we can figure out what the function of the behavior is, but other times it can be trickier. Typically, the function of every behavior is to help the child obtain something, such as a toy, attention, sensory need, or to get away from something, such as doing a task, unwanted attention, or sensory input. If we can remember that every behavior has a form and a function, and when we can understand the function, we can start to address it and give the child more appropriate replacement options for the form of the behavior.

The function of the behavior determines the intervention. You might have children who demonstrate the same behavior during an activity, but their motivations are different, and they may need different interventions. For example, two children are making lots of noise during circle time. Angela may be motivated by a desire to escape, while Deshawn is motivated by a need for attention. The way that you respond in each case is different. For Deshawn, you might try the "catch 'em being good" approach from chapter 6. But Angela may not respond to that; she might need a five-minute break from circle time instead. Gaining a better understanding of what the behavior means for the child can help the adult develop effective strategies that meet the child's needs.

When adults respond to children in a warm and supportive manner, children learn to understand, express, and regulate their emotions and behaviors. For example, Karlie tends to blurt out responses during circle time, and other children are missing out on the opportunity to share. Instead of saying, "That's rude!" her teacher could say, "Karlie, I know why you blurted out the answer. You have this awesome brain that's always filled with ideas, and you are excited to share them, so you want to say them right away before you forget. Unfortunately, when you do that, your friends don't have a chance to share their ideas. What can we do about that?"

When I was a preschool teacher, I had a child in my classroom who suddenly began exhibiting some aggressive behaviors. They seemed to show up out of the blue! Sometimes he would cling to me and seek attention, while at other times he would sit in a corner and refuse to engage. Then, at what seemed like random moments, he would act aggressively toward other children. It was difficult to predict those times, so it was a struggle to figure out how to prevent the behaviors. When my coteacher and I talked with his mom about it, we learned that his parents were going through a divorce and that home life was tense. Those feelings of fear and anxiety that he felt at home had started to show up as aggressive behaviors in the classroom. Once we talked with the family and better understood the situation, it became easier to empathize with him and put a plan into action. He really needed some extra care, love, and reassurance, and we provided predictability for him through a consistent classroom routine. We did what we could to make the classroom feel as safe as possible for him and gave him control over the situation by providing lots of opportunities to make choices throughout the day. I taught him to use a special thumbs-down signal when he started to feel overwhelmed so that I would know that he needed a hug and a play break. We also were able to refer the family to some community mental-health services. After this careful planning with the family, we noticed a big difference in school and his aggressive behaviors decreased over time.

Successful educators approach challenging behaviors with curiosity, almost in the same way that detectives go about their work. Children don't come to us with tidy labels and operating instructions. By approaching children who are experiencing stress with compassionate curiosity, you can build trust and connection. Children will feel as though they matter to you. In addition, you will learn a lot about the child, and the practice can help you to challenge your own potential biases or assumptions about the child. This practice also makes teaching more rewarding and enjoyable!

TEACHING SOCIAL-EMOTIONAL SKILLS

There is no sweeter child than my son, Ricky. I know that many parents out there would disagree and would insist, "No, *my* child is the sweetest child!" But let me just make my case. When he was three years old, I was angry with him—I can't remember what I was angry about, but I was really, really angry with him. I sat him down with me on the couch and said, "Ricky, I'm really angry with you." He stroked my cheek and said, "Gentle, gentle." It really made me laugh because this was a strategy that I used when teaching him how to be gentle with our pet cat!

When he was in kindergarten, the school play had just finished. All the children came out to take a final bow. Then, as they all ran off the stage, one little girl tripped and fell down. The crowd gasped, and before any adult could react to help her, my son ran back on stage and helped her up and

The National Center on Pyramid Model Innovations (NCPMI) is a treasure trove of resources on supporting children's social-emotional development. The Pyramid Model includes a set of practices that research has shown to be effective in reducing challenging behavior in young children with and without disabilities. The website offers hundreds of resources including tip sheets, handouts to share with families, visuals, scripted stories, and more. Many of the materials have been translated into Spanish. (See appendix B for a list of resources for this chapter.)

they both ran off, hand in hand. It was the perfect intersection between impulsivity and kindness.

Both of these instances are examples of times that Ricky used strategies that we had talked about and practiced on earlier occasions that he was able to generalize to occasions that we had not discussed or practiced. I truly believe that kindness is a skill that can be taught because, ultimately, kindness is a way of interacting with others. When you think about it, children aren't born with the ability to understand how their actions might affect others. That is a skill developed over time and is also a skill that can be taught. Social and emotional development affects just about every aspect of a child's life and their ability to learn. The thing is, we often neglect this area of development and then get frustrated when children don't have the skills that we expect them to have. We need to treat social-emotional skills just like anything else that we hope that children will learn through our guidance—with intentionality.

SOCIAL-EMOTIONAL FRAMEWORKS

In chapter 7, I introduced the MTSS framework that describes a continuum of evidence-based practices that provide intensive support to children with the most urgent needs. The tiers include the services provided to all children, then services provided to some children, and the most intensive supports to a few children. For many years, kindergarten to twelfth-grade schools have used a form of MTSS called *positive behavioral interventions and supports* (PBIS) to address social-emotional and behavior issues. The research base for PBIS is strong and shows that it can be effective in addressing children's social and emotional concerns. PBIS has been adapted for use in early childhood through the Pyramid Model for Supporting Social Emotional Competence in Infants and Young Children ("Pyramid Model").

The Pyramid Model offers a range of strategies that educators can use to prevent challenging behaviors and promote positive social-emotional development. The NCPMI site describes the model as "a promotion, prevention, and intervention framework early childhood educators can use to support young children's social emotional competence and prevent or reduce challenging behaviors." In addition, research from Hemmeter and colleagues (2016) has found that the practices improve classroom quality and are effective at supporting the social and emotional skills for children with, at risk for, and without disabilities. At least twenty-nine states have adopted the Pyramid Model as their accepted social-emotional framework, and many of the practices are widely used across the country.

THE TIERS OF THE PYRAMID MODEL

Source: Created by and available from the National Center for Pyramid Model Innovations (NCPMI) at ChallengingBehavior.org

This image details the Pyramid Model framework that is organized in this way:

- Yellow: The yellow tier, effective workforce, is the foundation of the model. It represents national, regional, state, and program systems and policies that support quality practices for children, families, and all of those who support them.

- Blue: The blue tiers describe key elements that are essential for all children. Nurturing and responsive relationships and high-quality engaging environments are instrumental for a child's well-being. When these elements are in place, typically the social and emotional development needs of 80 percent of children can be met (Hemmeter et al., 2016).

- Green: For children who are at risk of challenging behavior, targeted social-emotional supports are added. Intentional instruction around the social skills and emotional literacy is particularly important for children who may exhibit challenging behavior that may interfere with their development in many areas, but all children benefit from additional instruction around social and emotional skills. Children need to be taught throughout the day rather than in response to challenging behavior. This level of intentional support can mean a significant shift in practices for some teachers and programs.

- Orange: For children with persistent challenges, intensive, individualized interventions are added to the other tiers. This means individualized intervention of the right intensity, with the right focus, and with the right consistency to address the needs of a child whose challenging behavior is beginning to, or already is, interfering with her development.

Research has found that children who have social and emotional competence:

- tolerate frustration better,
- engage in less destructive behavior,
- are healthier,
- are less lonely,
- are less impulsive,
- are more focused, and
- have greater academic achievement

(Shonkoff and Phillips, 2000; Denham et al., 2003; Leerkes et al., 2008; Nelson, Kendall, and Shields, 2013).

The evidence-based practices within the Pyramid Model are profoundly useful for educators in high-quality inclusive programs. The practices benefit children with and without disabilities and can be adapted for use across a wide variety of settings. As educators, we can make a huge difference by teaching children skills in three distinct areas of social-emotional competence: the ability to understand and regulate emotions, the ability to make friends, and the ability to solve problems.

FUNCTIONAL BEHAVIOR ASSESSMENT AND BEHAVIOR SUPPORT PLANS

As we figure out strategies to address behaviors that challenge us, it's helpful to start with observation and assessment. NCPMI recommends a process for identifying behavior interventions using a functional behavior assessment to gather information to develop a behavior support plan. Check out the free online guide *Facilitating Individualized Interventions to Address Challenging Behavior*. (See appendix B for a list of resources for this chapter.) As described in chapter 4, a functional assessment is a collaborative, team approach, including the family, that uses observations of the child in everyday routines across multiple settings and situations. A *functional behavior assessment* is focused on analyzing a specific behavior that the family and educators hope to understand and modify. The word *understand* is key here. This is all about understanding the function of the behavior. Why does it occur? Is there a specific place or time that it occurs? What happens before the behavior occurs? What does the child gain by behaving this way?

FUNCTIONAL BEHAVIOR ASSESSMENT

A functional behavior assessment breaks down the situation in which the behavior happened, considering events before and after the behavior occurs. The assessment considers the environment, people, interactions, materials, and demands that may have something to do with why the child uses that behavior to communicate. Team members collect information about the following:

- Specific details about the challenging behavior
- Events or conditions that increase the likelihood of challenging behavior (called *setting events*)
- What happens before the behavior occurs (called *triggers* or *antecedents*)
- How often, how long, and how intense the behavior is
- Times when the behavior does *not* occur
- Conditions that make the behavior worse or more likely to occur
- Events that typically follow the behavior (called *consequences*)
- Child preferences and strategies tried in the past

A shorthand for this approach is called the ABC Observation. This stands for:

A: Antecedent

B: Behavior

C: Consequence

Collecting this information provides clues about all of the factors frequently related to the occurrence of the challenging behavior. The child is observed in routines, activities, or situations when the behavior is most likely to occur. The team tries to think like detectives about the child's behavior, and usually the team finds that the behavior occurs at specific times, with certain people, or in particular environments. Sometimes there are signs that the child is becoming more tense, anxious, or frustrated, and usually the challenging behavior will follow. Of course, every child is different, so these warning signs are very individual, can be influenced by the child's culture, and can be subtle, such as a foot tapping or heavy breathing or even rosy cheeks or red ears. The team will also uncover if there are events or activities that make the behavior more likely to occur, such as the child being hungry or tired. The assessment itself can help the team members to learn to recognize these early signs and actually prevent the behavior from occurring.

The team completes the assessment process by developing a *hypothesis statement*, a description of everything that is known about the behavior, triggers, and warning signs learned through the assessment. It also includes an informed guess about the purpose or function of the challenging behavior. Sometimes behaviors serve more than one function. In this case, the team will need to sort out all of the circumstances that might lead to the challenging behavior.

BEHAVIOR SUPPORT PLAN

The team then uses the hypothesis statement to develop a behavior support plan. This serves as the action plan for the team and will define the strategies to be used, skills to teach, and new ways to respond to the behavior. NCPMI suggests that behavior support plans contain the following components:

- **Behavior hypothesis statements:** statements that include a description of the behavior, setting events, triggers or antecedents for the behavior, maintaining consequences, and the purpose of the problem behavior

- **Prevention strategies:** strategies that may be used to reduce the likelihood that the child will have problem behavior. These may include environmental arrangements, personal support, changes in activities, new ways to prompt a child, changes in expectations, and more. This part of the plan may include positive reinforcement strategies for promoting the child's use of new skills or appropriate behavior, which may also be included in consequence strategies.

- **Replacement skills:** skills to teach that will replace the problem behavior

- **Consequence strategies:** guidelines for how the adults will respond to problem behaviors in ways that will not maintain the behavior. This part of the plan may include positive reinforcement strategies for promoting the child's use of new skills or appropriate behavior, which may also be included in prevention strategies.

- **Long-term strategies:** This section of the plan may include long-term goals that will assist the child and family in meeting their vision for the child: for example, the child will develop friends or attend a community preschool program.

For the behavior support plan to be most effective, the team should monitor it regularly. What is working well? What challenges have arisen? Which strategies should be adjusted or modified? Is the team using the strategies consistently? What are we learning about the child, the learning environments, and the adults in the child's life through this process?

At this point, you are probably wondering about those strategies and replacement skills that the team includes in a behavior support plan. There are lots of examples, and usually they can be considered within three key social-emotional skill areas: emotional literacy and emotional regulation, friendship skills, and problem-solving skills. Let's dive in!

Emotional Literacy and Emotional Regulation

Have you ever heard the expression that you have to "name it to tame it"? This is the concept behind emotional literacy as a first step to helping children learn how to manage and regulate their emotions. Children, just like adults, have big feelings. Unlike adults, however, children don't have the communication skills or years of experience to know how to cope with those big feelings. This is easy to see when you think about emotions in infants and toddlers. Six-month-old Marie doesn't know why she is sad, but she definitely feels it, and her mother can feel it, too, when she cries.

Learning how to manage our emotions begins very early! Infants begin to learn about self-regulation by first experiencing it through a caring adult in a process called *coregulation*. Our calm demeanor teaches the infant about how it feels to be calm and eventually how to calm herself. Marie is able to calm herself when her mother holds her close and makes sure that all of her needs are met. Coregulation happens when the adult provides support to the child in a nurturing relationship. Even adults need support from others to regulate ourselves sometimes. Think about the times that you meet a friend for lunch or call your mom at the end of a tough day. That's coregulation at work.

Preschool-aged children are typically ready to learn more strategies for how to regulate their emotions on their own. But the time to teach emotional regulation is *not* during the middle of an outburst. The most effective strategies start with prevention. Teaching happens during the day when children are calm, relaxed, and ready to understand new information.

The Pyramid Model: Steps for Teaching Social Skills

- Describe the skill.

- Demonstrate the skill the "right way" with an adult.

- Demonstrate the skill the "wrong way" with an adult.

- Have a child practice the skill with an adult.

- Have a child practice the skill with another child.

- Provide positive feedback and support for children attempting and successfully using the skill.

  (Fox and Lentini, 2006)

When we give children words to describe what they are feeling, we are helping strengthen their emotional literacy. Emotional literacy includes the ability to read facial expressions, nonverbal cues, language, and body cues in yourself and in other people. Emotional literacy is a foundation for children's ability to control their emotions, develop relationships, interact with others, and become effective problem solvers. It is one of the most important areas of development during a child's early years. When children learn how to understand and use these cues, they are on the path to being able to understand the difference between feelings and thoughts and can make decisions about how they want to respond to a situation rather than just reacting based on their emotions.

> *"For news of the heart, ask the face."*
>
> **—WEST AFRICAN PROVERB**

We can start by teaching children the words for different emotions and then teach them to use these words to label their own feelings and the feelings of others. We also can teach children to understand that their feelings can change. I may wake up grumpy, but I don't have to stay grumpy all day. Feelings come and feelings go, and it's important for young children to know that feelings don't last forever. In addition, we can teach children that they can have more than one feeling about something. They can feel differently about something than someone else feels. And all feelings are valid. As children's emotional vocabularies grow, their ability to accurately read their own and other's emotions grows, too. Here are some strategies for teaching emotional literacy in early childhood.

➤ Talk about Emotions

Talk about emotions in everyday life. Label your own emotions and the child's emotions as they happen throughout the day. You might say, "Wow! You look surprised! Do you know how I can tell? Your mouth is open, and your eyes are wide." Or "I feel sad. Yesterday, I was happy that Aunt Ellen came to visit, but now I feel sad that it is time for her to go." Start with a few simple emotions such as happy and sad, then move to the more complex emotions such as calm and anxious. Make sure to talk about a range of emotions, including those that feel comfortable and those that feel uncomfortable.

➤ Talk about Facial Expressions

Explain to children that most people can tell how you are feeling by looking at the expression on your face. Use a mirror so children can practice making faces that go with the different feeling words. What does your face look like when you are feeling frustrated? Excited? Worried? Calm? Elated? Embarrassed? Scared? Hopeful?

Cut out pictures of different feeling faces from magazines, and then talk about how they think that the person in the picture feels. NCPMI offers Feeling Faces cards, which are free to download and print, on its website. (See appendix B for a list of resources for this chapter.) You can use them to talk about the different emotions that we all feel. You can also use them as a way to check in with each other at the start of the day or during a circle-time activity. Children can also use the feeling faces cards to let adults know how they are feeling throughout the day.

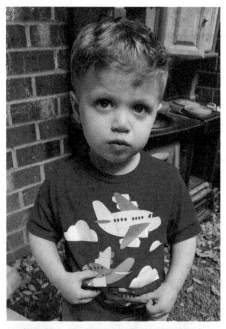

➤ Talk about Sensations in the Body

Talk with children about the fact that sometimes we can feel our feelings in our bodies, even before we know what we are feeling. Together with the child, practice closing your eyes and noticing sensations in the body. Ask the child where she feels big feelings: "What does angry feel like in your tummy?"

➤ Practice Describing Feelings

Ask children to describe their feelings often. Use questions such as, "What happened that surprised you?" "Did that make you feel angry?" "Why do you think Grandma was happy when she saw you? How can you tell that she was happy?"

Children should know that it's okay to have strong feelings such as anger or frustration, but that we all should manage those feelings in a positive way. For example, "I know it made you mad when George took the shovel from you. Next time you can ask an adult to help you."

➤ Practice Identifying Feelings Clues

Reflect on the fact that some emotions look the same but feel different. For example, we might cry out of happiness or out of sadness. How confusing! Talk with children about how we get clues about emotions from lots of different forms of information. In this classroom, the educator posted a feelings poster with a mirror beside it. This way, children can practice making the feeling faces to better understand the way they look to others.

➤ Read Books about Emotions

Use children's books that focus on building emotional literacy, either as material for circle-time reading or for small-group book sharing. When reading a story, ask children to imagine what the different characters are feeling. Ask questions such as, "Why do you think she feels that way?"

**Children's Books
with a Focus on Feelings**

Bang, Molly. *When Sophie Gets Angry—Really, Really Angry . . .* New York: Scholastic.

Emberley, Ed, and Anne Miranda. 1997. *Glad Monster, Sad Monster: A Book About Feelings*. New York: LB Kids.

Kachenmeister, Cherryl. 2001. *On Monday When It Rained*. New York: HMH Books for Young Readers.

As children become more and more competent with learning to recognize and name their own emotions and feelings, they can begin to learn how to control their emotions. We have to know what angry feels like before we are able to control our anger. We need to understand what calm looks like and feels like before we are able to calm down. Once children have the words to use, they can verbalize their feeling rather than having to act it out.

We all feel strong emotions in different ways, and as adults, we have likely learned ways to manage these strong emotions. If so, you are already on your way to helping young children to manage their emotions, because serving as a calm role model is the most important practice of all. Even at a very young age, children learn by watching adults. When we respond calmly to situations or show kindness to others, we are teaching children how to behave through our actions. We truly invite calm into our space by being calm. Your sense of calm creates a safe harbor for children.

- Invite calm by being calm.
- Pay attention to your own body language. Are your posture, tone, and pace communicating a sense of calm?
- Slow down and allow children time to process their own thoughts and feelings.
- Limit your words, especially when children are upset. They can't process what you are saying until they feel calmer.
- Take deep breaths and remember to consider the child's perspective.

Most of us as adults know how to calm ourselves down, use our words carefully, get help when we need it, and choose to walk away as needed. At least we try to do these things, most of the time. Young children haven't learned these skills yet and need support to learn important strategies and time to practice the new skills. Successful educators are intentional about teaching children how to express the emotions that they are feeling. When we don't teach children how to express emotions in a positive way, they might get carried away with the feeling and express the emotions in inappropriate ways, such as hitting or grabbing a toy, crying and rolling around on the floor, or just plain not following directions. When children learn ways to communicate emotions appropriately, they are less likely to resort to behaviors that are challenging to adults. The following are some strategies for teaching young children about how to express and regulate their emotions.

- **Practice using emotional vocabulary:** Use the new emotional vocabulary that children have acquired to help them manage difficult situations. For example, Cody's teacher noticed that another child was rough with him on the playground. His teacher said, "Are you sad because Derrick pushed you? Do you feel frustrated? Angry? Embarrassed? Gloomy? Should we go and tell him how that made you feel?" She told him the story about what was upsetting him and gave him the words for how to describe his feelings. His teacher also served as a role model for self-regulation. This type of calm response can turn down the intensity of the situation, help the child feel understood, and provide a chance to teach the child a helpful next step for dealing with the emotion.

- **Talk about ways to manage emotions:** Use circle time or small-group time to talk about how children can manage their emotions. You can read books about difficult situations and can talk about how children might respond, use puppets to act out the sequence of events, or engage children in a role-play activity. Ask children to close their eyes and imagine themselves in a place of calm: Are you in a garden surrounded by flowers? Are you in a fort that you made with blankets and pillows? Are you snuggled in the arms of your grandmother? Practice what it feels like to "go" to a calm place, and then later, during a stressful time, that can be a place that you suggest to the child as a way to center themselves.

- **Practice paying attention to body sensations:** Try using the NCPMI Relaxation Thermometer visual so that children can see how their bodies change when they feel strong emotions and when they are relaxed. When children are feeling calm, practice using it as a way for children to describe how they are feeling. Once they know how to use it, the thermometer can be a great tool for children to use to let adults know how they are feeling when they are upset. (See appendix B for a list of resources for this chapter.)

- **Use a Big Feelings Box:** Fill a box with materials, such as the following, that can help children regulate their emotions.

  ➢ Bubbles to blow—a great distraction and calming activity

  ➢ A jump rope—exercise can be an effective stress-management practice

- Scented hand lotion—if allergies are not an issue, it can be soothing to have someone rub your hands with lotion; this is also a good self-soothing technique
- Bubble packing material—popping the bubbles is soothing, or children can stomp on the bubble wrap as a safe way to express strong feelings
- Art supplies—children can draw a picture of what happened to make them upset. What happened before you were sad? Then what happened? Ask them to describe the episode by telling you about their picture and what they were thinking and feeling along the way.
- Musical instrument—shaking a tambourine can distract children and serve as a stress reducer
- Paper—ripping it into tiny pieces is a great stress reliever
- Beads and string—make a necklace or garland as a way to calm and distract the mind
- Fidget toys—there are lots of options to choose from! Fidget spinners, stress balls, sensory rings, and other squishy toys can be great for relieving anxiety
- Playdough—squish it out and flatten it like a pancake to express strong feelings

From a Distance: Supporting Emotional Regulation at Home

Children with disabilities who are receiving remote services might have feelings associated with isolation or other strong emotions. In these times, opportunities to engage in calming behaviors become especially important, so talk with families about how to schedule coping and calming activities into a child's day. Also consider ways to introduce new calming behaviors.

You can use Feelings Faces during virtual check-ins with the child and family, as well as during interactive peer activities. Families might even want to create a Big Feelings Box for home. Talk about it on a video call and share some ideas for what they might include. Once they have a week or so to collect their materials, come back together and share how the strategy is working.

Deep breathing stimulates the vagus nerve, which is located on both sides of the voice box. This practice can interrupt the fight, flight, or freeze response that we all go into during a stressful event. In addition, when we're anxious, we tend to take rapid, shallow breaths; deeper breaths from the tummy trigger the relaxation response. Ask the child, "Would it help to take some deep breaths together?" Show them how to rest their hand on their stomach to watch and count their breaths. Or encourage the child to lie down on their back on the carpet, put a stuffed animal on their belly, and practice belly breathing. You know that it's working when the stuffed animal goes up and down on their belly as they breathe. Other breathing strategies include blowing bubbles; blowing into a pinwheel; visualizing smelling flowers and blowing out candles; breathing in through the nose and out through the mouth; and breathing in for a count of three, holding it for a count of three, and letting out the breath slowly, slowly, slowly.

In addition to deep-breathing exercises, try some of the following calming techniques:

- Listen to music.
- Go for a walk.
- Count to ten.
- Get a drink of water.
- Read a story together.
- Take a break in a cozy spot.
- Draw a picture.
- Play with playdough.
- Swing.
- Rock back and forth.
- Hug a favorite toy.
- Do a puzzle together.

Ask families about calming strategies that work at home and try those out at school too! In one classroom, children could visit this poster, select one of the "calm-down choices", and hold onto the laminated card while they used the strategy to calm their body.

If a stressful event is coming up and you are able to prepare the child for it, you can help her create a calming ritual. Just like athletes who engage in a set of activities that are centering to them before a big game, rituals can work for young children as well. Rituals can provide a sense of stability, something familiar that is within the child's control that can ease anxiety and give the child more confidence as she approaches the event. For example, Matthew reads a comic book before he goes in for his doctor's appointment. Crystal does ten jumping jacks before her basketball game.

Activating muscles and joints can also bring on a sense of calm in young children. My son really benefitted from this approach with increased focus and attention. His therapist taught me the term

heavy work, which basically involves pushing around heavy things, such as a vacuum cleaner, pulling a wagon around, or even picking up and moving a piece of furniture from one place to another. It sounds kind of strange, but it's effective!

When children are in full-on cry mode, it can help to distract them with silliness or humor. My mother used to tell me, "Don't smile or your face will crack!" which of course made me smile or laugh. Laughter really does relieve anxiety by releasing endorphins, which are known to combat stress. Keep a silly joke at the ready for these occasions or cue up a comical video on your cell phone. Who doesn't love a funny cat video? Ask, "What did one toilet say to the other toilet? Are you okay? You're looking a little bit *flushed*?"

Pay attention to the learning environment. Sometimes, the environment itself causes stress for young children. Do you need to create a quiet space? As much as you can, remove distracting or disturbing items in the environment, such as flickering fluorescent lights.

Each child is unique—one child may want to have a conversation to help her calm down; another may need a hug or deep breaths.

Keep in mind that managing emotions in a skill that takes many years to practice. Even adults often have to work hard to self-regulate. Hopefully, we are able to manage our emotions most of the time, but it is not easy! For some children, the expectations that adults have are just too difficult to manage. We need to be patient while children navigate these waters. Reflect on the child's perspective, and try to be "gentle, gentle" as much as possible.

"The single best childhood predictor of adult adaptation is not school grades and not classroom behavior, but rather the adequacy with which the child gets along with other children."

**—WILLARD HARTUP,
PRESIDENT OF THE INTERNATIONAL
SOCIETY FOR THE STUDY OF
BEHAVIORAL DEVELOPMENT**

Friendship Skills

Developing close relationships is the best part of the human experience, and when relationships develop with people outside of the family, children truly flourish. It's one thing to be loved by a parent, grandparent, or sibling, but when a child is loved by a peer, the feeling is truly remarkable. The benefits of friendship in young children are the same that we feel as adults. The research backs this up as well and shows how important friendships are for young children. Friends look out for each other. Friends encourage each other to explore the world and learn new things. According to Geisthardt, Brotherson, and Cook (2002), friendships give us a sense of security and belonging and can even be great stress reducers! In fact, having a friend in preschool correlates with important factors in later life and is an important developmental goal (Rubin, Bukowski, and Parker, 1998). Catherine Bagwell and Michelle Schmidt (2011) write that friendships provide emotional support, practice with compromise, and opportunities to take someone else's perspective.

Friendships are important for all of us, and they are especially important for children with disabilities or suspected delays. Guralnick and colleagues (2007) found that children with disabilities in inclusive classrooms who have opportunities to interact with typically developing peers demonstrate higher levels of social competence. Yet friendships do not always come naturally, and research by Geisthardt, Brotherson, and Cook (2002) found that it can be especially difficult for children with disabilities. Guralnick and colleagues (2007) found that children with developmental disabilities are often the least preferred play partners of typically developing children. As we learned earlier, play is the way that young children learn, and when children have delayed social skills, their ability to engage in play activities with their peers is affected (Nelson et al., 2007). Making friends is a tricky business. It involves complex verbal and nonverbal social interactions that can sometimes be elusive for certain children. Fortunately, friendship skills can be taught! With encouragement and coaching from family members and educators, children can learn skills that will help them form strong, mutual friendships.

I remember one summer day at the playground when Ricky was around four years old. A group of children were playing an elaborate game of pirate ship, and Ricky was very interested in all the activity. He walked over to the group and watched for a while. They continued to play and barely noticed that he was standing there. After about ten minutes or so, Ricky came back over to me and sat down. He seemed to be considering his options. Finally, he looked up at me and said, "Mommy, can you introduce me to them?" This was a good first step! He definitely knew that introductions should be made. I think that I did take him over that time and said something along the lines of,

Important Friendship Skills to Teach

- How to share toys and other materials
- How to take turns
- How to suggest ideas for what to play
- How to work together as a team
- How to give compliments
- How and when to say, "I'm sorry"
- How to understand what my friend is feeling

(See appendix B for a list of resources for this chapter.)

"Hi guys! This is Ricky. Can he play with you all?" Later on, we talked about how he could introduce himself in the future. These types of experiences and practice with social relationships are a huge benefit that inclusive programs can have for children with disabilities. Through positive peer influences, children with disabilities can learn how to initiate social interactions, respond to social cues, practice giving compliments to peers, and find out how to engage in group-play activities.

As educators, we can make this learning possible for children of all abilities. When we support the development of peer relationships, children learn to understand differences and how they are our greatest assets. This learning happens in high-quality, inclusive classrooms, not just by the fact that children are learning and growing side by side, but also due to the actions of the educators. For example, Stanton-Chapman and Snell (2011) used an intervention of shared storybook reading along with pretend-play activities that encouraged children with disabilities to interact with their peers. These were children with language or developmental delays or behavior concerns. This simple intervention led to an increase in children with and without disabilities playing together—even on the playground!

By modeling prosocial behaviors and friendship skills and by teaching social-emotional strategies, educators can create an environment that fosters the development of friendships between children with and without disabilities. Researchers have found that visual supports can be helpful when teaching children how to enter into play with other children (Johnston and Nelson, 2016). A visual support might be a gesture, a word expressed with sign language, or a picture or graphic intended to let others know that the child wants to play. This strategy has been found to help nonverbal children communicate as their language skills develop (Groskreutz et al., 2015). Visuals are most helpful when they are used by the whole group and not just the child or children with communication delays. This way, everyone in the group understands the concept, and children with and without disabilities can use the visuals to engage with others and model the targeted skills. Try using visuals such as those available from Head Start Center for Inclusion. (See appendix B for a list of resources for this chapter.) These visual supports help children understand friendship skills by breaking down the steps involved. For example, if I want to ask a friend to play:

1. I can tap my friend on the shoulder.

2. When she looks at me, I can say, "Let's play!"

3. I can gently take my friend by the hand.

4. I can give my friend a toy that I want to share.

The following are some examples of effective teaching practices to foster friendships.

- **Teach children prosocial skills.** You can teach skills such as sharing classroom materials and even set up situations where there are not enough of a desired toy, so that a child who is working on that skill can practice asking for a turn. For example, Murray and Jacquetta are playing with playdough, but there is only one rolling pin on the table. The teacher notices that Murray really wants the rolling pin, so she suggests, "Let's tap Jacquetta on the shoulder and ask, 'May I have a turn?'" Teaching children how to ask for a turn, giving them the exact words to use, and then providing opportunities to practice the skill are all important steps.

- **Create activities intended to be carried out collaboratively.** Suggest games that take two people, such as rolling a ball back and forth. Encourage a typically developing peer to buddy up with a child who is struggling. This can be a useful strategy for all sorts of classroom activities. A peer can sit with a child and hold her hand during circle time. Peers can help each other during transition times. If a child is nonverbal, a peer can help a friend respond to comments from other children. She can show a friend how to play with a new toy or give suggestions for a play activity. She can give a compliment for a job well done or marvel over a beautiful art project.

- **Use circle time or small-group activities to teach and practice social skills.** Puppets are great for this! Pretend that two puppets are just getting to know each other. Ask children what one puppet should say to the other one. How might this puppet ask his friend to play? What should he do? What should she say?

"Inclusion . . . is important, not just educationally, but socially. You make friends and you get to know people and you learn how to navigate through life by being with the peers in your community."

—DAN HABIB, DIRECTOR AND PRODUCER OF THE DOCUMENTARY FILM *INCLUDING SAMUEL*

- **Use role-play to practice these skills.** It can start by having the child role-play with an adult, but children can role-play together as well. This is a great way to work through common situations such as asking to use a toy or inviting a friend to play when there is no chance for a social slight.

- **Create social stories.** Take notes about the behaviors you'd like to see in the early childhood environment. Then, write social stories to use when teaching new skills. For example, write social stories about such friendship skills as taking turns, giving compliments, and so on. In each story, describe a situation that the child may encounter and the behaviors the child should use in that situation. When children have information that helps them understand the expectations of a situation, we are less likely to see associated challenging behaviors. Social stories can be illustrated with photographs of the child or graphics found online. Often, social stories are written to highlight "challenging" behaviors that adults want to modify. For example, a child who is especially loud in circle time might benefit from reading a story about herself:

> *Last November, Gabby was loud during circle time. But she learned that yelling hurts her friends' ears. Now Gabby knows to use a quieter voice in circle time and raise her hand when she wants to speak.*

Her teacher could enhance the story with details about the daily routine, Gabby's friends, and so on and illustrate it with images of Gabby as the lead character.

- **Observe children to find common interests.** Adults can foster friendships just by pointing out these shared interests with children. "Look, Emily! Rodrigo is wearing a shirt with a bulldozer on it. You like bulldozers too! Maybe you could play together in the sandbox today."

- **Give feedback and celebrate effort.** Give children feedback and celebrate their efforts when they initiate interactions with peers. "Jorge, I just overheard you when you asked Margo to play with you in the block area. That was really being a good friend." The children involved in the interaction will learn from this feedback that they are on the right track, and other children will hear you as well and may be likely to try that strategy themselves. You can take this strategy a step further by writing a note of thanks that the child can share with family members at the end of the day. One educator used to have a "Super Friend" cape in the classroom for the purpose of recognition. And we shouldn't stop with only recognizing kindness in children; adults appreciate recognition, too. Use a bulletin board as a space where adults can post notes to one another to show appreciation. For example, a note could say thanks to the maintenance man for putting in a wheelchair ramp at the entrance to the building.

Problem-Solving Skills

The ability for children to persist when faced with obstacles grows over time. The areas of the brain that help children to persist and regulate themselves is still growing in preschool-aged children. Most children under the age of five will likely give up on a problem if their first opportunities to solve it aren't successful. But Webster-Stratton and Hammond (1997) found that preschool-age children can effectively be taught problem-solving skills. As educators, we can support children as they are learning to persist by giving them tools to come up with a solution when faced with a challenge. Developing their own problem-solving skills can be empowering for children!

With younger children, teachers start by working alongside them and showing that we're enthusiastic about their efforts. When they have difficulties, we convey our confidence that they'll be able to figure this out eventually. We also let them know that some problems take time to solve and that, when you're stuck, it's okay to come back later and try again. Older children benefit when we put feelings of frustration into words, understanding that the feeling shouldn't be a barrier to continuing to try or to come back and try later.

How do you teach these practices? First, spend time during circle time using puppets, books, or other teaching tools to model the practices. Then, use the visuals to spark conversation about typical problems that children encounter in the classroom. For example, when children are struggling with waiting and taking turns, a suggested strategy is the use of a timer. The educator would introduce the timer to the class, explain how it can be used, and then add an image of the timer to the problem-solving kit. Children might even discuss the specifics for using the timer, such as where it is stored, how many minutes to set, and so on. The collaborative approach to problem solving addresses

RESOURCE SPOTLIGHT

NCPMI recommends that educators create classroom solution kits as a way to teach children problem-solving strategies. The website includes visuals that children can use as they consider how they might resolve a tricky situation such as sharing toys or taking turns. You can laminate the cards and put them on an O-ring for children to consult when a conflict arises. The visuals are available in numerous languages, including Spanish, Hmong, and Somali. (See appendix B for a list of resources for this chapter.)

an issue up front, *before* conflict has occurred, and gives children a sense of ownership over the solution.

Educators can teach problem solving step by step. The Pyramid Model suggests four essential problem-solving steps for young children to learn and act on. Every conflict becomes a problem to solve.

1. **Name the problem:** "We have four kids in the sandbox and only one shovel."

2. **Brainstorm solutions:** Children can think of solutions in the moment, or they could consult a solution kit or problem-solving solution cards. The strategies might include, "Take Turns," "Use a Timer," "Get a Teacher for Help," "Say, 'Please Stop,'" "Use Kind Words," and others.

3. **Consider each solution:** Ask, "What would happen if we tried it?" "Would it be safe?" "Would it be fair?" "How would it make everyone feel?"

4. **Try one!** Try out a solution that everyone thinks will work.

This strategy encourages children to explore the problem together, rather than an adult stepping in to solve it. The child finds the answer on her own and develops a skill that can applied to other areas of life. The approach encourages teamwork, independent thinking, and curiosity. It also builds in the practice of giving children choices, which can give them a sense of autonomy and control over the situation. Children are more likely to buy in to the solution when they can choose which solution to try. Educators might ask questions to stimulate thinking, such as, "What do you think might work?" or "Is this a big problem or a little problem?" or "Should we find out what or who can help us?" This is also a way to engage children in problem solving about their challenging behaviors, if they are developmentally ready to do so. Rather than shaming children for inappropriate behaviors, we can use the opportunity to think about how our behavior affects others and can consider alternatives.

Once children are in the habit of using this strategy, educators can ask children to consider problems that occur in children's stories. Children's books have lots of examples of how people get along, or don't get along, with each other. During circle time or small-group book sharing, choose books that relate to the social skills that you are trying to teach. Give children the opportunity to ask questions and pose some of your own. For example, you can point out that children are helping each other, that children are taking turns, or that children are sharing in a book. After you read the book, give children opportunities through role-play activities in which they actually practice the skills. Use multiple times throughout the daily routine to talk about the social skills you are working on so that children have time to process the information, get feedback on their own behavior, and practice the skills with their friends.

TOXIC STRESS AND TRAUMA

Of course, each child comes with a unique set of experiences, abilities, and needs, and the degree to which children's home environments have been supportive can vary tremendously. Children with disabilities who are also experiencing stress in their home or community due to violence, trauma, abuse, or neglect have additional needs beyond their disability. Unfortunately, research shows that children with disabilities are at increased risk for abuse as compared to the general population (Legano et al., 2021). National data from 2015 show that child victims with a disability accounted for 14.1 percent of all victims of abuse and neglect (Children's Bureau, 2018). The rate of child abuse and neglect is at least three times higher in children with disabilities than in the typically developing population (Jones et al., 2012). Helton and colleagues (2019) found that nearly one-half of children investigated by child protective services (CPS) were not typically developing. Families caring for a child with a disability are often placed under higher emotional, physical, economic, and social demands than other families (Peer and Hillman, 2014). Stress is a huge factor, and researchers have found that the financial stress of raising a child with disabilities is often high (Murphy, 2011).

It's important for educators to understand typical behaviors of children who have experienced trauma and to think about the best strategies to support the child given these special circumstances. As we have explored throughout this chapter, young children often do not have the skills or ability to use words to express how they are feeling. However, there are certain signs to look for and typical behaviors that children exhibit that can help us recognize the need for additional supports.

RESOURCE SPOTLIGHT

NCPMI has developed a checklist of Pyramid practices that can be used during times of virtual learning. (See appendix B for a list of resources for this chapter.)

> "Out of suffering have emerged the strongest souls; the most massive characters are seared with scars."
>
> **—KAHLIL GIBRAN, AUTHOR AND VISUAL ARTIST**

ADVERSE CHILDHOOD EXPERIENCES

You may have heard about *adverse childhood experiences* (ACEs), a term that came from a study carried out by the Centers for Disease Control and Kaiser Permanente in 1995. Researchers found that there were three types of adversity that children face that are experienced as potentially traumatic and could have an effect on them later in life: physical and emotional abuse, neglect, and household dysfunction (Felitti et al., 1998). These experiences undermine children's ability to feel

safe and secure. Many studies have been conducted since then using the ACEs framework, and we have learned that ACEs are quite common. In fact, over two thirds of the US population have experienced at least one ACE, and almost one quarter of the population have experienced three or more. The higher numbers of ACEs in childhood are linked to problems later in life such as depression, heart disease, and early death (Center on the Developing Child, 2021).

The National Scientific Council on the Developing Child (2014) introduced the term *toxic stress* to describe the way that ACEs can affect children and lead to those later-life problems. The council described that when children are exposed to a large number of ACEs over time without the benefit of having a supportive, caring adult in their lives, the experience is truly toxic. Children faced with toxic stresses, such as severe poverty, child abuse, or violence in their community, suffer long-lasting effects on their bodies and in their brains.

The Harvard Center on the Developing Child describes *trauma* as "an experience of serious adversity or terror—or the emotional or psychological response to that experience" (Center on the Developing Child, 2021). For children with disabilities, the disability itself may be experienced as a traumatic event, especially if they have to undergo difficult medical procedures or experience exclusion or bullying.

In the brief *Preventing Adverse Childhood Experiences: Leveraging the Best Available Evidence* (CDC, 2019), the CDC suggests that prevention is the key to addressing ACEs. What are the most effective prevention strategies? The report confirms that high-quality early childhood programs and educators who work to teach social-emotional skills can make a difference for children who are experiences ACEs. In addition to the Pyramid Model practices outlined earlier in this chapter, educators can use a trauma-informed care approach.

TRAUMA-INFORMED CARE

Trauma-informed care is an approach we can use to support children and families through these difficult situations. We don't need to know about the experience to be able to help. The Pyramid Model practices are structured in a way that support all children and reflect the trauma-informed care approach. Trauma is often marked by fear and unpredictability. When we offer a place of safety and predictability, where children are nurtured and caregivers are responsive, we can counter some of those effects. As NCPMI guidance suggests, a trauma-informed care approach shifts thinking from "What is wrong with you?" to "What happened to you?" Certain strategies and supports can help children who have experienced traumatic events adapt to program activities more easily so that they feel safe and ready to learn. Some trauma-informed strategies to add to your toolbox are outlined below.

What Are the Signs of Trauma in Early Childhood?

- **Infants and Toddlers:**
  » Problems eating
  » Trouble sleeping
  » Clinginess or difficulty in separating from parent
  » Fearfulness
  » Easily startled
  » Aggression
  » Loss of skills or regression from developmental milestones

- **Preschoolers:**
  » Avoiding adults
  » Anxious or clingy
  » Helpless or passive
  » Restless or impulsive
  » Aggressive
  » Sad or irritable
  » Peer-relationship issues
  » Difficulty focusing
  » Physical symptoms, such as headaches or other aches and pains

(Head Start, 2020)

Children who have experienced trauma often feel like their world is out of control. The early childhood program can be an environment that is manageable and predictable when there are clear expectations, routines, and a consistent daily schedule. Minimize, plan, and prepare children for transitions, even if they seem insignificant to you. For example, when a special visitor is coming to the class, give children fair warning. You might say, "Tomorrow we will have a special visitor come to talk to us about books available at the library. Who do you think that visitor might be?" Place a visual of a book on the daily schedule.

Educators themselves can be a source of predictability by following through on promises, being open and transparent, and providing nurturing care and consistent boundaries. We can also model our own self-regulation skills and flexibility throughout daily events. If you are stressed and anxious yourself, find ways to ground yourself before engaging with the child.

The National Child Traumatic Stress Network is a great source of information related to trauma-informed care, culture and trauma, families and trauma, and secondary traumatic stress. The Pyramid Model also has a resource on trauma informed care called *A Guide for Early Childhood Professionals to Support Young Children's Resilience*. (See appendix B for a list of resources for this chapter.)

The Center of Excellence for Infant and Early Childhood Mental Health Consultation is home to many resources, tutorials, videos, and briefs for educators and families. Topics include stress and relaxation, challenging behaviors, and promoting social-emotional development. (See appendix B for a list of resources for this chapter.)

Help children feel seen and heard. Give them choices throughout the day so that they feel empowered in decision making. Create opportunities for children to be helpers. For example, one child could be the door holder and another child could help with snacks.

Provide a safe place in the classroom, and give children guidance for when and how to use it. This may simply be a cozy corner set up with soft furniture, pillows, stuffed animals, and blankets. Give children headphones to help block noise as needed. You might include books and other quiet activities that children can use when they go to this safe place to take a time out from a fast-paced classroom environment.

The Pyramid Model practices related to emotional literacy, friendship skills, and problem-solving skills are important to use as prevention strategies in a trauma-informed classroom.

COLLABORATION WITH MENTAL HEALTH EXPERTS

More and more, states are creating programs to address social-emotional issues in young children in comprehensive ways. An effective approach is infant and early childhood mental health consultation (IECMHC). IECMHC places mental-health professionals in early childhood settings to work closely with educators to address behaviors that are challenging to adults. This is typically a holistic approach that includes supports to families as well. Educators can learn strategies to support young children's social and emotional development. Consultants build partnerships with educators and families so that together they can

uncover underlying issues and develop a behavior support plan. Results have been promising, and the partnerships formed through IECMHC programs often lead to reductions in suspensions and expulsions and lower levels of teacher stress.

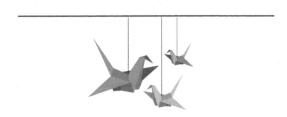

REFLECTION QUESTIONS

- How might you plan activities to build emotional literacy and strategies for emotional regulation?

- What aspects of your program are most likely to present self-regulation challenges to children? What could you modify to help children with these challenges?

- What can you do to foster the development of friendships between children?

- What resources are available in your community to meet the mental-health needs of children in your program? Where might you turn if you need help or support?

CHAPTER 9

Culturally and Linguistically Responsive Practices

A nation's culture lies in the hearts and in the soul of its people.

**—MAHATMA GANDHI,
HUMAN-RIGHTS ADVOCATE**

We are fortunate that the United States is home to families and children from diverse racial, ethnic, and cultural backgrounds. This diversity is a benefit because families from different backgrounds bring a wealth of strengths, knowledge, and values to our country. As educators, we should strive to be aware of children's cultural backgrounds because their family's beliefs, attitudes, and behaviors have a big effect on the child's development and learning. It is important to respect each child's culture, to learn as much as you can about a child's family, and to foster a close connection with the child and family by seeking to care for the child in a way that's consistent with the family's values and how they care for the child.

In the following pages, we'll explore the role that language and culture plays in children's lives and in our own work as early childhood educators. We'll think about our own biases and reflect on our practice, as well as discover strategies to promote an equitable and culturally responsive learning environment.

As indicated in the principles of child development and learning highlighted in NAEYC's equity position statement, "Children's learning is facilitated when teaching practices, curricula, and learning environments build on children's strengths and are developmentally, culturally, and linguistically appropriate for each child" (NAEYC, 2019).

WHAT IS CULTURE?

Merriam-Webster defines *culture* as "the customary beliefs, social norms, and material traits of a racial, religious, or social group" and "the characteristic features of everyday existence (such as diversions or a way of life) shared by people in a place or time" and the "set of shared attitudes, values, goals, and practices that characterizes an institution or organization" and the "set of values, conventions, or social practices associated with a particular field, activity, or societal characteristic" (Merriam-Webster, 2021). Basically, it's complicated. Culture can refer to our racial, ethnic, religious, or social group. It can also refer to the organization where we work and the field in which we work. Culture is learned rather than inherited through our genes. Families come to early childhood programs with their own set of cultural beliefs, values, and perceptions of the world. These influence the ways that families relate with educators and the ways that educators relate with families.

Culture Is . . .

- applicable to all people.
- value laden and rooted in belief systems.
- active and dynamic.
- multilayered and multidimensional.
- conscious and unconscious.
- tied to group member identity.
- an influence on our perceptions and behaviors.
- varied in expression both among and between individual group members.
- found in every aspect of life.

(Gullotta and Blau, eds., 2008)

THE CONCEPT OF DISABILITY ACROSS CULTURES

When supporting young children with disabilities or suspected delays, it's important to remember that different cultures vary in how they think about, define, and perceive what it means to have a disability. In some cultures, there is a real stigma associated with disability in general, and that can affect how a family views their child. Some families may even blame themselves for their child's disability, or they might think the disability is caused by something other than a medical issue, such as a family curse.

Do not make assumptions about the perspectives of an individual family based on their culture or language. For example, for some people in Latin American culture, the term *disability* is strictly associated with a visible disability such as an orthopedic impairment, rather than with a condition such as ADHD. Generally speaking, learning disabilities in Latin America are not necessarily considered disabilities because they aren't visible conditions. That said, we should never assume that every family with Latin American origins holds that viewpoint.

Regardless of the culture, families may wonder whether the child will grow out of the disability. Families who speak another language may also question whether or not the disability is something related to learning English.

Educators can prepare for these kinds of questions by being ready with information gathered through careful observation. Offer information about available resources through early intervention or early childhood special education systems, as well. It's also critical that conversations are framed with the fact that the disability or suspected delay is not a deficit in the child but is simply a difference. Families can be comforted by the fact that you know that their child has many strengths on which to build. Ask families to share information about the child's strengths at home and in the community.

Our own willingness and capacity to address cultural misunderstandings is essential, especially for children with disabilities and their families. Someone who may have different beliefs, different attitudes, or different behaviors than we do can often take us out of our cultural comfort zone. Given the importance of family partnerships, I would argue that a family's cultural beliefs and practices are more important than our own comfort. Successful educators identify, acknowledge, and address our own biases to make sure that they do not interfere with their capacity to serve families in a competent and respectful way.

This is good practice for working with all children, and it is especially important for working with children who have a disability or suspected delay and are also members of a cultural or racial group that is different from your own. We all have multiple social and cultural identities. Children with disabilities who also are part of a marginalized group face layers of potential bias. This concept is called *intersectionality,* "the overlapping and interdependent systems of oppression across, for example, race, gender, ability, and social status" (NAEYC, 2019). As early childhood educators, we play a critical role in helping children to grow and develop with a positive sense of self. Our first step is to recognize and discover how our own biases might affect our work with families.

IMPLICIT BIAS

Staats and colleagues (2015) define *implicit bias* as "the automatic and unconscious stereotypes that drive people to behave and make decisions in certain ways." Human beings use mental categories to sort the world as we try to make meaning out of all that we encounter. This tendency to sort people into categories in an unconscious way can bring along negative biases from our childhood into adulthood. Yale researcher Walter Gilliam and colleagues have studied implicit bias extensively in early childhood settings and have found a connection between implicit bias and racial disparities that we see in suspension and expulsion rates (2016). Children under the age of five suspended and expelled? Yes. Gilliam and colleagues (2005, 2006) found that children in public prekindergarten programs were expelled at a rate three times higher than children in K–12 education. Within these high rates of exclusionary practices, racial disparities exist as well. According to US Department of Education, Office of Civil Rights data, Black preschoolers are 3.6 times more likely to be suspended than their White peers (Office of Civil Rights, 2014). In 2016, these troubling findings led the US Department of Health and Human Services and Department of Education to release their joint "Policy Statement on Expulsion and Suspension Policies in Early Childhood Settings." The policy statement shares the research findings and provides guidance for states, territories, communities, and programs "to prevent, severely limit, and work toward eventually eliminating the expulsion and suspension—and ensure the safety and well-being—of young children in early learning settings." What is behind these disturbing trends?

There is no evidence that Black children are genetically predisposed to misbehave; rather, implicit bias may be the culprit. Research on implicit bias in early childhood is captured in the brief *Do Early Educators' Implicit Biases Regarding Sex and Race Relate to Behavior Expectations and Recommendations of Preschool Expulsions and Suspensions?* (Gilliam et al., 2016). Using eye-tracking technology, Gilliam and colleagues found that both White and Black early childhood educators tended to watch Black boys more closely and expected to see challenging behaviors from Black boys even when they did not occur. The research suggests that implicit bias affects the way that educators perceive behavior, which affects the decisions they make concerning discipline.

Disparities also exist for children with disabilities. The Children's Equity Project Report (2020) included research that revealed that children with disabilities are more likely to receive harsh discipline in school. In addition, children with disabilities are twice as likely to be excluded from K–12 settings than children without disabilities (Brobbey, 2018). This bias is compounded when young children are Black and have a disability. Black children with disabilities are most likely to be excluded (Brobbey, 2018). As educators, we have the opportunity to break this cycle through equitable learning opportunities and culturally and linguistically responsive practices. It starts with our ability to recognize our own biases.

RECOGNIZING OUR OWN BIASES

We each have multiple cultural identities. One of our cultures is the field of early childhood education. We view the world and interpret reality though that lens, and our perspective changes over time as we learn and grow. Our cultural identities influence how we deliver services and supports to children with disabilities and their families. But our cultural lenses also contribute to biases and misunderstandings. What is the solution? It starts with our ability to recognize bias within ourselves and then reflect on how our biases might influence our work with children, families, and colleagues.

> *"Not everything that is faced can be changed. But nothing can be changed until it is faced."*
>
> **—JAMES BALDWIN, AUTHOR**

When I was a disability services coordinator for a Head Start program that serves the children of migrant and seasonal farmworkers, I recognized bias in myself. Part of my role was to visit the Head Start centers and support the educators in their efforts to identify and serve children with disabilities. Many of the educators were themselves immigrants from Mexico. This was an enormous benefit to the program for many reasons, including the fact that the children were surrounded by adults who spoke Spanish as well as English. However, there were definitely cultural differences that sometimes led to misunderstandings.

On one particular visit, I remember walking into a classroom of toddlers and being surprised by the way the educators carried the children around the room. I watched as one educator in particular picked up a toddler and carried him to the changing table by holding him in the crook of her arm, with her arm wrapped around his waist. His arms and legs dangled freely as she carried him across the room. In my mind, she was carrying the toddler like a sack of potatoes. When I asked her about it, she said, "This is how we all carry the babies." The toddler wasn't harmed and even talked and laughed on his trip to the changing table. At the time, I was trying to form relationships with the educators, so I checked myself, made a conscious decision to withhold judgement, and filed the situation away to think about how I might address it later.

On a future visit, we sat down together to discuss these practices. We talked about asking a toddler, "Is it okay if I pick you up?" or simply letting him walk to the changing table himself if he is capable of doing so. Together, we reflected about the best way to carry a child. What if there are physical issues that we might not yet know about? Could some ways of carrying a child be painful? If a toddler doesn't yet have the capacity to let us know their preference, what is the "right" way? How does the child's parent carry him? These conversations turned out to be helpful to both of us, TA provider and educator. I learned about a cultural difference that was new to me, and the educator reflected on her own practice. She started asking the toddlers about their own preferences, and as you might imagine, they responded with, "I do it!"

"Do the best you can until you know better. Then when you know better, do better."

—MAYA ANGELOU, AUTHOR AND CIVIL-RIGHTS ACTIVIST

You can probably tell that the situation stuck with me over the years. It served as a reminder that we all are brought up differently and culture plays a huge role in our development and practices. As much as possible, children benefit from consistency among the important adults in their lives. I have learned over time that there are no easy answers in resolving cultural differences, but the first and most important practice is to withhold judgment and talk about these differences with families and colleagues. Together, you can come to agreement on how you choose to care for and interact with children, families, and each other.

CULTURALLY RESPONSIVE PRACTICES AND EQUITABLE LEARNING OPPORTUNITIES

"All children have the right to equitable learning opportunities that enable them to achieve their full potential as engaged learners and valued members of society" (NAEYC, 2019).

Culturally responsive practices ensure equitable treatment of children, because culturally responsive educators work to connect the activities in the learning environment to the child's daily life, home experiences, and cultural background. In chapter 3, we discussed the way that successful educators take the time to view the world from the child's and family's point of view. If your cultural perspectives dominate the interaction and are a mismatch with the family's preferences, the family may distance themselves from your program and may not be fully engaged. Families are our most powerful allies! The way around this problem is by taking an active role in ensuring that your practices are culturally responsive and equitable. All

Reflections on Culture for Early Childhood Educators

Self-reflection is an important part of our job as early childhood educators. To better understand the children and families we serve, our first step is to reflect on our own culture and how it shaped our own upbringing and values. This concept of self-reflection is further explored in the book *When Teachers Reflect: Journeys toward Effective, Inclusive Practice* (Tertell, Klein, and Jewett, eds., 1998). Think about these questions as you reflect on the role that culture plays in your day-to-day work:

- What do you remember about your own childhood and how you were brought up?

- How might your own childhood experiences influence your thinking about children's development?

- What cultural groups live in your community?

- What do you know about the communication styles, beliefs, and values held by these cultural groups?

- What do you know about the different beliefs about raising children that are held by these cultural groups? How did you learn this information?

- How do you react to people from cultural groups different from your own? Why do you think that you react in that way?

- How can early childhood education be an asset to the families from different cultures in your community?

early childhood educators have a professional obligation to advance equity.

DEFINING *EQUITY*

Equality is not the same as equity. You may have seen the graphic depicting three people looking over a fence to see a ballgame. Equality is depicted by an image of the people, each standing on one box. This solution works for the two taller people, but the shortest still can't see the game. Equity is depicted by an image in which the tallest person doesn't stand on a box at all, the second-tallest stands on one box, and the shortest stands on two. Now, all three can see the game. It's a great visual to explain the distinction between equality and equity, and it makes a lot of sense to me. You can imagine that as a little person myself, my world is very stepstool oriented. The image reminds us that equity isn't about everyone getting the same supports, because everyone does not need the same supports. Equity is about giving the *just right* supports. It's a way to think about how we can address disparities that exist due to racism, ableism, poverty, and other barriers that are faced by many children and families.

I remember a time that I was on a panel at an early childhood event, and we were all seated at a table. One by one we were expected to go up to the podium to share some remarks. I usually cannot see over the top of a podium, so in my mind I was already trying to figure out how I might take the microphone off of the stand so I could stand beside the podium. But the microphone looked pretty much wrapped around the stand. I was quite nervous, not about giving remarks but about podium management. But wouldn't you know it? When it came time for me to speak, I looked down and a stepstool was just there. The event planner was ready with the support I needed to meet the moment.

In early care and education, equity is in our blood. It's our nature. And given that this is so, we have the ability to generalize to all needs and to expect inclusion and equity even when the child's needs may not be as visible. We know that children differ in many ways. They have different needs, different interests, and different abilities. If we were to try to achieve equality, we would give every child the same thing, regardless of their differences. Every child would use the same materials and receive the same instructional approach. Equity is an approach that is responsive to children's differences. Rather than treating each child in the same way, an equitable approach considers the child's interests, strengths, challenges, and needs and provides the *just right* resources and materials necessary to ensure that they achieve success.

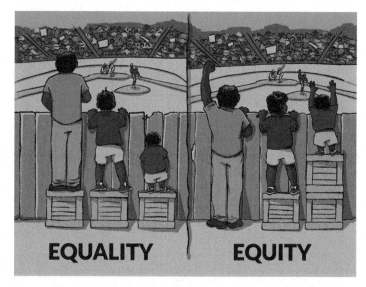

Source: Interaction Institute for Social Change, artist Angus Maguire.

What do culturally responsive and equitable practices look like in early childhood programs? The National Association for the Education of Young Children (2019) has developed a position statement to guide our work in this regard. The position statement recommends the following practices:

1. Uphold the unique value and dignity of each child and family.

2. Recognize each child's unique strengths, and support the full inclusion of all children.

3. Develop trusting relationships with children and nurture relationships among them while building on their knowledge and skills.

4. Consider the developmental, cultural, and linguistic appropriateness of the learning environment and your teaching practices for each child.

"Fairness doesn't mean giving every child the same thing; it means giving every child what they need."

—RICK LAVOIE, AUTHOR AND TEACHER

5. Involve children, families, and the community in the design and implementation of learning activities.

6. Actively promote children's agency.

7. Scaffold children's learning to achieve meaningful goals.

8. Design and implement learning activities using language(s) that the children understand.

9. Recognize and be prepared to provide different levels of support to different children depending on what they need.

10. Consider how your own biases (implicit and explicit) may be contributing to your interactions and the messages you are sending children.

11. Use multitiered systems of support.

Do you notice themes that we've explored in this book? references to differentiation? developing responsive and trusting relationships with children and families? recognizing children's strengths? allowing children to make choices? scaffolding children's learning? using multitiered systems of support? The reason there are so many overlapping principles is because, when you use inclusive practices and build inclusive learning environments, you are working toward equity for the children you serve by being responsive to their individual needs. Inclusion means *all* children, of all abilities, all races, all cultures, all genders, just all.

CHILDREN WHO ARE DUAL LANGUAGE LEARNERS

One clear point of intersection between ability and culture rises to the forefront when we serve children with disabilities who are also dual language learners (DLLs). Children who are DLLs are learning English in addition to the language that is spoken in their home environment. Sometimes, educators are unsure if the behaviors they are seeing are due to a developmental delay or are a temporary adjustment to being placed in an environment where everyone is speaking a different language. Although those behaviors may be similar to those seen in children with disabilities, the reasons for the behaviors are different. When should a teacher refer the child to early intervention or early childhood special education? It's important for educators to team up with specialists who have experience with second-language acquisition to sort it all out. Some behaviors that DLLs exhibit that can be misinterpreted include the following:

- Speaking infrequently
- Refusing to answer questions
- Confusing words that sound similar

- Being unable to tell or retell stories
- Seeming forgetful or unable to remember classroom routines

Together, educators, family members, and specialists can determine the underlying issue and identify the right supports for the child. Keep in mind that bilingualism is an enormous gift! Bilingualism is associated with cognitive advantages, including strong executive-functioning skills, attention, perspective taking, and self-regulation (Bialystok, Craik, and Luk, 2012). Research has shown that young children are perfectly capable of learning more than one language in early childhood and will not suffer long-term language delays by doing so (Byers-Heinlein and Lew-Williams, 2013). Sometimes educators and specialists mistakenly assume that a child with a disability will be confused by being exposed to more than one language. Research by Zoran (2004) showed that children with disabilities can learn more than one language and can function bilingually as effectively as their peers without disabilities. Delays are unrelated to growing up while learning two languages. In these situations, communication with the child's family is of utmost importance.

RESOURCE SPOTLIGHT

Traditions in American Indian and Alaska Native (AIAN) populations are important to understand and support children from these cultures in early childhood education. The Making it Work resource can help educators teach children about traditional cultural skills, values, and beliefs. (See appendix B for a list of resources for this chapter.)

- **Establish a system of coordination for all of the adults in the child's life.** This coordination will help to determine the most appropriate strategies for learning activities and peer relationships as well as which language will be used when working toward IFSP or IEP goals.

- **Ensure that the child has access to an adult who speaks the child's home language,** if possible, such as a teacher assistant or volunteer if the primary teacher is not bilingual. This practice will provide a comforting and reassuring presence to a child who is just learning English.

- **Learn a little bit of the child's home language yourself.** Even if you don't have access to someone who speaks a child's home language, it is relatively easy for educators to learn some basic words and phrases to use when communicating with the child. Duolingo (https://www. duolingo.com/) is a free app for your smartphone or tablet that provides easy and fun activities for learning the foreign language of your choice. Keep in mind that three- and four-year-olds don't have an extensive vocabulary to begin with! Educators who learn enough words or phrases to foster communication will give the child a sense of security in the classroom.

- **Provide multiple opportunities for children to interact with their peers** in English and in their home language.

- **Consider universal design approaches** by providing multiple ways to communicate and engage with the environment during the course of the day. Will the child use sign language?

visual supports? props? voice output devices? For example, in chapter 6 we discussed the use of visuals such as PECS, which is a set of pictures that represent items or actions used frequently during the course of an everyday routine. Many assistive technology devices can be adapted as well. This strategy can be useful for children who are dual language learners so that they can communicate with peers and adults while learning English.

- **Provide lots of open-ended activities** that can be used by children regardless of the language that they use or speak at home like paints, clay, blocks, crayons, and manipulatives.

- **Use "real" items from everyday life that a child who is a DLL already knows and understands.** For example, in their book *Universal Design for Learning in the Early Childhood Classroom*, authors Brillante and Nemeth (2018) suggest that children learn how to sort different colored socks rather than plastic toys. Sorting socks is a real-life skill, and children already are comfortable and familiar with socks, so their focus can be immediately directed to the different colors rather than becoming distracted by a plastic object that is unfamiliar to them.

- **Appeal to all the senses** (vision, hearing, touch, taste, and smell) when introducing and presenting new concepts.

- **Vary and adapt the amount of adult guidance** according to children's abilities so that each child is in charge of his own learning as much as possible.

- **Offer adapted or specialized materials.** Provide materials such as recorded books, Braille books, and other printed material, large and bold print, and adapted handles on various materials throughout the classroom to enhance active participation.

- **Make appropriate environmental changes.** For example, provide color contrast in materials, good lighting, a reduced noise level, comfortable seating, and work spaces to support children's learning.

EMBRACING CULTURAL DIVERSITY AND EQUITY IN EARLY CHILDHOOD ENVIRONMENTS

In addition to being sensitive to the needs of children who are dual language learners and their families, what are some other strategies that we can use to embrace cultural diversity and promote equity in our programs?

- **Let families know that you value their culture**, expertise, contributions they make as members of your program's community, and the role they play as experts on their own children.

- **Provide activities that allow families to participate regardless of language**, like painting a mural or helping in the school garden.

- **Let families know that you value the language they speak at home.** It is such an advantage to be multilingual! Families may not be aware of how their child will benefit from speaking more than one language. In my experience with my own father and with the families in the migrant and seasonal Head Start program, families have a strong desire to make sure that their child learns English. My dad never spoke Spanish at home, because he wanted to practice his own English. As a result, my Spanish-speaking abilities are not so hot. Let families know that by speaking a second language at home, they are giving their child a tremendous gift.

RESOURCE **SPOTLIGHT**

Learn about how to support young children who are DLLs by using helpful resources such as those listed on the Head Start website. (See appendix B for a list of resources for this chapter.)

- **Ask families to share photographs from home** or significant places in their community that can be used to create a shared book to be used in the classroom. Acknowledging the fact that children have busy lives outside of the program helps to foster connections and shows families that you value the rich learning experiences they provide for their children outside of school.

- **Build on cultural traditions by celebrating the cultural identities of families.** Children benefit from knowing who they are and where they come from. For example, families in tribal communities often strive to maintain their children's connection to traditional indigenous practices and the use of Native languages. Do what you can to support these efforts and to learn about culturally-grounded practices.

- **Create a culturally responsive learning environment** that includes photos, books, music, and other materials that represent the children's culture, because we know that children learn best in environments in which they are surrounded by materials that are familiar to them. This doesn't have to be expensive! You can find culturally relevant materials at yard sales, flea markets, or thrift shops, and just having those materials in the classroom will go a long way because it will help children build on their prior knowledge and experience.

- **Provide opportunities for families to share their culture** with the group by including books, stories, toys, visuals, songs, and food that reflects the rich diversity of the children in the program.

- **Display pictures of the children and their families themselves**—make sure to include representation of different genders, abilities, family compositions, ages, and lifestyles.

- **Provide books and audiobooks in the child's home language** to help to create a sense of belonging as well and can often be found at the public library or online. A vast collection is available from free at the International Children's Digital Library. (See appendix B for a list of resources for this chapter.)

- **Offer culturally relevant props and objects in the dramatic play area of the classroom.** This can be a great space to use when teaching children about other cultures. For example, you can create a restaurant theme with menus from restaurants that serve all different kinds of food—Indian, Thai, Chinese, Ethiopian, Mexican—the possibilities are endless! Ask each family to take a photograph of a plate of food that best represents the food of their culture. Enlarge the photos and laminate them to create props for the dramatic play restaurant.

- **Teach children to respect differences.** For example, read books that show examples of different people and abilities as well as different cultures and traditions around the world.

Another idea is to teach children greetings from other countries. For example, you might say to the group, "Did you know that in India, people bow, put their hands together, and say *namaste* when they greet each other? How does your family greet each other?" During morning circle time, pass around a mirror and ask children to share one thing they see about themselves. Part of respecting differences is also about finding similarities among the children in your program. Be open about this and talk about differences and similarities. For example, Myla and Xavier have different hair colors, but they both like to dip their cookies in milk during snack time. Some things are the same and some are different and we are friends!

As we celebrate diversity in this way, we build a nurturing and supportive community in our programs in which everyone is valued. If we create this type of community, it will be less likely that children will bully or say hurtful things to one another. In this place, in this space, we value and support one another. The more time that you spend learning about other cultures, the more your mindset widens and your teaching practices are enriched. We have much to learn from the families in our programs, and the partnerships we build with them will continue to be held dear long after their child transitions on.

> *"Children are better able to learn when the classroom climate is positive, warm, and inviting. Part of being welcomed is seeing your language and culture reflected throughout all aspects of the classroom"* *(López and Páez, 2021).*

REFLECTION QUESTIONS

- How does my culture and identity shape my thinking about the world? How does it affect my practices as an early childhood educator?
- What am I doing to make sure that the practices I use are ones that foster equity? How might I reflect on my own implicit biases?
- Are the materials in my classroom meaningful and relevant to my unique group of children? Do they also reflect the broader experiences of children from other cultures and ethnic groups?
- Does my approach support continuity of care between the contexts of home and the program?
- Do I encourage cultural and linguistic continuity between home and my program?

CHAPTER 10

Self-Care for the Early Childhood Educator

The soul is healed by being with children.

—FYODOR DOSTOEVSKY, AUTHOR

Apparently, Dostoevsky never worked as an early childhood educator. I'm joking! Children are amazing, fun, and can really lift you up, but they can also exhaust you to the bone. I remember a particular dental appointment. At the time, I was working as a preschool teacher, and my days were filled with laughter, crayons, circle time, and play. It was a joyous time, but I had never known such exhaustion. So there I was, lying in the chair as the hygienist organized her tools, and all I could think about was how wonderful it was to lie back and relax for a bit—and on a workday! Yes, going to the dentist was relaxing. How crazy is that?

Remember Danny, a spirited child with red hair and smudged glasses, from the introduction? Every day, Danny would come in to the classroom, drop his backpack on the floor, find the nearest child, and either bop the child on the head as if he was playing whack-a-mole, knock down a block tower, or yank away a toy. I could feel my blood pressure rise every time I heard the sound of him coming down the hall—usually the scraping sound of him dragging his backpack. It's funny to think back on it now, but at the time, it was seriously stressful. It took time to teach Danny about the expectations of my classroom, where his backpack belonged, how to greet other children, why his actions were hurtful, and how to make good choices at the start of the day. But all of that was possible only because I learned how to manage my own emotions first. How can we teach children the joy of feeling calm when we aren't calm ourselves?

Reflecting on those days reminds me that being an early childhood educator is fabulous work, but it also can sap your strength. What is the solution to this? We need to learn strategies to strengthen our own mental health and ways to continue to grow as professionals. We can't drink from an empty cup, so we need to find ways to fill up our own cups so we can give our best to the children we care about. In the following pages, we'll explore ways to strengthen our own resources and integrate self-care into our daily routines through wellness strategies, such as mindfulness and grounding techniques, and the use of professional-learning communities.

One thing I have learned over the years is that the mental state that I bring to my work or to my relationships is basically a similar or the same mental state that gets reflected back to me by the people I encounter. It's almost creepy. It's generally true that when we put positivity, strength, and happiness into the world, we typically get those "vibes" back in return. Sometimes, I wake up in the morning, and it's like I'm Cinderella on the day the shoe fits. I feel like Snow White with all of the woodland animals gathering around and the birds chirping sweetly as I yawn and stretch. Those days go really well. And then there are other days. I wake up with a headache. My sweet husband was snoring loudly all night long, and I couldn't really sleep. Instead of waking up to chirping birds, I wake up to the sound of the cat vomiting on the floor beside my bed. Ick. Or even better, I *don't* hear the cat vomiting, and I step in it as I climb out of bed. Those are the days that make dealing with a classroom full of young children a major challenge. Those are the days that hearing a backpack scraping down the hallway would create, let's just say, tension.

Our work is tough. Wonderful much of the time, but tough, nevertheless. The research backs me up on this. In 2012, a group of researchers funded by the CDC had an idea that being an early childhood educator was a stressful and sometimes physically taxing occupation. Whitaker and colleagues (2013) surveyed more than two thousand Head Start teachers in Pennsylvania about their physical and mental health. Guess what. The researchers found that early childhood education actually *is* physically and mentally taxing work. In fact, they concluded that "women who work in Head Start programs have poorer physical and mental health than do US women who have similar sociodemographic characteristics." The Head Start staff reported frequent migraines and lower-back pain. And that wasn't all.

- 23.5 percent of the teachers reported that they had diagnosed depression, compared to just 17 percent of the general population.

- 28.3 percent of the teachers reported that they frequently had "unhealthy days" versus 14.5 percent of the general population.

Other research by Johnson and colleagues (2021) report that teacher stress is common and leads to high turnover rates in the early childhood field. Think about it. A typical day for an early childhood educator includes:

- engaging in many interactions with lots of different people—colleagues, families, administrators, specialists—who all require our attention and emotional-regulation skills.
- shifting focus between the classroom as a whole to an individual child's needs and back again.
- problem solving on the fly as we interact with children who have different needs and abilities.
- using socially appropriate emotions, language, and nonverbal communication to show empathy toward colleagues as well as a diverse group of children while regulating our own emotions such as frustration or fear.

As early childhood educators, we use all of these skills to support and help the children and families in our programs. We lift other people up, and when they succeed, we rise and fly with them! In fact, we can't wait to go tell somebody. "Do you know what happened to Sophia in my class? She is doing amazingly well! Last week, she transitioned from circle time to centers without a meltdown!" We celebrate the successes of the children in our programs, but when they struggle, unfortunately, we struggle too. Inclusion has many rewards, but it means we spend much emotional energy when we collaborate with our colleagues, specialists, and families. Sometimes, we end up being the only source of emotional support that a child or family knows or receives.

"Life is not so much what you accomplish, as what you overcome."

—ROBIN ROBERTS, NEWSCASTER

Teaching is such an important role, but it can be very stressful. This has been especially true during the COVID-19 pandemic. Educators played a huge part in helping children and families maintain a sense of safety and connection during a time of tremendous stress and isolation. Supporting young children's social and emotional development depends largely on our ability to build relationships with children and families, to nurture others, and manage our own emotions. Our ability to do all of this is related to our own physical and emotional well-being. Our emotional investments are necessary to be successful educators, but they also cause us to be vulnerable to disappointment, hurt, or worry if a child or family is not doing so well.

Educators are often people who feel deep empathy for the children and families in our programs. We want to fix things. But much of the time, the struggles that families face are outside of our control. This can lead us to feeling down, stressed, and exhausted. There are terms for this phenomenon: *the cost of caring*, *emotional labor*, *compassion fatigue*, and *vicarious trauma*, all of which can lead to burnout and many other symptoms. These are times to remind ourselves to focus on what we can control and to let go of what we can't. What is the solution? We can use phrases such as, "I will do everything in my power to do what I can to be with you through this." It's also important that we take good care of ourselves so that we have the stamina, positivity, and emotional resources so we can help others.

> *"If I am not good to myself, how can I expect anyone else to be good to me?"*
>
> **—MAYA ANGELOU, AUTHOR AND CIVIL-RIGHTS ACTIVIST**

In addition to the emotional toll of our jobs, early childhood educators also face financial stressors because we work in a historically underpaid field. Educators who work with families experiencing poverty can be under the same economic stresses as the families they serve. As noted in the *Early Childhood Educator Workforce Index 2020* released by the University of Berkeley Center for the Study of Child Care Employment (CSCCE):

> *The historical and pervasive undervaluing of labor performed by people of color and especially women in the United States, combined with reliance on a market-based system that depends mostly on parents' ability to pay, has made early care and education one of the most underpaid fields in the country. As a result, early educators face severe pay penalties for working with younger children in all states, with poverty rates an average of 7.7 times higher than teachers in the K–8 system (McLean et. al, 2021).*

The CSCCE also notes that there are disparities that exist within our field. Educators who work with infants and toddlers make up to $8,375 less per year than those who work with preschool children (McLean, et. al, 2021). Racial disparities exist as well. Known as the "race gap," the index says that Black, Latina, and immigrant women are more likely than White women to work with infants and toddlers and in home-based settings, which are lower-wage segments of the field. However, this isn't just an infant-toddler versus preschool care issue, because McLean and colleagues also found that racial disparities exist across program settings and ages of children. A recent CSCCE study found that "Black early educators are paid on average $0.78 less per hour than their White peers" (Austin et al., 2019).

All of these issues lead to stress. Do you know that phrase, "If mama ain't happy, ain't nobody happy"? It's true for early childhood educators as well! Strategies for stress management, self-care, and physical health are keys to our effectiveness. Good nutrition, exercise, and adequate sleep are foundational to combating the effects of physical, emotional, and mental stress. When educators engage in healthy behaviors, they cope more effectively and experience less stress. Teachers who are happy and healthy enjoy greater job satisfaction and are less likely to get burned out and leave their jobs. What can we do to promote wellness and self-care in our busy lives?

Wellness is not simply the absence of illness. Researcher Bill Hettler (1976) defined *wellness* as "an active process of becoming aware of and learning to make choices that lead toward a longer and more successful existence." The National Wellness Institute website suggests that we consider wellness in a holistic way and think about how we are doing in the various dimensions of our lives, including physical, social, intellectual, occupational, emotional, and spiritual wellness. In my time spent with other early childhood educators, I have found that key coping strategies fall within the social, emotional, intellectual, and spiritual dimensions. I have collected coping strategies that seem to work as a way of managing stressful situations common to early childhood educators. The important thing is that you pay attention to your stress levels and have a plan for how you will manage stress. Think of it as putting together a toolbox of coping strategies to go along with your toolbox of teaching practices. Let's explore some strategies that might work for you.

SOCIAL WELLNESS

Friendship and belonging are important for children, but they are also incredibly important for adults. We need people in our lives who care about us, can listen to us, and accept all of who we are. We need people who remind us that we are not alone. Relationships outside of work give us a chance to disconnect from the drama that can sometimes build when groups of people are around each other consistently. These relationships can give us perspective when we think through the concerns we may be facing in our work with children and families. Social support is key for our well-being, and having these supports can increase positive feelings such as connectedness and community.

Friendships keep us from feeling alone in the world and can be lifesavers after a full day of being around young children. Sometimes we are able to build these kinds of relationships at work, but not always. Consider the following strategies for social wellness.

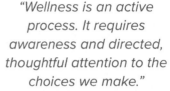

"Wellness is an active process. It requires awareness and directed, thoughtful attention to the choices we make."

—NATIONAL WELLNESS INSTITUTE

- **Build a supportive community** of early childhood educators to learn and share ideas with each other. We keep our work from getting stale when we have relationships that provide us with new and fresh ideas to try. The community you build can be a formal professional-learning community or just a group that gets together informally on a regular basis. Organize a regular gathering, such as a book club or monthly potluck, with a group of friends who make you laugh and give you support. Whatever you decide to do as an activity, the main thing is that you have each other to lean on. When work gets stressful, it is truly helpful to have a network of people who have been or are going through a similar experience.

- **Reach out to others** through online communities hosted by Facebook or other platforms. I've found a group of early childhood education professionals on Facebook who give me wonderful ideas to try! Meetup.com is another online source for finding friends in your area or around the world. You can search events in your area or start your own group.

- **Find a mentor** through your local or state child-care resource and referral agency. A mentor can help you work through issues in your program and provide the support you need when you might question yourself. They may have implemented something you haven't tried before or have resources to share that could be helpful. Most importantly, a mentor is able to listen to you and give you encouragement.

- **Ask for help when you need it.** This can be difficult, especially at first. It takes bravery to say, "I really need a friend right now." But think about it: how would you react if someone said those words to you? When you ask for help directly, most people feel warmth and care toward you and appreciate the vulnerability that it takes to put yourself out there in that way. Be ready to offer specifics about what others might do to help. Do you need a moment alone? Would it be a lifesaver to have someone care for your own children on a Saturday afternoon? Ask! Would a home-cooked meal for your family give you a much-needed break? Ask! Would it be a relief to have someone pick up a few things at the grocery store for you? Ask! They can always say no. Reach out for help and then be prepared to give help when your friend reaches out for help, too.

EMOTIONAL WELLNESS

When I was a child, I learned a trick from a nun who visited patients in the hospital where I was recovering from surgery. She happened to be in my hospital room when the phlebotomist came in to take a sample of blood. You may know how it is in a hospital—people are poking and prodding you all the time. This nun could tell that I was a little bit anxious about the whole thing. This is the strategy she taught me: When you start to feel anxious or stressed, take a moment for some deep breathing. When you breathe in, think, "I am," and when you breathe out, think, "at peace." Try it! I use this trick all the time, and it does help to bring down the temperature on my stress levels.

As educators, we spend time teaching children skills to manage their emotions. These strategies can be useful for our own emotional wellness too. As adults, we're able to understand our emotions in an intellectual way that children aren't quite ready to understand. We can learn the relationships among our thoughts, our emotions, and our behavior. For example, we might feel a certain way, which leads us to think about the situation a certain way, which leads us to behave a certain way. We don't have to be yanked around by our emotions if we change the way that we think about them! Changing the way we think changes the way we act. Stress comes from our perception of the situation, because technically, the actual situation is not stressful. Our thoughts about it *make it* stressful, so if we just change our thoughts. . . Easier said than done, right? Try these emotional wellness strategies in addition to your efforts to weed out those pesky unhelpful thoughts.

- **Start by asking yourself, "Is this thought true? Is it helpful?"** Sometimes our thoughts are based on an accurate perception of the situation, and sometimes they are just plain wrong. For example, a coworker and I were having a discussion, and she suddenly put her head in her hands and began rubbing her eyes. My immediate reaction was panic and stress. Oh no! What did I say? Did I offend her? Have I hurt her feelings? I could feel the stress build as I started to ramble on and backtrack from whatever I had been saying. She suddenly looked up and said, "Jani, I am so sorry. Did I tell you that my uncle passed away last week? Please forgive me, but I didn't hear what you were just saying because I started thinking about him and felt sad." Boom! This new information showed me that my perception of the situation was entirely wrong. The stress I had been feeling a moment before just evaporated, and my emotions turned to care for my colleague. This kind of thing happens in all kinds of situations, within relationships at work and just in everyday life. Taking a moment to pause and question your thoughts in this way can break the spell that the emotion is creating and make space for your reaction to be based on what is really going on,

- **Try using grounding strategies when difficult emotions arise.** Grounding, or centering, refers to a set of simple strategies that can help you detach from emotional pain, such as anxiety, anger, sadness, or frustration. You consciously distract yourself temporarily from the emotions. This approach won't solve the problem, but it will give you temporary control over your feelings and provide a bit of space between your emotions, thoughts, and how you choose to act on those thoughts. There are two types of grounding strategies—mental and physical.

Mental grounding involves focusing your mind elsewhere. For example, you might focus on your environment and in your mind describe to yourself everything you see or hear in great detail. Or you might count down from ten to one, or you might think about a pleasant or comforting place or meal or person. You can also try to focus your mind on soothing things or soothing words. For example, you might say to yourself, "You are a good person and you're trying really hard. This is just a difficult day." Say kind words to yourself as if you were talking to a friend or small child. Picture a favorite person in your mind and imagine that person smiling at you or giving you a caring hug. Think of things you are looking forward to in the next week, or think about a saying or quotation that brings you peace, such as, "This too shall pass," or the serenity prayer. I like this quotation by Eleanor Roosevelt: "No one can make you feel inferior without your consent." I think about it sometimes as a way to ground myself and to serve as a reminder that I am in control of my own feelings, especially those feelings about my own self-worth.

Physical grounding involves focusing on your senses. For example, you might grab tightly to the arms of the chair you're sitting in and really focus on that sensation. Or you might go to the bathroom and run cool water over your hands. Or you might touch various objects around you and pay close attention to the texture, temperature, or weight of each object. Or you might wiggle your toes and focus on that sensation, or breathe deeply and pay attention to each inhale and exhale (just as my friendly nun taught me to do!). When I attend a long meeting, I often put a familiar object, such as a seashell or a smooth stone, in my pocket to help me center if necessary. Have you heard of emotional eating? It isn't necessarily a bad thing if you understand the reason behind it. We do this as a form of physical grounding because emotional eating distracts us from the stressful emotion we are experiencing. It's the unconscious way our body is trying to help us distract and remove ourselves from the situation. This is a good reminder that *you* are in control of how you choose to respond to the emotions that you feel.

Which grounding method do you like best? Choose one or a few and practice using them. Like any other skill, grounding takes practice, and it's helpful to practice during nonstressful situations so you can become comfortable with it. Then, when you need to use the skill, you'll be ready with it in your coping strategies toolbox!

Unhelpful thoughts can sap the energy we need to do our best work. We need to save our energy for doing things that will help and that are within our control. Another strategy to provide space before unhelpful thoughts take over is called "thought stopping." The idea is to notice your own unhelpful thoughts and practice using a trigger word to stop the thoughts. For example, if you start to think, "What's the point in even trying?" interrupt the thought by telling yourself, "Stop!" or "Hold on now!" This gives you a moment to get back on track and replace the unhelpful thought with one that is supportive and helpful, such as "You are smart! You got this!" You might even visualize the unhelpful thought in a hot air balloon floating away.

INTELLECTUAL WELLNESS

In 1988, Carol Dweck and Ellen Leggett introduced the notion that the way people think about the limitations of their own intelligence affects their ability to learn and reach goals. They found that students either maintain a fixed mindset or a growth mindset about their own intelligence. The students with a fixed mindset believed that their intelligence was something already set and predetermined and that, no matter how hard they tried or how much they studied, they would only get so far because of the limitations on their own intelligence. The students with a growth mindset, on the other hand, believed that their intelligence was changeable and could grow with hard work and persistence. As you might imagine, Dweck and Leggett found that students with a growth mindset tended to be more successful in their ability to reach learning goals and embrace challenges.

This research can tell us a great deal about our own mindsets and how we tend to view our own competence, intelligence, and capacity for overcoming challenges. Early childhood educators who maintain a growth mindset will be more likely to seek strategies that foster intellectual wellness and, as a result, will be able to learn from the mistakes we make and persist in the face of challenges. They will take pleasure in learning new information and will strive to grow and learn throughout their careers. Consider the following strategies we can use to foster intellectual wellness.

RESOURCE SPOTLIGHT

Taking Care of Ourselves is a free booklet that educators can use to learn about how to identify your sources of stress and implement stress-reduction strategies. (See appendix B for a list of resources for this chapter.)

- **Joining professional learning communities:** Learning communities (or communities of practice) are not just a strategy to support social wellness. They also promote intellectual wellness by providing opportunities to share experiences, exchange perspectives on common problems of practice, and learn from other educators in a supportive environment. By being involved with a community of learners, educators have a chance to reflect on their own practice. As a result, we discover new information and new meaning to the work that improves our own teaching practices. Virtual professional learning communities are becoming increasingly popular because they are easy to access and can connect educators with others without regard to distance. Not sure about how to approach a situation with a child in your classroom? There may be an educator across the country who has figured out some solutions!

- **Connecting with a coach:** Many programs offer free coaching for educators who are looking to build their skills and to benefit from feedback. Head Start uses a model called Practice-Based Coaching. This model is a collaborative partnership build on rapport, trust, and a shared understanding of the goals of the relationship. Typically, a coach will provide a safe space for the educator to ask questions, discuss problems, get support, gather feedback, reflect on practice, and try new ideas. Sometimes the coach is a master or lead teacher who serves in an "expert" role, while other times the coach is a peer. The coaching can be delivered in person or virtually using technology. Together, the partners work on shared goals and develop an action plan. The coach observes the teaching practices, and together they work through challenges. Sometimes, videotaping is used, which can be really effective because it can help the educator and coach look at the teaching practice together and have a conversation about what went well or what didn't go well. The coach provides constructive feedback in a supportive way to help the educator achieve identified goals and improve or refine practice. When new skills are honed, the partners can celebrate that success!

- **Reflecting on your own practice:** Whether it is with a coach or on your own, it's always helpful to reflect on your practice as an educator. By reflecting on your teaching, you can identify any barriers to learning that might exist and problem solve strategies for providing the best supports. Through assessing the strengths and weaknesses in your own practice, you will develop an awareness of the factors that you can control and how your actions can foster a rich learning experience for children. The reflection process will also help you to understand yourself and the way you teach. Keep the growth mindset in mind. Instead of thinking, "I just can't do this," think, "Up until now, I haven't learned how to do this." Instead of thinking,

"This isn't working," think, "What am I missing?" or "What else can I try?" Asking yourself questions will help you understand what your strengths are and recognize any areas where you might benefit from professional development.

- **Writing in a journal:** In her book *Writing as a Way of Healing*, Louise DeSalvo (2000) shares that writing our deepest thoughts and feelings in a personal journal is linked with "improved immune function, improved emotional and physical health, and positive behavioral changes." Some educators find that a journal is helpful to keep track of the teaching practices that have been most successful, as well as progress they are making with a child or group of children. Your journal might include notes about what is and what isn't working in your program. It can also be a place where you reflect on your life outside work and the personal growth you are making over time.

SPIRITUAL WELLNESS

Spirituality is a very personal thing. Spiritual wellness, however, it isn't necessarily about religion. The National Wellness Institute (n.d.) suggests that spiritual wellness is about forming a positive perception of meaning and purpose in life. This can arise just from being open to different cultures and religions or from giving your time to volunteer or participate in community-service activities. Spiritual wellness also can be built through spending time alone in personal reflection, as you think about your own values and how you might make decisions that are complementary to your values. A key strategy that I use to promote spiritual wellness is through the practice of mindfulness.

WHAT IS MINDFULNESS?

Mindfulness has been growing in popularity. Researcher Jon Kabat-Zinn (2003) defines this practice as "the awareness that emerges through paying attention on purpose, in the present moment, and non-judgmentally to the unfolding of experience moment by moment." Through nonjudgmental awareness of the present moment, we are able to recognize our own thoughts, feelings, and behaviors as they arise, without getting stuck in our usual, automatic responses. And there are many benefits! First of all, it's free. You don't need any books or gadgets to practice mindfulness, and through the practice we are able to "wake up" to what we are really experiencing in the moment. Most importantly, it is backed by science. Kabat-Zinn found that mindfulness helps us to:

- experience life clearly, as it happens, without an emotional charge;
- discover what is the wisest and kindest way to respond in the moment;
- connect with ourselves and with the children in our lives;

- slow down when we need to; and
- become more aware of our choices in a situation and reduce impulsive reactions.

If you aren't already convinced, you will be when you learn that mindfulness has been shown to be an effective intervention for symptoms related to illness and mental health problems (Davis and Hayes, 2012). It is scientifically proven to improve mental and physical health. And you don't have to sit crisscross applesauce to do it! Research has found that mindfulness can reduce blood pressure, help us to manage pain, decrease stress and anxiety, treat clinical depression, and increase our ability to manage our emotions and impulses (Davidson et al., 2003; Grossman et al., 2004).

Mindfulness requires us to be fully present and focused. The practice involves bringing awareness to something specific, such as your breath. The focused attention brings our thoughts into view, but the practice requires that we simply notice our thoughts and keep from analyzing them or trying to think about what they mean. We pay attention to thoughts and feelings without trying to distinguish whether they are right or wrong. Over time, you start to recognize unhealthy patterns of thinking. There is mindful sitting, mindful standing, mindful journaling, mindful breathing, mindful walking, and even mindful eating.

Now, some of you might be thinking, "Jani, you're getting too 'woo woo' for me." I'm telling you, though, it works! Let's think about a typical day that has built-in time for mindfulness.

MINDFULNESS THROUGHOUT THE DAY

First, start off your day right. Researchers have found that we release the most stress hormones within minutes after waking (Hirotsu, Tufik, and Anderson, 2015). Why? Because thinking of the day ahead triggers our fight-or-flight instinct and releases the stress hormone cortisol into our blood. Instead, try this: When you wake up, spend two minutes in your bed simply noticing your breath. As thoughts about the day pop into your mind, let them go and return to your breath.

Later, when you get to the school or your first home visit of the day, take ten minutes in your car to boost your brain with a short mindfulness practice before you dive into activity. Close your eyes, relax, and sit upright. Place your full focus on your breath. Simply maintain an ongoing flow of attention on the experience of your breathing: inhale, exhale, inhale, exhale. To help your focus stay on your breathing, count silently at each exhalation. Any time you find your mind distracted, simply release the distraction by returning your focus to your breath. Most important, allow yourself to enjoy these minutes. Throughout the rest of the day, other people and competing urgencies will fight for your attention, but for these ten minutes, your attention is all your own.

As an educator, you have the opportunity to apply focus and awareness to everything you do from the moment you enter the school or workplace. Focus on the task at hand, and recognize distractions if they arise. Focus on what is important, and maintain awareness of what is merely noise. To avoid entering a meeting with a wandering mind, take two minutes to practice mindfulness. You can do this while you're walking to the meeting.

Try mindful eating during lunch with all or some of your food. Pay attention to the colors, smells, textures, flavors, temperatures, and even the sounds of your food. What are you feeling in your body? Where in the body do you feel hunger? Where do you feel satisfaction? What does half- or three-quarters full feel like? Watch the impulses that arise in your mind after taking a few sips or bites. Your mind might suggest that you grab a book, call someone on your cell phone, or get some additional work done. Simply notice the impulse and return your awareness to the act of eating. When you are finished eating, explore your thoughts and sensations. Is there a lingering taste from lunch? How do you feel physically and emotionally? Take a little while to consider the experience. There are no rights or wrongs, just individual experiences. This may be your first experience of eating lunch without that feeling of being on autopilot. Research by Killingsworth and Gilbert (2010) showed that people spend almost 47 percent of their waking hours thinking about something other than what they're doing. Break the spell and enjoy the feeling of being present while eating lunch!

As the day progresses and your brain starts to tire, mindfulness can help you stay sharp and avoid poor decisions. After lunch, set a timer on your phone to ring every hour. When the timer rings, stop what you're doing and do one minute of mindfulness practice. Another option is to use the regular transitions that are built into your typical routine as mindfulness-break reminders. Circle time? Take a mindfulness break. Time to go outside? Practice mindfulness as you walk from the inside environment to the outdoors. When you do the activity in your routine, focus completely on what you are doing: the body movements, the tastes, the touch, the smells, the sights, the sounds, and so on. When thoughts arise, acknowledge them, let them be, and bring your attention back to the activity. You'll find that, again and again, your attention will wander. As soon as you realize this has happened, gently acknowledge it, note what distracted you, and bring your attention back to your senses.

Finally, as the day comes to an end and you start your commute home, apply mindfulness. For at least ten minutes of the commute, turn off your phone, shut off the radio, and simply be. Let go of any thoughts that arise. Attend to your breath. Pay attention to how you are feeling internally as you drive. Notice the physical sensations of driving. How does your grip feel on the steering wheel? How is your body supported by the seat? A mindful commute will allow you to let go of the stresses of the day so you can return home and be fully present with your family.

MENTAL-HEALTH SUPPORTS

Hopefully, some of these strategies will resonate with you, and you will add some coping skills to your toolkit. Keep in mind that sometimes it is best to seek support from a mental-health provider. There's help out there, and it's okay to ask for it. This in itself is a form of self-care! You are not alone. Many people are in similar situations, so there are national hotlines available to help.

- **Alcoholics Anonymous:** (https://www.aa.org/) Online information on help and resources, including local AA resources, for alcohol addiction and abuse.

- **Childhelp Hotline:** Live, toll-free hotline with resources to aid in every child abuse and neglect situation. Text and live chat are also available: 800-4-ACHILD (800-422-4453)

- **Disaster Distress Helpline:** Live, toll-free crisis counseling and referral support for people experiencing emotional distress related to natural or human-caused disasters: (800-985-5990)

- **FindTreatment.gov:** SAMHSA online resource for learning about and finding treatment for substance use disorders

- **National Association for Children of Addiction (NACoA):** (https://nacoa.org/) Online information, help, and resources for children, teens, and adults: 888-554-COAS (888-554-2627) (toll-free)

- **National Domestic Violence Hotline:** Free, confidential, 24/7 help for those experiencing domestic violence: 800-799-SAFE (800-799-7233) (toll-free)

- **Parent Helpline:** Trained parent advocates provide support to empower parents: 855-4A PARENT (855-427-2736) (toll-free)

- **SAMHSA National Helpline:** Substance Abuse and Mental Health Services Administration (SAMHSA) offers this free, confidential helpline 24/7, 365 days a year. Find treatment referral and information for individuals and families facing mental or substance use disorders: https://www.samhsa.gov/

- **StrongHearts Native Helpline:** Safe, confidential, and anonymous help for American Indians and Alaska Natives experiencing domestic, dating, or sexual violence. Culturally appropriate support: 844-7NATIVE (844-762-8483) (toll-free)

- **Suicide Prevention Lifeline:** The Lifeline provides 24/7, free, and confidential support for people in distress. Find prevention and crisis resources for you or your loved ones, and best practices for professionals: 800-273-TALK (800-273-8255) (toll-free)

YOUR ROLE AS AN ADVOCATE FOR INCLUSION IN EARLY CHILDHOOD

At this point, my friend, I hope that you are wondering how you can be an advocate for inclusion. You may be having a "the sea is so wide, and my boat is so small" moment yourself. It is going to take each of us to build a system of inclusion for each and every child. We can do it, though! Consider the following strategies for next steps in your journey to foster inclusion in early childhood education.

First, we foster inclusion by being inclusive. Think about the children in your program. How can you create a learning environment that is as inclusive as possible? Do you need to talk with families about this goal? school administrators? funders? Be prepared to share concrete examples of what you hope to achieve as you create inclusion within your classroom or program. Try to have an impact on the things that you can control in the little part of the world where you live and work. How we respond to others is the thing that we can control the most.

Reflect on your current practice and think about areas that you might work on. Are you using inclusive language? Are there teaching practices that you hope to fine-tune? Do you believe that *each and every child* belongs in your program?

Advocacy itself can take many forms. Some advocates donate money. Others show up at protests or set up meetings with elected officials. Still others advocate for inclusion on social media or take time to educate friends and family members. We all can share stories and engage others in conversation. All of these efforts matter.

Remember that you are now part of that mighty fleet. You are not the only one thinking about inclusion, and when you talk with others and share your stories, you are creating a ripple on the water that will become a wave. Find others who share your values and passion. Lean on each other and build each other up. You will need those members of your fleet, because there are plenty of people out there who do not yet understand. Together we are strong. We have resilience and energy and grit that is matched only by those qualities in the children we love.

> *My boat is small, but I also know that my boat is not the only boat. I have many partners in this work, including you. Together we make a mighty fleet on behalf of children and families.*

Dandelions are definitely my favorite weed. Doesn't this image just sing childhood to you? Such a lovely experience, teaching children about the fun of blowing dandelion seeds for the first time. I think that I love dandelions because they remind me of us, this mighty force of early childhood educators. Just like a child blowing the seeds from a dandelion, we, too, provide the same little push, the lightest puff of air, that can make all of the difference in the world for a child. Our empathy, understanding, and care can mean the difference between shame and pride for a child with a disability. Inclusion versus exclusion. Thank you for joining in this work with me. The children we love are worth the fight, and if we work together, every child can fly.

Appendix A: Glossary of Terms

504 Plan: "a plan that specifies the accommodations and modifications necessary for a student with a disability to attend school with her or his peers; named for Section 504 of the federal Rehabilitation Act of 1973, which prohibits discrimination against individuals with disabilities, ensuring that children with disabilities have equal access to public education; students with 504 plans do not meet the eligibility requirements for special education under IDEA" (IRIS Center, 2021)

Ableism: "a set of beliefs or practices at the individual, community, or systemic level that devalues and discriminates against people with physical, intellectual, or psychiatric disabilities and often rests on the assumption that disabled people need to be 'fixed' in one form or the other" (Smith, n.d.)

Access: "providing a wide range of activities and environments for every child by removing physical barriers and offering multiple ways to promote learning and development" (DEC and NAEYC, 2009)

Accessibility: "the extent to which a facility is readily approachable and usable by individuals with disabilities, particularly such areas as the personnel office, worksite, and public areas" (University of Massachusetts Lowell, 2019)

Accommodation: "an adaptation or change to educational environments and practices designed to help students overcome the challenges presented by their disabilities and to allow them to access the same instructional opportunities as students without disabilities. An accommodation does change the expectations for learning or reduce the requirements of the task" (IRIS Center, 2021)

Acquisition: the stage of the learning cycle when the child has begun to learn how to complete the target skill correctly but is not yet accurate or fluent in the skill. The goal in this phase is to improve accuracy (Haring, et al., 1978).

Activity Matrix: a chart that lists the classroom schedule of activities down the left-hand column and the child's current objectives or target behaviors across the top. A matrix can also have the schedule of activities down the left-hand column and different children's names across the top. Within the boxes is a description of how the objective or target behavior would be embedded into each of the activities (NCPMI, n.d.).

Adaptation: a "term used to describe allowable changes in educational environments or practices (i.e., supports or services) that help a student overcome the barriers imposed by a disability and provide them with opportunities to achieve the same outcomes and obtain the same benefits as students without disabilities" (IRIS Center, 2021)

Adverse Childhood Experiences (ACEs): "preventable, potentially traumatic events that occur in childhood (0–17 years), such as neglect, experiencing or witnessing violence, and having a family member attempt or die by suicide. Also included are aspects of a child's environment that can undermine their sense of safety, stability, and bonding, such as growing up in a household with substance use; mental health problems; or instability due to parental separation or incarceration of a parent, sibling or other member of the household" (CDC, 2019).

Antecedents (or Triggers): the "events that happen right before a behavior occurs" (FPG, UNC, n.d.)

Assessment: the process of gathering information to make decisions. Assessment informs intervention, and as a result, is a critical component of services for children who have or are at risk for delays/disabilities and their families. In early intervention and early childhood special education, assessment is conducted for the purposes of screening, determining eligibility for services, individualized planning, monitoring child progress, and measuring child outcomes (DEC, 2014).

Assistive Technology: "any item, piece of equipment, or product system, whether acquired commercially off the shelf, modified, or customized, that is used to increase, maintain, or improve functional capabilities" (Sandall et al., 2005).

At-Risk: "term used to describe students whose condition or situation makes it probable for them to develop disabilities" (IRIS Center, 2021).

Attention Deficit Hyperactivity Disorder (ADHD): one of the most common mental disorders affecting children. Symptoms of ADHD include inattention (not being able to keep focus), hyperactivity (excess movement that is not fitting to the setting), and impulsivity (hasty acts that occur in the moment without thought) (American Psychiatric Association, 2021).

Augmentative and Alternative Communication (AAC): the supplementation or replacement of natural speech and/or writing using aided and/or unaided symbols . . . The use of aided symbols requires a transmission device (Lloyd, Fuller, and Arvidson, 1997).

Authentic Assessment: practices include methods and strategies for identifying the contextual and adult behavior that promote a child's participation and learning in everyday activities. The assessment practices involve observing children's engagement in everyday activities, the learning opportunities that occur in the activities, child strengths and abilities displayed in the activities, and the adult behavior that can support child participation and learning in the activities (ECTA, 2020b).

Autism Spectrum Disorder (ASD): a "developmental disability that can result in significant delays and developmental differences in a number of areas, including communication, social interaction, and behavior" (IRIS Center, 2021)

Behavior Hypothesis Statements: include a description of the behavior, triggers or antecedents for the behavior, maintaining consequences, and the purpose of the problem behavior (NCPMI, n.d.)

Behavior Support Plan: a team's action plan outlining the specific steps to be used to promote a child's success and participation in daily activities and routines. Essential components of the behavior support plan are prevention strategies, the instruction of replacement skills, new ways to respond to problem behavior, and lifestyle outcome goals (NCPMI, n.d.).

Cerebral Palsy: "a nonprogressive, neuromotor impairment that affects body movements and muscle coordination" (IRIS Center, 2021)

Child Find: "this law requires all school districts to identify and evaluate all children ages birth through 21 who have or are suspected of having a disability, regardless of severity, to determine if they need special education services" (IRIS Center, 2021)

Collaboration: "any collective action in which two or more individuals work together toward a common goal of planning, implementing, or evaluating a specific aspect of an educational program for a student or group of students" (IRIS Center, 2021)

Communication Board: "a form of assistive technology consisting of photographs, symbols, words/phrases, or any combination of these designed to make language visible and accessible for individuals with speech impairments" (IRIS Center, 2021)

Consent: within "IDEA has a very specific meaning that rises out of, and is closely tied to, its provisions regarding prior written notice. *Consent,* in IDEA, means informed written consent . . . intended to inform parents fully about a specific issue. Only by building that foundation of understanding can informed consent be given" (Küpper and Rebhorn, 2007).

Consequence Strategies: guidelines for how the adults will respond to problem behaviors in ways that will not maintain the behavior; may include positive reinforcement strategies for promoting the child's use of new skills or appropriate behavior (this may also be included in prevention strategies) (NCPMI, n.d.)

Coregulation: "reciprocal process between child and caregiver characterized by warm, responsive interactions . . . the process by which children develop social and emotional capacities via the caregiving relationship. Close physical contact, calming touch, supportive vocalizations, and modeling are primary modes of coregulation. Over time and with support, a child internalizes the caregiver's regulatory capacities through practice and reinforcement" (Gehl and Hackbert, 2019).

Cross-Sector: includes the major organizations, agencies, and institutions in a state that provide services and support the development and learning of young children, their families, and the practitioners who serve them (ECTA, 2015)

Culture: the languages, customs, beliefs, rules, arts, knowledge, and collective identities and memories developed by members of all social groups that make their social environments meaningful (American Sociological Association, n.d.)

Cultural Responsiveness: an awareness of the various cultures represented by a program's population and effort to align practices with the values and beliefs of these cultures.

Practices and products that are culturally responsive are communicated in a way that is both understandable and relevant to constituent groups (NCPMI, n.d.).

Curriculum: the plans for the learning experiences through which children acquire knowledge, skills, abilities, and understanding (NAEYC, 2020)

Curriculum Modification: "a change to the ongoing classroom activity or materials in order to facilitate or maximize a child's participation in planned activities and routines" (Sandall and Schwartz, 2008)

Developmental Milestones: the behaviors that mark stages of typical growth . . . most children pass through specific changes at approximately the same time as they get older (Cleveland Clinic, 2021)

Differentiated Instruction: an instructional approach that accommodates the diversity of students by coping with student diversity, adopting specific teaching strategies, invoking a variety in learning activity, monitoring individual student needs, and pursuing optimal learning outcomes (Suprayogi and Valcke, 2016)

Down Syndrome: "a disorder arising from chromosome defect (i.e., an extra chromosome on the twenty-first pair) that often results in identifiable physical characteristics (e.g., short stature, broad facial profile) and that usually causes delays in physical and intellectual development." (IRIS Center, 2021)

Early Intervention Services: "specialized services provided to very young children at risk for or showing signs of developmental delay" (IRIS Center, 2021)

Embedded Instruction: multiple, brief teaching interactions between a teacher and child during everyday activities. By identifying functional behavior targets, selecting classroom activities best suited for embedded learning opportunities, and using planned and intentional instructional strategies, teachers can help children learn new behavior for participating in classroom activities throughout the day (ECTA Center, 2017).

Emotional Literacy: the ability to give word meaning, such as *angry*, *frustrated*, *happy*, and *proud*, to one's emotions. Children who have larger emotional vocabularies tend to have less problem behavior (NCPMI, n.d.)

Emotional Regulation: "the ability to control one's state or behavior in order to achieve individual goals, handle everyday stress, and deal with various social situations appropriately" (IRIS Center, 2021)

Equality: "in the context of instructional supports and accommodations, term used to describe a state in which each student is given precisely the same tools to complete a learning task or assignment, even at the expense of their ability to do so" (IRIS Center, 2021)

Equity: "in the context of instructional supports and accommodations, term used to describe a state in which each student is given what he or she needs to successfully complete a learning task or assignment" (IRIS Center, 2021)

Equitable Learning Opportunities: "learning opportunities that not only help each child thrive by building on each one's unique set of individual and family strengths—including cultural background, language(s), abilities and disabilities, and experiences—but also are designed to eliminate differences in outcomes that are a result of past and present inequities in society" (NAEYC, n.d.)

Ethnicity: groups that share a common identity-based ancestry, language, or culture; often based on religion, beliefs, and customs as well as memories of migration or colonization (Stanford University, n.d.)

Evidence-Based Practices: interventions or supports that have published research documenting their effectiveness. Practices that are considered evidence based are ones that have been demonstrated as effective within multiple research studies that document similar positive outcomes. In this guide, the term "evidence-based practices" is used interchangeably with "recommended practices" and in some cases "targeted practices" when describing statewide initiatives to improve child outcomes (NCPMI, n.d.)

Executive Functions: "the mental processes that control and coordinate activities related to learning, including processing information, retaining and recalling information, organizing materials and time, and using effective learning and study strategies" (IRIS Center, 2021)

Fading: strategy of "gradually reducing the prompt by reducing the intensity, increasing the response interval, or [changing] the location of the prompt" (FPG, UNC, n.d.)

Fidelity: the degree to which an intervention or practice is delivered as intended by the developers and achieves expected results. Fidelity implies strict and continuing faithfulness to the original innovation or practice and can be measured and compared to previous or future efforts to deliver the intervention or practice (NCPMI, n.d.)

Flow: a highly focused mental state conducive to productivity (Csikszentmihalyi, 1990)

Fluency: the stage of the learning cycle when a child is able to complete a target skill accurately but works slowly. The goal of this phase is to increase the child's speed of responding (Haring et al., 1978)

Free Appropriate Public Education (FAPE): "ensures that each eligible student with a disability receives an individualized education that meets his or her unique needs and is provided in conformity with the student's IEP at no cost to the child or family" (IRIS Center, 2021)

Functional Behavior Assessment (FBA): "a process used to develop an understanding of a child's challenging behavior. The goal of functional behavioral assessment is to identify the function of the child's behavior—the reason or purpose why a child behaves as he/she does in specific situations" (NCPMI, n.d.)

Generalization: the stage of the learning cycle when a child is accurate and fluent in using the skill; the child is not yet able to modify or adapt the skill to fit novel task demands or situations. Here the goal is for the child to be able to identify elements of previously learned skills that they can adapt to the new demands or situation (Haring et al., 1978).

Historical Trauma: "the cumulative emotional and psychological wounding over the lifespan and across generations, emanating from massive group trauma experiences. Examples of historical trauma include the multigenerational effects of White supremacy reflected in colonization, genocide, slavery, sexual exploitation, forced relocation, and incarceration based on race or ethnicity" (NAEYC, n.d.)

Home visit: "term used to describe instruction delivered primarily in a student's home rather than in a school or center" (IRIS Center, 2021)

Hypothesis Statement: within the context of a behavior support plan, a description of everything that is known about the behavior, triggers, and warning signs learned through a functional behavioral assessment process; also includes an informed guess about the purpose or function of the challenging behavior (NCPMI, n.d.)

Implicit Bias: "the automatic and unconscious stereotypes that drive people to behave and make decisions in certain ways" (Staats et al., 2015)

Inclusion: "embodies the values, policies, and practices that support the right of every infant and young child and his or her family, regardless of ability, to participate in a broad range of activities and contexts as full members of families, communities, and society. The desired results of inclusive experiences for children with and without disabilities and their families include a sense of belonging and membership, positive social relationships and friendships, and development and learning to reach their full potential. The defining features of inclusion that can be used to identify high-quality early childhood programs and services are access, participation, and supports" (DEC and NAEYC, 2009).

Individualized Education Program (IEP): "a written education plan for a child with disabilities (ages 3–21) developed by a team of professionals (e.g., teachers, therapists) and the child's parents; it is reviewed and updated yearly and describes how the child is presently doing, what the child's learning needs are, and what services the child will need" (CONNECT and DEC, 2018)

Individualized Family Service Plan (IFSP): "a written plan for an infant or toddler with disabilities (birth-3) developed by a team of professionals (e.g., teachers, therapists) and the child's family; it is reviewed and updated yearly and describes how the child is presently doing, what the child's learning needs are, and what services the child will need" (CONNECT and DEC, 2018)

Individualized Instruction: refers to the idea that each student learns differently and thus in order to accommodate these differences, instruction should be personalized, matched, or adapted to the experiences, aptitudes, and interests of each student. (Waxman, Alford, and Brown, 2013)

Infant and Early Childhood Mental Health: "the developing capacity of the child from birth to 5 years of age to form close and secure adult and peer relationships; experience, manage, and express a full range of emotions; and explore the environment and learn—all in the context of family, community, and culture" (Zero to Three, 2016)

Interdisciplinary Team: "group of professionals from different disciplines who work together to plan and manage a student's IEP" (IRIS Center, 2021)

Intersectionality: the "overlapping and interdependent systems of oppression across, for example, race, gender, ability, and social status. Intersectionality encourages us to embrace and celebrate individuals' multiple social identities . . . [and] highlights the complex and cumulative effects of different forms of structural inequity that can arise for members of multiple marginalized groups" (NAEYC, n.d.)

Itinerant Teacher: an educator who teaches students or who consults with others in more than one setting (IRIS Center, 2021)

Learning Cycle: a sequential process for both learning and instruction. It places focus on a series of steps that encourage a more thorough understanding and a deeper application of content. The learning cycle has four stages: acquisition, fluency, maintenance, and generalization (Haring et al., 1978).

Least Restrictive Environment (LRE): "requires that students with disabilities be educated with their non-disabled peers to the greatest appropriate extent" (IRIS Center, 2021)

Least to Most Prompts (also called "the system of least prompts"): "a hierarchy of prompts that are ordered from the least to the most assistance needed for the child to perform a behavior. For each trial, the adult initially gives the child an opportunity to perform the behavior without prompts; if the child does not respond correctly, the adult delivers the least controlling prompt and gives the child another opportunity to respond. Again, if the child does not respond or starts to respond incorrectly, the adult delivers the next more controlling prompt. This continues on each trial until the child responds correctly or the most controlling level of prompt is provided" (NCPMI, n.d.)

Maintenance: stage of the learning cycle when the child is accurate and fluent in using the target skill but does not typically use it in different situations or settings (Haring et al., 1978)

Mediation: "process through which a neutral party facilitates a meeting between parents and school officials to resolve disagreements about a student's individualized education program and questions about his or her placement and services" (IRIS Center, 2021)

Medically Fragile: "term used to describe children whose medical conditions are subject to sudden change or that place them at risk for developmental delays" (IRIS Center, 2021)

Mentoring: "a method of ongoing support in which a more-experienced or more-knowledgeable person helps a less-experienced or less-knowledgeable person to learn or refine skills" (IRIS Center, 2021)

Modeling: "an instructional strategy in which an adult demonstrates a response. There are two types of modeling: verbal and nonverbal. In verbal modeling, an adult uses language to demonstrate how to say or do something . . . . In nonverbal modeling, an adult uses physical movements, signs, or gestures to demonstrate how to say or do something" (CONNECT and DEC, 2018)

Modifications: "any of a number of services or supports that allow a student to access the general education curriculum but in a way that fundamentally alters the content or curricular expectations in question" (IRIS Center, 2021)

Most to Least Prompts: "a series of two or more prompts that provide progressively decreasing amounts of assistance. This strategy always begins with the most help a child needs in order to be able to do something with few or no errors. Over time, as the child learns the skill, the amount of support the adult provides decreases until the child is able to do the skill independently" (NCPMI, n.d.).

Multidisciplinary Team: "a team of teachers, educational professionals (e.g., related services personnel, school psychologist), administrators, specialists, and parents or guardians who assess the individual needs of students to determine eligibility for special education and develop individualized education programs (IEP); often called IEP teams" (IRIS Center, 2021)

Multitiered Systems of Support (MTSS): "data-driven, problem-solving framework to improve outcomes for all students. MTSS relies on a continuum of evidence-based practices matched to student needs." PBIS and the Pyramid Model are examples of MTSS centered on social behavior. RTI is another example of a MTSS. A MTSS typically includes three tiers: tier 1, Universal Prevention (All); tier 2, Targeted Prevention (Some); and tier 3, Intensive, Individualized Prevention (Few) (Center on PBIS, 2021).

Observation: "the act of careful watching and listening; the activity of paying close attention to someone or something in order to get information" (Merriam-Webster, 2021b)

Participation: using a range of instructional approaches to promote engagement in play and learning activities and a sense of belonging for every child (DEC and NAEYC, 2009)

Peer-Mediated Intervention: a systematic teaching strategy in which typically developing children are taught to deliver specific social and communicative behavior to children with social-skill deficits (NCPMI, n.d.)

People-First Language: "a preferred method for referring to individuals with disabilities that emphasizes a word order placing mention of the individual before her or his disability (e.g., 'a person who is blind' rather than 'a blind person'), current terminology, and positive or neutral descriptions" (IRIS Center, 2021)

Physical Environment: "the overall design and layout of a classroom, including its learning centers, materials, and furnishings" (IRIS Center, 2021)

Picture Exchange Communication System (PECS): behavior-based intervention that teaches the learner to use visual-graphic symbols to communicate with others. Learners with ASD are taught to give a picture or graphic symbol of a desired item to a communicative partner in exchange for the actual item through a six-phase process (National Professional Development Center on ASD, 2019)

Placement: "term used to specify the educational setting in which special education services will be provided" (IRIS Center, 2021)

Positive Behavioral Interventions and Supports (PBIS): an individualized process for understanding and resolving the problem behavior of children, based on values and empirical research. It offers an approach for developing an understanding of why the child engages in problem behavior and strategies for preventing the occurrence of problem behavior while teaching the child new skills. Positive behavior support offers a holistic approach that considers all factors that impact a child and the child's behavior. It can be used to address problem behaviors that range from aggression, tantrums, and property destruction to social withdrawal (NCPMI, n.d.).

Practices: "what professionals do with, and for, children and their families to support optimal development in young children and family capacity to support their children" (ECTA, 2020c)

Practice-Based Coaching (PBC): focuses on the implementation of specified practices; occurs in the context of a collaborative partnership and uses a cyclical process of action planning, observation, reflection, and feedback for supporting practitioners' use of recommended practices (NCPMI, n.d.)

Prior Written Notice: "the public agency's obligation to inform parents a reasonable time before it proposes to take specific actions or refuses to take specific actions" (Küpper and Rebhorn, 2007)

Procedural Safeguards Notice: "the comprehensive written explanation that public agencies must provide parents on specific occasions to, among other things, fully inform them of IDEA's procedural safeguards. 'Upon initial referral or parent request for evaluation' are two occasions that trigger the provision of the procedural safeguards notice" (Küpper and Rebhorn, 2007).

Prompts: "instructions, gestures, demonstrations, touches, or other things we can do to increase the likelihood that children will respond how we want them to. Prompting helps children complete tasks that might otherwise be too difficult or contain multiple or complex steps. Supporting children using prompts (and providing positive descriptive feedback) helps them learn to complete tasks independently" (Barton Lab, n.d.)

Pull-Out Program: an "educational program in which instruction and related services are delivered to students with disabilities outside the general education classroom" (IRIS Center, 2021)

Pyramid Model for Supporting Social Emotional Competence in Infants and Young Children ("Pyramid Model"): "a promotion, prevention, and intervention framework early childhood educators can use to support young children's social emotional competence and prevent or reduce challenging behaviors" (NCPMI, n.d.)

Race: a social and political construction—with no inherent genetic or biological basis—used by social institutions to arbitrarily categorize and divide groups of individuals based on physical appearance (particularly skin color), ancestry, cultural history, and ethnic classification (Wijeysinghe, Griffin, and Love, 1997)

Racial Disparity: an unequal outcome one racial group experiences as compared to the outcome for another racial group (Fong, McCoy, and Detlaff, 2014)

Reliability: scores on a developmental screening tool will be stable regardless of when the tool is administered, where it is administered, and who is administering it. Reliability answers the question: Is the tool producing consistent information across different circumstances? Reliability provides assurance that comparable information will be obtained from the tool across different situations (US Department of Health and Human Services, 2014).

Referral: "process through which a student is sent to another professional for services to support his or her academic, social, or behavioral needs" (IRIS Center, 2021)

Related Services: "part of special education that includes services from professionals (e.g., occupational therapist [OT], physical therapist [PT], Speech-Language Pathologist [SLP]) from a wide range of disciplines typically outside of education, all designed to meet the learning needs of individual children with disabilities" (IRIS Center, 2021)

Replacement Skills: the skills to teach that will replace a problem behavior (NCPMI, n.d.)

Response Prompt: "teacher/parent behavior targeted at eliciting a child to present correct responding in a method appropriate to that child's communication capabilities. Response prompts are used to increase the probability of correct responding from the child" (Wolery, Ault, and Doyle, 1992)

Response to Intervention (RTI): "a multi-tier approach to the early identification and support of students with learning and behavior needs." For RTI implementation to work well, the following essential components must be implemented with fidelity and in a rigorous manner: high-quality, scientifically based classroom instruction, ongoing student assessment, universal screening and progress monitoring, tiered instruction, and parent involvement (RTI Action Network, n.d.)

Scaffolding: the practice of having an adult "provide the encouragement and the guidance to enable a child to reach beyond their current capacity. The model must be competent in order for the child to develop the skill" (Gehl and Hackbert, 2019).

Screen Reader Software: "any of a variety of computer programs or applications that enable a computer to convey information through non-visual means (e.g. text-to-speech, braille); a type of assistive technology commonly used by individuals who are blind, but also by those with low vision and learning disabilities" (IRIS Center, 2021)

Self-Contained Class: "a special classroom, usually located within a regular public school building, that exists only for students with disabilities" (IRIS Center, 2021)

Self-Regulation: the "capacity to be aware of and manage emotions to maintain a state and sense of calm . . . includes a wide range of internal processing such as inhibiting, initiating, and modulating of emotions and then choosing behaviors that make sense for the given situation" (Gehl and Hackbert, 2019)

Sensory Processing Disorder (also called **Sensory Integration Disorder):** "difficulty processing information from the senses . . . and responding appropriately to that information. These children typically have one or more senses that either over- or underreact to stimulation. Sensory processing disorder can cause problems with a child's development and behavior" (University of Michigan Health, 2021).

Sensory Reinforcers (or **Sensory Supports):** "activities or sensations the child enjoys experiencing, such as sitting in a rocking chair, getting lotion applied to hands, or playing with a favorite spinning top" (FPG, UNC, n.d.)

Service Coordination: "the process of facilitating students' access to services, and coordinating the services, supports, and resources as identified on the IFSP or IEP; assures that services will be provided in an integrated way and that they will not be needlessly duplicated" (IRIS Center, 2021)

Setting Events: the ecological events or conditions that increase the likelihood of challenging behavior (NCPMI, n.d.)

Social Environment: the "way that a classroom environment influences or supports the interactions that occur among young children, teachers, and family members" (IRIS Center, 2021)

Social Stories (also called **Scripted Stories):** "help children understand social interactions, situations, expectations, social cues, the script of unfamiliar activities, and/or social rules"; "brief descriptive stories that provide information regarding a social situation" (Broek, et al., 1994; NCPMI, n.d.)

Special Health-Care Needs: physical, intellectual, and developmental disabilities, as well as long-standing medical conditions, such as asthma, diabetes, a blood disorder, or muscular dystrophy (CDC, 2021b)

Specialized Services: "those services delivered to some children in a program, but not all, including early intervention, special education, related services and others" (ECTA, 2020b)

Specially Designed Instruction (SDI): "adapting, as appropriate to the needs of an eligible child . . . content, methodology, or delivery of instruction—[t]o address the unique needs of the child that result from the child's disability and [t]o ensure access of the child to the general curriculum" (Council for Exceptional Children, 2021)

Strength-Based Approach: an assumption that all children and families have resources, personal characteristics, and relationships that can be mobilized to enhance their learning, development, and well-being, no matter how many risk factors or challenges they face (Center for the Study of Social Policy, 2021)

Supports: "broader aspects of the system such as professional development, incentives for inclusion, and opportunities for communication and collaboration among families and professionals to assure high quality inclusion" (DEC and NAEYC, 2009)

Temporal Environment: "the timing, sequence, and length of routines and activities that take place in a classroom throughout the day" (IRIS Center, 2021)

Toxic Stress: "excessive or prolonged activation of stress response systems in the body and brain. Toxic stress response can occur when a child experiences strong, frequent, and/or prolonged adversity—such as physical or emotional abuse, chronic neglect, caregiver substance abuse or mental illness, exposure to violence, and/or the accumulated burdens of family economic hardship—without adequate adult support . . . [P]rolonged activation of the stress response systems can disrupt the development of brain architecture and other organ systems and increase the risk for stress-related disease and cognitive impairment well into the adult years" (Center on the Developing Child, 2021b).

Trauma: "an experience of serious adversity or terror—or the emotional or psychological response to that experience" (Center on the Developing Child, 2021a)

Trauma-Informed Care: an approach that focuses on prevention to help children manage symptoms and triggers that cause challenge and stress; an approach that "realizes the widespread impact of trauma and understands potential paths for recovery; recognizes the signs and symptoms of trauma in clients, families, staff, and others involved with the system; and responds by fully integrating knowledge about trauma into policies, procedures, and practices, and seeks to actively resist re-traumatization" (SAMHSA, 2014)

Universal Design: the philosophy of developing and designing physical environments to be accessible, to the greatest extent possible, to the people who use them, without the need for adaptation (Center for Applied Special Technology, 2008)

Universal Design for Learning: an educational framework based on the learning sciences, which informs the design and development of flexible instructional practices, materials, and tools that address the variability of all learners. This framework is essential to allow children with disabilities ways to engage with learning and to develop knowledge and skills in early childhood programs (Center for Applied Special Technology, 2008).

Validity: the scores on a screening tool accurately capture what the tool is meant to capture in terms of content. Validity answers the question: Is the tool assessing what it is supposed to assess? (US Department of Health and Human Services, 2014)

Vicarious Trauma: type of trauma that results when caregiving professionals are repeatedly exposed to the traumatic experiences or trauma stories of the clients they care for. Characterized by extreme symptoms with persistent heightened arousal at one end and emotional numbing and withdrawal at the other (Gehl and Hackbert, 2019)

Visual Supports (also called **Visual Cues):** concrete cues that are paired with, or used in place of, a verbal cue to provide the learner with information about a routine, activity, behavioral expectation, or skill demonstration (Sam et al., 2019)

Work Samples: collections of children's drawings, paintings, writing samples, or photographs that represent the best examples of what a child knows and is able to do at a given point in time

Zone of Proximal Development: the space between what a learner can do without assistance and what a learner can do with adult guidance or in collaboration with more capable peers (Vygotsky, 1978)

Appendix B: Online Resources to Support Inclusion

CHAPTER 1: INCLUSION: WHAT, HOW, AND WHY

Positions, Policy Statements and State-level Guidance

- California Department of Education: Inclusion Works!: https://www.cde.ca.gov/sp/cd/re/documents/inclusionworks2ed.pdf

- Delaware Early Childhood Inclusion Guide: https://ectacenter.org/~pdfs/topics/inclusion/de-inclusion-guide-final.pdf

- Head Start Disability Services Coordinator Orientation Guide: https://eclkc.ohs.acf.hhs.gov/children-disabilities/disability-services-coordinator-orientation-guide/disability-services-coordinator-orientation-guide

- Illinois Guidance Materials on Early Childhood Preschool Inclusion: https://www.isbe.net/Pages/Preschool-Inclusion-LRE.aspx

- Joint Position Statement on Inclusion (DEC and NAEYC): https://www.naeyc.org/sites/default/files/globally-shared/downloads/PDFs/resources/position-statements/ps_inclusion_dec_naeyc_ec.pdf

- OSEP Dear Colleague Letter on Preschool Inclusion: https://sites.ed.gov/idea/files/policy_speced_guid_idea_memosdcltrs_preschool-lre-dcl-1-10-17.pdf

- Policy Statement on Inclusion of Children with Disabilities in Early Childhood Programs: https://www2.ed.gov/policy/speced/guid/earlylearning/joint-statement-full-text.pdf

- Virginia Guidelines for Early Childhood Inclusion: https://ttaconline.org/Document/zxblhX_YCJOKW9RFGcsYls8GP00pSKNw/early-childhood-inclusion-guid-doc.pdf

Resources Related to Federal Legislation

- Facts about the Americans with Disabilities Act: https://eclkc.ohs.acf.hhs.gov/human-resources/article/facts-about-americans-disabilities-act

- IDEA: https://sites.ed.gov/idea/

- Institute for Human Centered Design. 2016. *ADA Checklist for Existing Facilities*. https://www.adachecklist.org/doc/fullchecklist/ada-checklist.pdf

- Mid-Atlantic ADA Center. 2012. *All Kids Count: Child Care and the ADA*. http://www.adainfo.org/sites/default/files/Child-Care-ADA-Resources.pdf

- Office of Special Education IDEAs That Work!: https://osepideasthatwork.org/

- Office of Special Education Programs (OSEP): https://www2.ed.gov/about/offices/list/osers/osep/index.html

- Section 504: Your Rights Under Section 504 of the Rehabilitation Act: https://www.hhs.gov/sites/default/files/ocr/civilrights/resources/factsheets/504.pdf

- US Department of Justice, Civil Rights Division, Disability Rights Section. 2020. "A Guide to Disability Rights Laws." https://www.ada.gov/cguide.htm

Research Compilations on Inclusion

- ECTA Compilation of Research and Studies on Inclusion: https://ectacenter.org/topics/inclusion/research.asp

- Fact Sheet of Research on Preschool Inclusion: https://ectacenter.org/~pdfs/topics/inclusion/research/Research_Supporting_Preschool_Inclusion_R.pdf

- Preschool Inclusion: Key Findings from Research and Implications for Policy: http://www.nccp.org/wp-content/uploads/2020/05/text_1154.pdf

- Research Synthesis Points on Early Childhood Inclusion: https://nceln.fpg.unc.edu/sites/nceln.fpg.unc.edu/files/resources/NPDCI_ResearchSynthesisPoints.pdf

- Resources within Reason: The Evidence for Preschool Inclusion: https://fpg.unc.edu/sites/fpg.unc.edu/files/resources/other-resources/ResourcesWithinReason-Jan2017.pdf

OSEP-Funded National Technical Assistance Centers

- Center for IDEA Early Childhood Data Systems (DASY Center): https://dasycenter.org/

- The Early Childhood Personnel Center: https://ecpcta.org/

- Early Childhood Technical Assistance (ECTA) Center: http://ectacenter.org

- ECTA Inclusion Resources: https://ectacenter.org/topics/inclusion/research.asp

- Indicators of High-Quality Inclusion: https://ectacenter.org/topics/inclusion/indicators.asp

- IRIS Center: https://iris.peabody.vanderbilt.edu/

- Office of Special Education Programs Technical Assistance Network: https://osepideasthatwork. org/sites/default/files/OSEPplacemat-508_updated%2004.01.20.pdf

Other Related National Centers

- Beach Center on Disability: https://beachcenter.lsi.ku.edu/

- Caring for Our Children: http://nrckids.org/CFOC

- Division for Early Childhood (DEC) of the Council for Exceptional Children: http://www.dec-sped.org

- DEC Recommended Practices: https://www.dec-sped.org/dec-recommended-practices

- Head Start Center for Inclusion: http://headstartinclusion.org/

- Head Start Early Childhood Learning and Knowledge Center (ECLKC): https://eclkc.ohs.acf.hhs.gov

- National Resource Center for Health and Safety in Child Care and Early Education: https://nrckids.org/

Information about Specific Conditions

- American Speech-Language-Hearing Association (ASHA): https://www.asha.org/

- American Association on Intellectual and Developmental Disabilities: https://www.vmrc.net/national-resources/

- Attention Deficit Hyperactivity Disorder (ADHD): https://www.psychiatry.org/patients-families/adhd/what-is-adhd and https://www.additudemag.com/

- The Autism Society: https://www.autism-society.org/

- Children and Families Affected by Parental Substance Use Disorders (SUDs): https://ncsacw.samhsa.gov/topics/parental-substance-use-disorder.aspx

- ECTA Compilation of Information, Specific Disability Populations: https://ectacenter.org/topics/earlyid/idspecpops.asp

- Easter Seals: https://www.easterseals.com/

- Fetal Alcohol Syndrome: https://www.cdc.gov/ncbddd/fasd/index.html

- Fragile X Syndrome: https://medlineplus.gov/genetics/condition/fragile-x-syndrome/

- Head Start Disability Guides: https://headstartinclusion.org/tip-sheets/disability-guides/

- Learning Disabilities: https://www.nichd.nih.gov/health/topics/learningdisabilities

- Little People of America (information about dwarfism): https://www.lpaonline.org/

- Muscular Dystrophy Association: https://www.mda.org/

- National Association of Councils on Developmental Disabilities: https://www.nacdd.org/

- National Center on Birth Defects and Developmental Disabilities (NCBDDD): https://www.cdc.gov/ncbddd/

- National Center on Deaf-Blindness: https://www.nationaldb.org/

- National Down Syndrome Society: https://www.ndss.org/

- National Institute on Deafness and Other Communication Disorders: https://www.nidcd.nih.gov/

- Prevent Blindness: https://preventblindness.org/your-babys-developing-sight/

- Spina Bifida Association: https://www.spinabifidaassociation.org/

- United Cerebral Palsy: https://ucp.org/

CHAPTER 2: UNDERSTANDING EARLY INTERVENTION AND SPECIAL EDUCATION

- Child Outcomes Infographic: https://ectacenter.org/~pdfs/eco/three-child-outcomes-breadth.pdf

- ECTA information on Part C eligibility: https://ectacenter.org/topics/earlyid/partcelig.asp

- Eligibility and Service Delivery Policies: Differences between IDEA Part C and IDEA Part B: http://www.infanthearing.org/earlyintervention/docs/aspect-idea-part-c-and-idea-part-b.pdf

- IFSP Process: Planning and Implementing Family-Centered Services in Natural Environments http://ectacenter.org/topics/ifsp/ifspprocess.asp

- Inclusion of Infants and Toddlers with Disabilities or Other Special Needs: https://childcareta.acf.hhs.gov/infant-toddler-resource-guide/inclusion-infants-and-toddlers-disabilities-or-other-special-needs

- List of State Part C Coordinators: http://ectacenter.org/contact/ptccoord.asp

- List of State Section 619 Coordinators: http://ectacenter.org/contact/619coord.asp

- Office of Head Start fact sheet, ideas for children who do not qualify for IDEA: https://eclkc.ohs.acf.hhs.gov/publication/services-children-who-do-not-qualify-idea-fact-sheet

- Office of Special Education IDEAs that Work!: https://osepideasthatwork.org/

- OSEP Part C Guidance and Training Resources: http://ectacenter.org/partc/OSEPresources.asp

- Parent Training and Information Center: https://www.parentcenterhub.org/find-your-center/

- Parent Training and Information Center, *Building the Legacy for Our Youngest Children with Disabilities:* https://www.parentcenterhub.org/legacy-partc/

- Parent Training and Information Center, Training Curriculum on Part B of IDEA 2004: https://www.parentcenterhub.org/legacy/

- Part C of IDEA: https://ectacenter.org/partc/partc.asp

- Transitions, Hospital to EI, EI to Part B Preschool Special Education: https://ectacenter.org/decrp/topic-transition.asp

- Transition from Part C to Preschool: http://ectacenter.org/topics/transition/transition.asp

- Transition from Preschool Services to Kindergarten: http://ectacenter.org/topics/transition/transtoK.asp

CHAPTER 3: WORKING WITH FAMILIES

- Building the Legacy for Our Youngest Children Training Modules: https://www.parentcenterhub.org/legacy-partc/

- Building the Legacy Training Modules: https://www.parentcenterhub.org/legacy/

- Center for Appropriate Dispute Resolution in Special Education (CADRE) Dispute Resolution—Part B Guide: https://www.cadreworks.org/sites/default/files/resources/Dispute%20Resolution%20Process%20Comparison%20Chart.pdf

- Center for Parent Information and Resources: https://www.parentcenterhub.org

- Child Care Aware of America: http://childcareaware.org/about/child-care-aware-of-america

- CONNECT Modules, Module 4: Family and Professional Partnerships: http://community.fpg.unc.edu/connect-modules/learners/module-4

- Culture and Language: https://eclkc.ohs.acf.hhs.gov/culture-language/article/cultural-backgrounders-various-refugee-cultural-groups-new-united-states

- DEC Recommended Practices, Guides for Families: http://ectacenter.org/decrp/type-pgfamily.asp

- Dispute Resolution—Part C Guide: https://www.cadreworks.org/sites/default/files/resources/Part%20C%20DR%20Comparison%20Chart-FINAL%208–23–18.pdf

- Encouraging Active Parent Participation in IEP Team Meetings: http://www.casenex.com/casenex/cecReadings/encouragingActive.pdf

- Fact Sheets About Specific Disabilities: https://www.parentcenterhub.org/specific-disabilities/

- List of Parent Centers Across the United States: https://www.parentcenterhub.org/find-your-center

- NCPMI, My Teacher Wants to Know: https://challengingbehavior.cbcs.usf.edu/docs/ttyc/TTYC_MyTeacherWantstoKnow.pdf
https://challengingbehavior.cbcs.usf.edu/docs/My-teacher-wants-to-know.pdf

- PACER Center (Parent Special Education Information): https://www.pacer.org/parent/

- Parent, Family, and Community Engagement Simulation: Boosting School Readiness through Effective Family Engagement Series: https://eclkc.ohs.acf.hhs.gov/family-engagement/article/parent-family-community-engagement-simulation-boosting-school-readiness-through-effective-family

- Parents' Guide to the Family Educational Rights and Privacy Act (FERPA): Rights Regarding Children's Educations Records https://studentprivacy.ed.gov/sites/default/files/resource_document/file/A%20parent%20guide%20to%20ferpa_508.pdf

- *Talking with Families about Their Child's Development:* https://eclkc.ohs.acf.hhs.gov/sites/default/files/pdf/talking-with-families-about-their-childs-development.pdf

- Team Decisions for Preschool Special Education Services: Guiding Questions: https://ectacenter.org/~pdfs/topics/inclusion/team-decisions-guiding-questions.pdf

- "Welcome to Holland" by Emily Perl Kingsley: https://www.dsasc.ca/uploads/8/5/3/9/8539131/welcome_to_holland.pdf

- Your Health Information Privacy Rights: https://www.hhs.gov/sites/default/files/ocr/privacy/hipaa/understanding/consumers/consumer_rights.pdf

CHAPTER 4: SCREENING, EVALUATION, AND ASSESSMENT

- Assessment Practice Guides for Practitioners: https://ectacenter.org/decrp/type-pgpractitioner.asp#pgpractitioner-assessment

- Birth to 5: Watch Me Thrive! https://www2.ed.gov/about/inits/list/watch-me-thrive/index.html

- Birth to 5: Watch Me Thrive! training: https://www.cdc.gov/ncbddd/watchmetraining/index.html

- *Birth to 5: Watch Me Thrive! A Compendium of Screening Measures for Young Children:* https://www2.ed.gov/about/inits/list/watch-me-thrive/files/screening-compendium-march2014.pdf

- Birth to 5: Watch Me Thrive! An Early Care and Education Provider's Guide for Developmental and Behavioral Screening: https://www2.ed.gov/about/inits/list/watch-me-thrive/files/ece-providers-guide-march2014.pdf

- Brazelton Center, Development Is a Journey: https://www.brazeltontouchpoints.org/wp-content/uploads/2021/05/Development-is-a-Journey-Roadmap-ECE-Providers-full-color.pdf

- CDC free materials: https://www.cdc.gov/ncbddd/actearly/freematerials.html

- CDC's Developmental Milestones https://www.cdc.gov/ncbddd/actearly/milestones/index.html

- Development Is a Journey Conversation Guide: https://www.brazeltontouchpoints.org/wp-content/uploads/2021/06/Development-is-a-Journey-Conversation-Roadmap-ECE-Providers-Implementation-Guide.pdf

- Developmentally Appropriate Practice Position Statement from the National Association for the Education of Young Children: https://www.naeyc.org/sites/default/files/globally-shared/downloads/PDFs/resources/position-statements/dap-statement_0.pdf

- Head Start Child Screening and Assessment Topic Page: https://eclkc.ohs.acf.hhs.gov/child-screening-assessment

- Head Start Early Learning Outcomes Framework: Birth to Five: https://eclkc.ohs.acf.hhs.gov/interactive-head-start-early-learning-outcomes-framework-ages-birth-five

- Learn the Signs, Act Early: https://www.cdc.gov/ncbddd/actearly/index.html

- Ongoing Child Assessment: Children with Disabilities: https://eclkc.ohs.acf.hhs.gov/video/children-disabilities

- Practice Improvement Tools: Assessment (ECTA): https://ectacenter.org/decrp/topic-assessment.asp

CHAPTER 5: WORKING ON IFSP OR IEP GOALS

- "Activity Matrix: Organizing Learning throughout the Day": https://eclkc.ohs.acf.hhs.gov/video/activity-matrix-organizing-learning-throughout-day

- "Break It Down: Turning Goals into Everyday Teaching Opportunities": https://eclkc.ohs.acf.hhs.gov/video/break-it-down-turning-goals-everyday-teaching-opportunities

- Effective Instruction: Embedding IEP Goals: https://eclkc.ohs.acf.hhs.gov/video/effective-instruction-embedding-iep-goals

- Embedded Instruction Practices: https://ectacenter.org/~pdfs/decrp/PGP_INS3_embedded_2018.pdf

- Embedded Instructional Practices Checklist: https://ectacenter.org/~pdfs/decrp/INS-2_Embedded_Instruction_2018.pdf

- Individualized Education Program (IEP) Basics: https://eclkc.ohs.acf.hhs.gov/children-disabilities/article/individualized-education-program-iep-basics

- Naturalistic Instruction Practices: https://ectacenter.org/~pdfs/decrp/PGP_INS1_naturalistic_2018.pdf

- Naturalistic Instructional Practices Checklist: https://ectacenter.org/~pdfs/decrp/INS-1_Naturalistic_Instruction_2018.pdf

- Practice Improvement Tools: Teaming and Collaboration (ECTA): https://ectacenter.org/decrp/topic-teaming.asp

CHAPTER 6: INCLUSIVE LEARNING ENVIRONMENTS

- AbleNet: https://www.ablenetinc.com/

- Assistive Technology Checklist from ECTA: https://ectacenter.org/~pdfs/decrp/ENV-5_Assistive_Tech_2018.pdf

- Cadan Assistive Technologies: http://tfeinc.com/

- Child Physical Activity Checklist from ECTA: https://ectacenter.org/~pdfs/decrp/ENV-3_Child_Phys_Activity_2018.pdf

- Classroom rules poster: https://challengingbehavior.cbcs.usf.edu/docs/Our-Preschool-Rules_Story.pdf

- Creating Inclusive Environments and Learning Experiences for Infants and Toddlers: https://childcareta.acf.hhs.gov/infant-toddler-resource-guide

- Early Care and Education Environment: Indicators and Elements of High-Quality Inclusion: https://ectacenter.org/topics/inclusion/indicators-ece.asp

- Environmental Adaptations Checklist from ECTA: https://ectacenter.org/~pdfs/decrp/ENV-4_Environmental_Adaptations_2018.pdf

- Environmental Arrangements Checklist from ECTA: https://ectacenter.org/~pdfs/decrp/ENV-2_Env_Arrangements_2018.pdf

- Measuring the Quality of Inclusion: The Inclusive Classroom Profile: https://npdci.fpg.unc.edu/measuring-quality-inclusion-inclusive-classroom-profile.html

- Natural Environment Learning Activities Checklist from ECTA: https://ectacenter.org/~pdfs/decrp/ENV-1_Natural_Env_Learning_Opps_2018.pdf

- The PACER Simon Technology Center: https://www.pacer.org/stc/

- Practice Improvement Tools: Environment (ECTA): https://ectacenter.org/decrp/topic-environment.asp

- Social stories: https://headstartinclusion.org/tools-and-supports/social-stories/

- STEM Innovation for Inclusion in Early Education ("STEMIE") Center: https://stemie.fpg.unc.edu/resources

- STEMIE Guide to Adaptations: https://stemie.fpg.unc.edu/guide-adaptations

- Stop and Go activity: https://challengingbehavior.cbcs.usf.edu/docs/Stop-Go_Activity.pdf

- Transition visuals: https://challengingbehavior.cbcs.usf.edu/docs/Transition-visual_cards.pdf

- Visuals for the block area: https://headstartinclusion.org/tools-and-supports/classroom-visuals-and-supports/

CHAPTER 7: INCLUSIVE TEACHING PRACTICES

- 15-Minute In-Service Suite: Additional Highly Individualized Teaching and Learning Suites https://eclkc.ohs.acf.hhs.gov/children-disabilities/article/highly-individualized-teaching-learning

- 15-Minute In-Service Suite: Highly Individualized Teaching and Learning: An Overview https://eclkc.ohs.acf.hhs.gov/video/highly-individualized-teaching-learning-overview

- 15-Minute In-Service Suite: Organizing Learning throughout the Day https://eclkc.ohs.acf.hhs.gov/video/activity-matrix-organizing-learning-throughout-day

- Autism Focused Intervention Resources & Modules (AFIRM): https://afirm.fpg.unc.edu/afirm-modules

- CONNECT Modules: http://community.fpg.unc.edu/connect-modules/learners

- Creating Social (Scripted) Stories: https://challengingbehavior.cbcs.usf.edu/docs/ScriptedStories_Home.pdf?cid=f7af3b43e857ce2921b1a26158a2a34a

- Curriculum Modification Planning Forms and Related Materials: https://headstartinclusion.org/training-materials/extended-professional-development-packages/curriculum-modifications-and-adaptations/

- Division for Early Childhood (DEC) Recommended Practices Performance Checklists: http://ectacenter.org/decrp/type-checklists.asp

- Head Start Center for Inclusion: Educator Resources: https://headstartinclusion.org/tools-and-supports/educator-resources/

- Highly Individualized Practices Webinar Series https://eclkc.ohs.acf.hhs.gov/children-disabilities/article/highly-individualized-practices-series

- Instructional Strategies Video Exemplars: https://headstartinclusion.org/training-materials/instructional-strategies-video-exemplars/

- Position Statement on Multitiered System of Support Framework in Early Childhood (DEC): https://www.decdocs.org/position-statement-mtss

- Practice Guides for Practitioners: http://ectacenter.org/decrp/type-pgpractitioner.asp

- Practice Improvement Tools—Instruction (ECTA): https://ectacenter.org/decrp/topic-instruction.asp

- Preschool During the Pandemic: Early Childhood Education in Extraordinary Times: https://ectacenter.org/topics/disaster/preschoolpandemic.asp

- Resources Supporting Individualization: https://eclkc.ohs.acf.hhs.gov/children-disabilities/article/resources-supporting-individualization

- Snack Talk Tip Sheet: https://haringcenter.org/wp-content/uploads/2020/12/Snack-Talk-Tip-Sheet.pdf

- SpecialQuest Multimedia Training Library: https://eclkc.ohs.acf.hhs.gov/children-disabilities/specialquest-multimedia-training-library/specialquest-multimedia-training-library

- Systematic Instruction Practices: https://ectacenter.org/~pdfs/decrp/PGP_INS4_systematic_2018.pdf

- Systematic Instructional Practices Checklist: https://ectacenter.org/~pdfs/decrp/INS-3_Systematic_Instruction_2018.pdf

- Using Visual Supports: https://afirm.fpg.unc.edu/visual-cues-introduction-practice

- *We Carry Kevan:* https://www.wecarrykevan.com/

CHAPTER 8: INCLUSIVE PRACTICES TO FOSTER SOCIAL-EMOTIONAL DEVELOPMENT

- Center of Excellence for Infant and Early Childhood Mental Health Consultation: https://www.ecmhc.org/index.html

- Children's Books with a Social-Emotional Theme: https://challengingbehavior.cbcs.usf.edu/docs/booknook/ChildrensBookList.pdf

- DEC Position Statement on Challenging Behavior and Young Children: https://challengingbehavior.cbcs.usf.edu/docs/DEC_PositionStatement_ChallengingBehavior.pdf

- Facilitating Individualized Interventions to Address Challenging Behavior: https://www.ecmhc.org/documents/CECMHC_FacilitatingToolkit.pdf

- Feeling Faces Cards: https://challengingbehavior.cbcs.usf.edu/docs/FeelingFaces_cards_EN-Blank.pdf

- Head Start Resources on Effectively Addressing Behaviors: https://eclkc.ohs.acf.hhs.gov/mental-health/article/effectively-addressing-behaviors

- *Including Samuel*, 2007 documentary film about inclusion: https://includingsamuel.com/

- Mental Health Consultation Tool: https://eclkc.ohs.acf.hhs.gov/mental-health/learning-module/mental-health-consultation-tool

- National Center for Pyramid Model Innovations (NCPMI): http://challengingbehavior.cbcs.usf.edu

- National Child Traumatic Stress Network: https://www.nctsn.org/

- NCPMI Behavioral Intervention Process: https://challengingbehavior.cbcs.usf.edu/Pyramid/pbs/process.html

- NCPMI Problem-Solving Solution Kits, classroom https://challengingbehavior.cbcs.usf.edu/docs/SocialEmotionalSkills_solution-kit_cue-cards.pdf

- NCPMI Problem-Solving Solution Kits, home edition: https://challengingbehavior.cbcs.usf.edu/docs/Solution_kit_cards_home.pdf

- NCPMI Relaxation Thermometer: https://challengingbehavior.cbcs.usf.edu/docs/Relaxation-Thermometer.pdf

- Peer-Mediated Skills: https://challengingbehavior.cbcs.usf.edu/docs/Peer-Mediated-Skills.pdf

- Pyramid practices that can be used during virtual learning: https://challengingbehavior.cbcs.usf.edu/docs/Pyramid-Virtual-Learning-Checklist.pdf

- The Pyramid Model and Trauma-Informed Care: A Guide for Early Childhood Professionals to Support Young Children's Resilience: https://challengingbehavior.cbcs.usf.edu/docs/Trauma-Informed-Care_Guide.pdf

- Teaching Friendship Skills (visual supports): https://challengingbehavior.cbcs.usf.edu/docs/Peer-Mediated-Skills.pdf

- *Tucker Turtle Takes Time to Tuck and Think*: https://challengingbehavior.cbcs.usf.edu/docs/TuckerTurtle_Story.pdf

- *Tucker Turtle Takes Time to Tuck and Think at Home*: https://challengingbehavior.cbcs.usf.edu/docs/TuckerTurtle_Story_Home.pdf

- Turtle Technique: https://challengingbehavior.cbcs.usf.edu/docs/TurtleTechnique_steps.pdf

- Visual Supports from the Head Start Center on Inclusion: https://headstartinclusion.org/tools-and-supports/classroom-visuals-and-supports/

CHAPTER 9: CULTURALLY AND LINGUISTICALLY RESPONSIVE PRACTICES

- Culturally Responsive Strategies to Support Young Children with Challenging Behavior: https://www.naeyc.org/resources/pubs/yc/nov2016/culturally-responsive-strategies

- Dual Language Learners Program Assessment: https://eclkc.ohs.acf.hhs.gov/sites/default/files/pdf/dllpa-collection-508-revised-v3.pdf

- Dual Language Learners Toolkit: https://eclkc.ohs.acf.hhs.gov/culture-language/article/dual-language-learners-toolkit

- Dual Language Learners With Disabilities: Supporting Young Children in the Classroom: https://iris.peabody.vanderbilt.edu/module/dll/#content

- Duolingo: https://www.duolingo.com/

- Equity Coaching Guide (NCPMI): https://challengingbehavior.cbcs.usf.edu/Implementation/Equity/Guide/index.html

- Head Start Resources on Culture and Language: https://eclkc.ohs.acf.hhs.gov/culture-language

- International Children's Digital Library at http://www.childrenslibrary.org/

- Making it Work: https://eclkc.ohs.acf.hhs.gov/culture-language/article/making-it-work-implementing-cultural-learning-experiences-american-indian-alaska-native-early

- Multicultural Principles for Early Childhood Leaders: https://eclkc.ohs.acf.hhs.gov/culture-language/article/multicultural-principles-early-childhood-leaders

- NAEYC Position Statement on Equity: https://www.naeyc.org/resources/position-statements/equity

- NAEYC Principles of Child Development and Learning: https://www.naeyc.org/resources/position-statements/dap/principles

- Office of Head Start Cultural Backgrounders: https://eclkc.ohs.acf.hhs.gov/culture-language/article/cultural-backgrounders-various-refugee-cultural-groups-new-united-states

- Outreach to Families with Limited English Proficiency and Disabilities (within the Fundamentals of Child Care Development Fund Administration): https://childcareta.acf.hhs.gov/ccdf-fundamentals/outreach-families-limited-english-proficiency-and-disabilities

- Reducing Suspension and Expulsion Practices in Early Childhood Settings: https://www.acf.hhs.gov/ecd/child-health-development/reducing-suspension-and-expulsion-practices

- Supporting the Development of Young Children in American Indian and Alaska Native Communities Who Are Affected by Alcohol and Substance Exposure: https://www.acf.hhs.gov/sites/default/files/documents/ecd/tribal_statement_a_s_exposure_0.pdf

CHAPTER 10: SELF-CARE FOR THE EARLY CHILDHOOD EDUCATOR

- 10 Percent Happier: https://www.tenpercent.com/

- Calm: https://www.calm.com

- Child Care Aware of America State-by-State Resources: https://www.childcareaware.org/resources/map/

- Early Childhood Workforce Index 2020: https://cscce.berkeley.edu/workforce-index-2020/

- Getting Started with Mindfulness: A Toolkit for Early Childhood Organizations: https://www.zerotothree.org/resources/2896-getting-started-with-mindfulness-a-toolkit-for-early-childhood-organizations

- Insight Timer: https://insighttimer.com/

- Head Start Resources on Staff Well-being: https://eclkc.ohs.acf.hhs.gov/mental-health/article/promoting-staff-well-being

- National Wellness Institute Six Dimensions of Wellness: https://nationalwellness.org/resources/six-dimensions-of-wellness/

- Practice-Based Coaching: https://eclkc.ohs.acf.hhs.gov/professional-development/article/practice-based-coaching-pbc

- Racial Wage Gaps in Early Education Employments: https://cscce.berkeley.edu/racial-wage-gaps-in-early-education-employment/

- Stop, Breathe and Think: https://www.stopbreathethink.com/about/

- Taking Care of Ourselves: https://www.ecmhc.org/documents/TakingCare_ProviderBk_final.pdf

- UCLA Mindful: https://www.uclahealth.org/ucla-mindful

References and Recommended Reading

20 USC 1400. 2004. Individuals with Disabilities Education Improvement Act of 2004.

42 USC 9801 et seq. 2007. Head Start Act. https://eclkc.ohs.acf.hhs.gov/sites/default/files/pdf/HS_Act_2007.pdf

Allen, K. Eileen, and Ilene Schwartz. 2001. *The Exceptional Child: Inclusion in Early Childhood Settings.* 4th edition. Albany, NY: Delmar Publishing.

Allen, Kris. 2018. "The Importance of Inclusive Play for All Children." We Build Fun blog. https://www.webuildfun.com/the-importance-of-inclusive-play-for-all-children

Almon, Joan. 2013. *Adventure: The Value of Risk in Children's Play.* Annapolis, MD: Alliance for Childhood.

Annamma, Subini A., Amy L. Boelé, Brooke A. Moore, and Janette Klingner. 2013. "Challenging the Ideology of Normal in Schools." *International Journal of Inclusive Education* 17(12): 1278–1294.

American Psychiatric Association. 2021. "What Is ADHD?" American Psychiatric Association. https://www.psychiatry.org/patients-families/adhd/what-is-adhd

American Sociological Association. n.d. "Culture." American Sociological Association. https://www.asanet.org/topics/culture

American Speech-Language-Hearing Association. 2021. "IDEA Part C: Evaluation and Assessment Definitions." ASHA. https://www.asha.org/advocacy/federal/idea/idea-part-c-evaluation-and-assessment-definitions/#:~:text=Evaluation%20means%20%22the%20procedures%20used,%C2%A7303.321(b)

The Annie E. Casey Foundation. 2021. "Child Population by Single Age in the United States." Baltimore, MD: Kids Count Data Center. https://datacenter.kidscount.org

Artiles, Alfredo J., Beth Harry, Daniel J. Reschly, and Philip C. Chinn. 2002. "Over-Identification of Students of Color in Special Education: A Critical Overview." *Multicultural Perspectives* 4(1): 3–10.

Austin, Lea J.E., et al. 2019. "Racial Wage Gaps in Early Education Employments." Center for the Study of Child Care Employment, University of California, Berkeley. https://cscce.berkeley.edu/racial-wage-gaps-in-early-education-employment/

Avramidis, Elias, Phil Bayliss, and Robert Burden. 2000. "A Survey into Mainstream Teachers' Attitudes Towards the Inclusion of Children with Special Educational Needs in the Ordinary School in One Local Education Authority." *Educational Psychology* 20(2): 191–211.

Avramidis, Elias, and Brahm Norwich. 2002. "Teachers' Attitudes Towards Integration/Inclusion: A Review of the Literature." *European Journal of Special Needs Education* 17(2): 129–147.

Bagwell, Catherine L., and Michelle E. Schmidt. 2011. *Friendships in Childhood and Adolescence.* New York: Guilford.

Banda, Devender R., Stephanie L. Hart, and Lan Liu-Gitz. 2010. "Impact of Training Peers and Children with Autism on Social Skills during Center Time Activities in Inclusive Classrooms." *Research in Autism Spectrum Disorders* 4(4): 619–625.

Barton, Erin E., and Barbara J. Smith. 2014. "Fact Sheet of Research on Preschool Inclusion." Denver, CO: Pyramid Plus: The Colorado Center for Social Emotional Competence and Inclusion.

Barton, Erin E., and Barbara J. Smith. 2015a. "Advancing High Quality Preschool Inclusion: A Discussion and Recommendations for the Field." *Topics in Early Childhood Special Education* 35(2): 69–78.

Barton, Erin E., and Barbara J. Smith. 2015b. *The Preschool Inclusion Toolbox: How to Build and Lead a High-Quality Program.* Baltimore, MD: Paul H. Brookes.

Barton Lab. n.d. "What Is a Prompt?" Barton Lab, Vanderbilt University. https://cdn.vanderbilt.edu/vu-web/lab-wpcontent/sites/96/2020/02/12211548/Prompting-Procedures.pdf

Bashan, James D., et al. 2015. *Equity Matters: Digital and Online Learning for Students with Disabilities.* Lawrence, KS: Center on Online Learning and Students with Disabilities. https://centerononlinelearning.ku.edu/wp-content/uploads/2017/04/2015_COLSD_Annual-Publication_FULL-2.pdf

Bialystok, Ellen, Fergus I.M. Craik, and Gigi Luk. 2012. Bilingualism: consequences for mind and brain. *Trends in Cognitive Sciences.* 16(4):240–250.

Blair, Kwang-Sun Cho, and Lise Fox. 2011. *Facilitating Individualized Interventions to Address Challenging Behavior.* Washington, DC: Center for Early Childhood Mental Health Consultation, Georgetown University Center for Child and Human Development.

Booth-LaForce, Cathryn, and Jean F. Kelly. 2004. "Childcare Patterns and Issues for Families of Preschool Children with Disabilities." *Infants and Young Children* 17(1): 5–16.

Boyle, Coleen A., et al. 2011. "Trends in the Prevalence of Developmental Disabilities in U.S. Children, 1997-2008." *Pediatrics* 127(6): 1034–1042.

Braun, Summer S., Kimberly A. Schonert-Reichl, and Robert W. Roeser. 2020. "Effects of Teachers' Emotion Regulation, Burnout, and Life Satisfaction on Student Well-Being." *Journal of Applied Developmental Psychology* 69(6): 101151.

Brillante, Pamela, and Karen Nemeth. 2018. *Universal Design for Learning in the Early Childhood Classroom*. New York, NY. Routledge.

Brobbey, Gordon. 2018. "Punishing the Vulnerable: Exploring Suspension Rates for Students with Learning Disabilities." *Intervention in School and Clinic* 53(4): 216–219.

Broek, E., et al. 1994. *The Original Social Story Book*. Arlington, TX: Future Education. https://carolgraysocialstories.com

Bruder, Mary Beth. 1998. "A Collaborative Model to Increase the Capacity of Childcare Providers to Include Young Children with Disabilities." *Journal of Early Intervention* 21(2): 177–186.

Bruder, Mary Beth. 2005. "Service Coordination and Integration in a Developmental Systems Approach to Early Intervention." In *A Developmental Systems Approach to Early Intervention: National and International Perspectives*. Baltimore, MD: Paul H. Brookes.

Burke, Jenene. 2012. "'Some Kids Climb Up; Some Kids Climb Down': Culturally Constructed Play-Worlds Of Children With Impairments." *Disability and Society* 27(7): 965–981.

Buysse, Virginia. 2011. "Access, Participation, and Supports: The Defining Features of High-Quality Inclusion." *Zero to Three* 31(4): 24–31.

Buysse, Virginia, Barbara D. Goldman, and Martie L. Skinner. 2002. "Setting Effects on Friendship Formation among Young Children with and without Disabilities." *Exceptional Children* 68(4): 503–517.

Buysse, Virginia, Patricia W. Wesley, Donna Bryant, and David Gardner. 1999. "Quality of Early Childhood Programs in Inclusive and Noninclusive Settings." *Exceptional Children* 65(3): 301–314.

Buysse, Virginia, Patricia Wesley, Lynette Keyes, and Donald Bailey, Jr. 1996. "Assessing the Comfort Zone of Child Care Teachers in Serving Young Children with Disabilities." *Journal of Early Intervention* 20(3): 189–203.

Byers-Heinlein, Krista, and Casey Lew-Williams. 2013. "Bilingualism in the Early Years: What the Science Says." *LEARNing Landscapes* 7(1): 95–112.

Campbell, Philippa H., and L. Brook Sawyer. 2007. "Supporting Learning Opportunities in Natural Settings through Participation-Based Services." *Journal of Early Intervention* 29(4): 287–305.

Carr, Edward G., et al. 2002. "Positive Behavior Support: Evolution of an Applied Science." *Journal of Positive Behavior Interventions* 4(1): 4–16.

Causton-Theoharis, Julie, et al. 2011. "Does Self-Contained Special Education Deliver on Its Promises? A Critical Inquiry into Research and Practice." *Journal of Special Education Leadership* 24(2): 61–78.

Center for Applied Special Technology. 2008. Universal Design for Learning Guidelines: Version 1.0. Wakefield, MA: CAST. https://udlguidelines.cast.org/more/downloads

Center for Early Childhood Mental Health Consultation. n.d. *Taking Care of Ourselves*. Washington, DC: Center for Early Childhood Mental Health Consultation, Georgetown University Center for Child and Human Development. https://www.ecmhc.org/documents/TakingCare_ProviderBk_final.pdf

Center for Parent Information and Resources. 2008. "Part B, Module 18: Options for Dispute Resolution." Center for Parent Information and Resources. https://www.parentcenterhub.org/partb-module18/

Center for Parent Information and Resources. 2017. "Parental Rights under IDEA." Center for Parent Information and Resources. https://www.parentcenterhub.org/parental-rights/

Center for Parent Information and Resources. 2019. "Five Options, 1-2-3." Center for Parent Information and Resources. https://www.parentcenterhub.org/disputes-overview/

Center for the Study of Social Policy. 2019. "Key Equity Terms and Concepts: A Glossary for Shared Understanding." Washington, DC: Center for the Study of Social Policy. https://cssp.org/resource/key-equity-terms-and-concepts-a-glossary-for-shared-understanding/

Center for the Study of Social Policy. 2021. "Strengthening Families." Center for the Study of Social Policy. https://cssp.org/our-work/project/strengthening-families/

Center on Positive Behavioral Interventions and Supports. 2021. "Tiered Framework." Center on PBIS. https://www.pbis.org/pbis/tiered-framework

Center on the Developing Child. 2021a. "ACEs and Toxic Stress: Frequently Asked Questions." Center on the Developing Child, Harvard University. https://developingchild.harvard.edu/resources/aces-and-toxic-stress-frequently-asked-questions/

Center on the Developing Child. 2021b. "Toxic Stress." Center on the Developing Child, Harvard University. https://developingchild.harvard.edu/science/key-concepts/toxic-stress/

Centers for Disease Control and Prevention. n.d. "Watch Me! Celebrating Milestones and Sharing Concerns." Centers for Disease Control and Prevention. https://www.cdc.gov/ncbddd/watchmetraining/index.html

Centers for Disease Control and Prevention. 2019. *Preventing Adverse Childhood Experiences: Leveraging the Best Available Evidence.* Atlanta, GA: National Center for Injury Prevention and Control, Centers for Disease Control and Prevention.

Centers for Disease Control and Prevention. 2021a. "CDC's Developmental Milestones." Centers for Disease Control and Prevention. https://www.cdc.gov/ncbddd/actearly/milestones/index.html

Centers for Disease Control and Prevention. 2021b. "Children and Youth with Special Healthcare Needs in Emergencies." CDC. https://www.cdc.gov/childrenindisasters/children-with-special-healthcare-needs.html

Child Welfare Information Gateway. 2018. *The Risk and Prevention of Maltreatment of Children with Disabilities.* Washington, DC: US Department of Health and Human Services, Children's Bureau.

Cleveland Clinic. 2021. "Child Development." Cleveland Clinic. https://my.clevelandclinic.org/health/articles/21559-child-development

CONNECT Modules and Division for Early Childhood. n.d. "Module 4: Family-Professional Partnerships." Connect: The Center to Mobilize Early Childhood Knowledge. https://connectmodules.dec-sped.org/connect-modules/learners/module-4/

CONNECT Modules and Division for Early Childhood. n.d. "Glossary." Connect: The Center to Mobilize Early Childhood Knowledge. https://connectmodules.dec-sped.org/glossary/

Cook, Clayton R., et al. 2018. "Positive Greetings at the Door: Evaluation of a Low-Cost, High-Yield Proactive Classroom Management Strategy." *Journal of Positive Behavior Interventions* 20(3): 149–159.

Council for Exceptional Children. 2021. "Specially Designed Instruction." Council for Exceptional Children. https://exceptionalchildren.org/topics/specially-designed-instruction

Cross, Alice F., et al. 2004. "Elements of Successful Inclusion for Children with Significant Disabilities." *Topics in Early Childhood Special Education* 24(3): 169–183.

Csikszentmihalyi, Mihaly. 1990. *Flow: The Psychology of Optimal Experience.* New York: Harper and Row.

Dabkowski, Diane M. 2004. "Encouraging Active Participation in IEP Team Meetings." *Teaching Exceptional Children* 36(3): 34–39.

Daugherty, Stefanie, Jennifer Grisham-Brown, and Mary Louise Hemmeter. 2001. "The Effects of Embedded Skill Instruction on the Acquisition of Target and Nontarget Skills in Preschoolers with Developmental Delays." *Topics in Early Childhood Special Education* 21(4): 213–221.

Davidson, Richard J., et al. 2003. "Alterations in Brain and Immune Function Produced by Mindfulness Meditation." *Psychosomatic Medicine* 65(4): 564–570.

Davis, Daphne M., and Jeffrey Hayes. 2012. "What Are the Benefits of Mindfulness?" *American Psychological Association* 43(7): 64.

Division for Early Childhood. 2017. *Position Statement on Challenging Behavior and Young Children*. Washington, DC: Division for Early Childhood. https://challengingbehavior.cbcs.usf.edu/docs/DEC_PositionStatement_ChallengingBehavior.pdf

DeGeorge, Katherine L. 1998. "Friendship and Stories: Using Children's Literature to Teach Friendship Skills to Children with Learning Disabilities." *Intervention in School and Clinic* 33(3): 157–162.

Denham, Susanne A., et al. 2003. "Preschool Emotional Competence: Pathway To Social Competence?" *Child Development* 74(1): 238–256.

Derman-Sparks, Louise, and Julie O. Edwards. 2009. *Anti-Bias Education for Young Children and Ourselves.* Washington, DC: National Association for the Education of Young Children.

DeSalvo, Louise. 2000. *Writing As a Way of Healing: How Telling Our Stories Transforms Our Lives.* Boston, MA: Beacon.

Diamond, Karen E., and Hsin-Hui Huang. 2005. "Preschoolers' Ideas about Disabilities." *Infants and Young Children* 18(1): 37–46.

Division for Early Childhood and the National Association for the Education of Young Children. 2009. "Early Childhood Inclusion: A Joint Position Statement of the Division for Early Childhood and the National Association for the Education of Young Children." Chapel Hill, NC: FPG Child Development Institute, the University of North Carolina at Chapel Hill.

Division for Early Childhood of the Council for Exceptional Children. 2014. "DEC Recommended Practices." https://divisionearlychildhood.egnyte.com/dl/7urLPWCt5U/?

Doran, George T., Arthur Miller, and James Cunningham. 1981. "There's a SMART Way to Write Management Goals and Objectives." *Management Review* 70(11): 35–36.

Dunlap, Glen, et al. 2013. *Prevent, Teach, Reinforce for Young Children: The Early Childhood Model of Individualized Positive Behavior Support.* Baltimore, MD: Paul H. Brookes.

Dunst, Carl J., Serena Herter, and Holly Shields. 2000. "Interest-Based Natural Learning Opportunities." In *Young Exceptional Children: Natural Environments and Inclusion.* Monograph Series No. 2. Longmont, CO: Sopris West.

Dunst, Carl J., et al. 2001a. "Contrasting Approaches to Natural Learning Environment Interventions." *Infants and Young Children* 14(2): 48–63.

Dunst, Carl J., et al. 2001b. "Natural Learning Opportunities for Infants, Toddlers, and Preschoolers." *Young Exceptional Children* 4(3): 18–25.

Dunst, Carl J., et al. 2006. "Everyday Activity Settings, Natural Learning Environments, and Early Intervention Practices." *Journal of Policy and Practice in Intellectual Disabilities* 3(1): 3–10.

Dweck, Carol S., and Ellen L. Leggett. 1988. "A Social-Cognitive Approach to Motivation and Personality." *Psychological Review* 95(2): 256–273.

Early Childhood Technical Assistance Center. n.d. "Team Decisions for Preschool Special Education Services: Guiding Questions." https://ectacenter.org/~pdfs/topics/inclusion/team-decisions-guiding-questions.pdf

Early Childhood Technical Assistance Center. 2012. "Understanding Procedural Safeguards: Examples of Explanations and Implications for Families." https://ectacenter.org/~pdfs/topics/procsafe/UnderstandingProcSfgrds-table-2012.pdf

Early Childhood Technical Assistance Center. 2015. *A System Framework for Building High-Quality Early Intervention and Preschool Special Education Programs.* Chapel Hill, NC: Frank Porter Graham Child Development Institute, University of North Carolina at Chapel Hill.

Early Childhood Technical Assistance Center. 2017. "Embedded Instruction Practices." https://ectacenter.org/~pdfs/decrp/PG_Ins_EmbeddedInstr_prac_print_2017.pdf

Early Childhood Technical Assistance Center. 2019. "Screening." https://ectacenter.org/topics/earlyid/screeneval.asp#:~:text=Under%20Part%20C%2C%20screening%20is,part%20of%20post%2Dreferral%20procedures.&text=The%20purpose%20of%20screening%20is,need%20of%20early%20intervention%20services

Early Childhood Technical Assistance Center. 2020a. "Embedded Instruction Practices." https://ectacenter.org/~pdfs/decrp/PGP_INS3_embedded_2018.pdf

Early Childhood Technical Assistance Center. 2020b. "Indicators of High-Quality Inclusion: Glossary." ECTA. https://ectacenter.org/topics/inclusion/indicators-glossary.asp

Early Childhood Technical Assistance Center. 2020c. "Practices." https://ectacenter.org/practices. asp#:~:text=Practices%20are%20what%20professionals%20do,outcomes%20for%20children%20 and%20families

Early Childhood Technical Assistance Center. 2021. "Early Care and Education Environment Indicators of High-Quality Inclusion." https://ectacenter.org/topics/inclusion/indicators-ece.asp

Elango, Sneha, Jorge L. García, James J. Heckman, and Andrés Hojman. 2015. *Early Childhood Education.* Chicago, IL: University of Chicago. https://heckmanequation.org/www/assets/2017/01/ FINALMoffitt-ECE-Paper2015.pdf

Fantuzzo, John, et al. 2007. "Investigation of Dimensions of Social-Emotional Classroom Behavior and School Readiness for Low-Income Urban Preschool Children." *School Psychology Review* 36(1): 44–62.

Feinberg, Emily, Michael Silverstein, Sara Donahue, and Robin Bliss. 2011. "The Impact of Race on Participation in Part C Early Intervention Services." *Journal of Developmental and Behavioral Pediatrics* 32(4): 284–291.

Felitti, Vincent J., et al. 1998. "Relationship of Childhood Abuse and Household Dysfunction to Many of the Leading Causes of Death in Adults: The Adverse Childhood Experiences (ACE) Study." *American Journal of Preventive Medicine* 14(4): 245–258.

Fialka, Janice, Arlene K. Feldman, Karen C. Mikus, and Ann Turnbull. 2012. *Parents and Professionals Partnering for Children with Disabilities: A Dance That Matters.* Thousand Oaks, CA: Corwin.

Fong, Rowena, Ruth McRoy, and Alan Detlaff. 2014. "Disproportionality and Disparities." Encyclopedia of Social Work. http://oxfordre.com/socialwork/view/10.1093/acrefore/9780199975839.001.0001/ acrefore-9780199975839-e-899

Forlin, Chris, Anne Jobling, and Annemaree Carroll. 2001. "Preservice Teachers' Discomfort Levels toward People with Disabilities." *The Journal of International Special Needs Education* 4: 32–38.

Fox, Lise, et al. 2003. "The Teaching Pyramid: A Model for Supporting Social Emotional Competence and Preventing Challenging Behavior in Young Children." *Young Children* 58(4): 48–52.

Fox, Lise, and Rochelle Lentini. 2006 "You Got It! Teaching Social and Emotional Skills." *Young Children* 61(6): 36–42.

Frank Porter Graham Child Development Institute (FPG) at the University of North Carolina at Chapel Hill (UNC). n.d. "Glossary." ASD Toddler Initiative. https://asdtoddler.fpg.unc.edu/glossary.html

García, Jorge Luis, James J. Heckman, Duncan Ermini Leaf, and María José Prados. 2016. "The Life-Cycle Benefits of an Influential Early Childhood Program." Working Paper 22993. https://www.nber.org/system/files/working_papers/w22993/w22993.pdf

Gehl, Maria, and Lucianne Hackbert. 2019. "Getting Started with Mindfulness: A Toolkit for Early Childhood Organizations." Zero to Three. https://www.zerotothree.org/resources/2896-getting-started-with-mindfulness-a-toolkit-for-early-childhood-organizations#chapter-1833

Geisthardt, Cheryl L., Mary Jane Brotherson, and Christine C. Cook. 2002. "Friendships of Children with Disabilities in the Home Environment." *Education and Training in Mental Retardation and Developmental Disabilities* 37(3): 235–252.

Gilbert, J., Tawara D. Goode, and C. Dunne. 2007. "Cultural Awareness." Curricula Enhancement Module Series. Washington, DC: National Center for Cultural Competence, Georgetown University Center for Child and Human Development.

Gilliam, Walter S. 2005. "Prekindergarteners Left Behind: Expulsion Rates in State Prekindergarten Systems." Foundation for Child Development. https://www.fcd-us.org/prekindergartners-left-behind-expulsion-rates-in-state-prekindergarten-programs/

Gilliam, Walter S., and Golan Shahar. 2006. "Preschool and Child Care Expulsion and Suspension: Rates and Predictors in One State." *Infants and Young Children* 19(3): 228–245.

Gilliam, Walter S., et al. 2016. *Do Early Educators' Implicit Biases Regarding Sex and Race Relate to Behavior Expectations and Recommendations of Preschool Expulsions and Suspensions?* Research study brief. New Haven, CT: Child Study Center, Yale School of Medicine.

Gillispie, Carrie. 2019. "Young Learners, Missed Opportunities: Ensuring That Black and Latinx Children Have Access to High-Quality State Funded Pre-K." The Education Trust. https://s3-us-east-2.amazonaws.com/edtrustmain/wp-content/uploads/2014/09/05162154/Young-Learners-Missed-Opportunities.pdf

Glenn-Applegate, Katherine, Jill Pentimonti, and Laura M. Justice. 2011. "Parents' Selection Factors when Choosing Preschool Programs for Their Children With Disabilities." *Child and Youth Care Forum* 40(3): 211–231.

Goode, Tawara D., Wendy A. Jones, and Joan Christopher. 2017. "Responding to Cultural and Linguistic Differences among People with Intellectual Disability." In *A Comprehensive Guide to Intellectual and Developmental Disabilities*. 2nd edition. Baltimore, MD: Paul H. Brookes.

Green, Katherine, Nicole P. Terry, and Peggy A. Gallagher. 2014. "Progress in Language and Literacy Skills Among Children with Disabilities in Inclusive Early Reading First Classrooms." *Topics in Early Childhood Special Education* 33(4): 249–259.

Greenberg, Mark T., Joshua L. Brown, and Rachel M. Abenavoli. 2016. *Teacher Stress and Health: Effects on Teachers, Students, and Schools.* Issue brief. State College, PA: Edna Bennett Pierce Prevention Research Center, Pennsylvania State University. https://www.prevention.psu.edu/uploads/files/rwjf430428.pdf

Grisham-Brown, Jennifer, and Mary Louise Hemmeter. 2005. *Blended Practices for Teaching Young Children in Inclusive Settings.* Baltimore: Paul H. Brookes.

Grisham-Brown, Jennifer, et al. 2009. "Addressing Early Learning Standards for All Children within Blended Preschool Classrooms." *Topics in Early Childhood Special Education* 29(3): 131–142.

Grisham-Brown, Jennifer, et al. 2010. "Differences in Child Care Quality for Children with and without Disabilities." *Early Education and Development* 21(1): 21–37.

Groskreutz, Mark P., Amy Peters, Nicole Groskreutz, and Thomas Higbee. 2015. "Increasing Play-Based Commenting in Children with Autism Spectrum Disorder Using a Novel Script-Frame Procedure." *Journal of Applied Behavior Analysis* 48(2): 442–447.

Grossman Paul, Ludger Niemann, Stefan Schmidt, and Harald Walach. 2004. "Mindfulness-Based Stress Reduction and Health Benefits: A Meta-Analysis." *Journal of Psychosomatic Research* 57(1): 35–43.

Gullotta, Thomas, and Gary Blau, eds. 2008. *Family Influences on Childhood Behavior and Development: Evidence-Based Approaches to Prevention and Treatment Approaches.* New York: Routledge.

Guralnick, Michael J. 2001. "A Developmental Systems Model For Early Intervention." *Infants and Young Children* 14(2): 1–18.

Guralnick, Michael J., Brian Neville, Mary A. Hammond, and Robert T. Connor. 2007. "The Friendships of Young Children with Developmental Delays: A Longitudinal Analysis." *Journal of Applied Developmental Psychology* 28(1): 64–79.

Hampshire Patricia K., and Patrick Mallory. 2021. "A Tiered Approach to Implementing Universal Symbols for Entering Inclusive Early Childhood Playgroups." *Teaching Exceptional Children* 53(6): 414–423.

Haring, Norris G., Thomas Lovitt, Marie Eaton, and Cheryl Hansen. 1978. *The Fourth R: Research in the Classroom.* Columbus, OH: Charles E. Merrill.

Head Start. 2020. "Signs and Symptoms of Childhood Trauma." Head Start Early Childhood Learning and Knowledge Center. https://eclkc.ohs.acf.hhs.gov/publication/signs-symptoms-childhood-trauma

Health Resources and Services Administration's Maternal and Child Health Bureau. 2020. "National Survey of Children's Health." NSCH Data Brief. https://mchb.hrsa.gov/sites/default/files/mchb/Data/NSCH/nsch-data-brief.pdf

Heckman, James J., et al. 2010. "Analyzing Social Experiments as Implemented: A Reexamination of the Evidence from the HighScope Perry Preschool Program." *Quantitative Economics* 1(1): 1–46.

Helton, Jesse J., Elizabeth Lightfoot, Q. John Fu, and Christina Bruhn. 2019. "Prevalence and Severity of Child Impairment in a US Sample of Child Maltreatment Investigations." *Journal of Developmental and Behavioral Pediatrics* 40(4): 285–292.

Hemmeter, Mary Louise, Michaelene Ostrosky, and Lise Fox. 2006. "Social and Emotional Foundations for Early Learning: A Conceptual Model for Intervention." *School Psychology Review* 35(4): 583–601.

Hemmeter, Mary Louise, Patricia A. Snyder, Lise Fox, and James Algina. 2016. "Evaluating the Implementation of the *Pyramid Model for Promoting Social Emotional Competence* in Early Childhood Classrooms." *Topics in Early Childhood Special Education* 36(3): 133–146.

Hettler, Bill. 1976. "Six Dimensions of Wellness." National Wellness Institute. https://nationalwellness.org/resources/six-dimensions-of-wellness/

Hirotsu, Camila, Sergio Tufik, and Monica L. Andersen. 2015. "Interactions Between Sleep, Stress, and Metabolism: From Physiological to Pathological Conditions." *Sleep Science* 8(3): 143–152.

Holahan, Annette, and Virginia Costenbader. 2000. "A Comparison of Developmental Gains for Preschool Children with Disabilities in Inclusive and Self-Contained Classrooms." *Topics in Early Childhood Special Education* 20(4): 224–235.

Innes, Fiona K., and Karen E. Diamond. 1999. "Typically Developing Children's Interactions with Peers with Disabilities: Relationships Between Mothers' Comments and Children's Ideas About Disabilities." *Topics in Early Childhood Special Education* 19(2): 103–111.

IRIS Center. 2021. "Glossary." The IRIS Center, Peabody College, Vanderbilt University. https://iris.peabody.vanderbilt.edu/resources/glossary/

Johnson, Anna D., et al. 2021. "To Whom Little Is Given, Much Is Expected: ECE Teacher Stressors and Supports as Determinants of Classroom Quality." *Early Childhood Research Quarterly* 54(1): 13–30.

Johnston, Susan S., and Catherine Nelson. 2016. "Using Graphic Symbols to Teach Children with Autism to Enter into Playgroups." *Intervention in School and Clinic* 52(2): 85–91.

Jones, Damon E., Mark Greenberg, and Max Crowley. 2015. "Early Social-Emotional Functioning and Public Health: The Relationship Between Kindergarten Social Competence and Future Wellness." *American Journal of Public Health* 105(11): 2283–2290.

Jones, Lisa, et al. 2012. "Prevalence and Risk of Violence Against Children with Disabilities: A Systematic Review and Meta-Analysis of Observational Studies." *Lancet* 380(9845): 899–907.

Justice, Laura M., Jessica A. R. Logan, Tzu-Jung Lin, and Joan N. Kaderavek. 2014. "Peer Effects in Early Childhood Education: Testing the Assumptions of Special-Education Inclusion." *Psychological Science* 25(9): 1722–1729.

Kabat-Zinn, Jon. 2003. "Mindfulness-Based Interventions in Context: Past, Present, and Future." *Clinical Psychology: Science and Practice* 10(2): 144–156.

Kaczmarek, Louise, Ruth Pennington, and Howard Goldstein. 2000. "Transdisciplinary Consultation: A Center-Based Team Functioning Model." *Education and Treatment of Children* 23(2): 156–172.

Kasari, Connie, Stephanny F. N. Freeman, Nirit Bauminger, and Marvin C. Alkin. 1999. "Parental Perspectives on Inclusion: Effects of Autism and Down Syndrome." *Journal of Autism and Developmental Disorders* 29(4): 297–305.

Killingsworth, Matthew, and Daniel Gilbert. 2010. "A Wandering Mind Is an Unhappy Mind." *Science* 330(6006): 932.

Knoche, Lisa, Carla A. Peterson, Carolyn P. Edwards, and Hyun-Joo Jeon. 2006. "Child Care for Children with and without Disabilities: The Provider, Observer, and Parent Perspectives." *Early Childhood Research Quarterly* 21(1): 93–109.

Küpper, Lisa. 2007. "Module 1: Top 10 Basics of Special Education." Newark, NJ: Center for Parent Information and Resources. https://www.parentcenterhub.org/partb-module1/

Küpper, Lisa, and Theresa Rebhorn. 2007. "Module 10: Initial Evaluation and Reevaluation." *Building the Legacy: Training Curriculum on IDEA*. https://www.parentcenterhub.org/wp-content/uploads/repo_items/legacy/10-trainerguide.pdf

Lawrence, Sharmila, Sheila Smith, and Rashida Banerjee. 2016. *Preschool Inclusion: Key Findings from Research and Implications for Policy.* Child Care and Early Education Research Connections. New York: National Center for Children in Poverty, Columbia University. http://www.nccp.org/wp-content/uploads/2020/05/text_1154.pdf

Leatherman, Jane. 2007. "'I Just See All Children as Children': Teachers' Perceptions about Inclusion." *The Qualitative Report* 12(4): 594–611.

Leerkes, Esther, et al. 2008. "Emotion and Cognition Processes in Preschool Children." *Merrill-Palmer Quarterly* 54(1): 102–124.

Legano, Lori A., et al. 2021. "Maltreatment of Children with Disabilities." *Pediatrics* 147(5): e2021050920. https://doi.org/10.1542/peds.2021-050920

López, Lisa M., and Mariela Páez. 2021. *Teaching Dual Language Learners: What Early Childhood Educators Need to Know*. Baltimore, MD: Paul H. Brookes.

Lloyd, Lyle L., Donald R. Fuller, and Helen H. Arvidson. 1997. *Augmentative and Alternative Communication: A Handbook of Principles and Practices*. Boston: Allyn and Bacon.

Macy, Marisa G., and Diane D. Bricker. 2007. "Embedding Individualized Social Goals into Routine Activities in Inclusive Early Childhood Classrooms." *Early Child Development and Care* 177(2): 107–120.

Maushart, Susan. 2000. *The Mask of Motherhood: How Becoming a Mother Changes Our Lives and Why We Never Talk About It*. New York: Penguin.

McLaughlin, Tara, and Patricia Snyder. 2014. "Using Embedded Instruction to Enhance Social-Emotional Skills." In *Friendship 101: Helping Students Build Social Competence*. Arlington, VA: Council for Exceptional Children.

McLean, Caitlin, et al. 2021. *Early Childhood Workforce Index 2020*. Berkeley, CA: Center for the Study of Child Care Employment, University of California, Berkeley. https://cscce.berkeley.edu/workforce-index-2020/report-pdf/

Meek, Shantel, et al. 2020. *Start with Equity: From the Early Years to the Early Grades*. Tempe, AZ: Children's Equity Project, Sanford School of Social and Family Dynamics, Arizona State University, and Washington, DC: Bipartisan Policy Center. https://childandfamilysuccess.asu.edu/cep/start-with-equity

Merriam-Webster. 2021a. "Culture." Merriam-Webster Dictionary. https://www.merriam-webster.com/dictionary/culture

Merriam-Webster. 2021b. "Observation." Merriam-Webster Dictionary. https://www.merriam-webster.com/dictionary/observation

Morgan Chelsea W., and Gregory Cheatham. 2021. "Rationale for Change: Reconceptualizing Inclusive Early Childhood Education through Practice." *Young Exceptional Children* 24(3): 115–123.

Mulvihill, Beverly, Darlene Shearer, and M. Lee Van Horn. 2002. "Training, Experience, and Child Care Providers' Perceptions of Inclusion." *Early Childhood Research Quarterly* 17(2): 197–215.

Murphy, Nancy. 2011. "Maltreatment of Children with Disabilities: The Breaking Point." *Child Neurology* 26(8): 1054–1056.

Najavits, Lisa M. 2002. *Seeking Safety: A Treatment Manual for PTSD and Substance Abuse.* New York: Guilford Press.

National Association for the Education of Young Children. n.d. "Definitions of Key Terms." NAEYC. https://www.naeyc.org/resources/position-statements/equity/definitions

National Association for the Education of Young Children. 2003. *Early Childhood Curriculum, Assessment, and Program Evaluation.* Position statement. Washington, DC: NAEYC. https://www.naeyc.org/sites/default/files/globally-shared/downloads/PDFs/resources/position-statements/CAPEexpand.pdf

National Association for the Education of Young Children. 2019. *Advancing Equity in Early Childhood Education.* Position statement. Washington, DC: NAEYC. https://www.naeyc.org/sites/default/files/globally-shared/downloads/PDFs/resources/position-statements/advancingequitypositionstatement.pdf

National Association for the Education of Young Children. 2020. *Developmentally Appropriate Practice.* Position statement. Washington, DC: NAEYC. https://www.naeyc.org/sites/default/files/globally-shared/downloads/PDFs/resources/position-statements/dap-statement_0.pdf

National Association for the Education of Young Children and National Association of Early Childhood Specialists in State Departments of Education. 2002. *Early Learning Standards: Creating the Conditions for Success.* Joint position statement. Washington, DC: National Association for the Education of Young Children. https://www.naeyc.org/sites/default/files/globally-shared/downloads/PDFs/resources/position-statements/position_statement.pdf

National Center for Hearing Assessment and Management. 2016. "Eligibility and Service Delivery Policies: Differences Between IDEA Part C and IDEA Part B." http://www.infanthearing.org/earlyintervention/docs/aspect-idea-part-c-and-idea-part-b.pdf

National Center for Pyramid Model Innovations. n.d. "Glossary of Terms." NCPMI. https://challengingbehavior.cbcs.usf.edu/Pyramid/overview/glossary.html

National Center on Parent, Family, and Community Engagement. 2020. *Talking with Families About Their Child's Development.* US Department of Health and Human Services, Administration for Children and Families, Office of Head Start, National Center on Parent, Family, and Community Engagement. https://eclkc.ohs.acf.hhs.gov/sites/default/files/pdf/talking-with-families-about-their-childs-development.pdf

National Center on Pyramid Model Innovations. n.d. "Pyramid Model Overview." NCPMI. https://challengingbehavior.cbcs.usf.edu/Pyramid/overview/index.html

National Center on Response to Intervention. 2010. *Essential Components of RTI—A Closer Look at Response to Intervention*. Washington, DC: National Center on Response to Intervention.

National Child Traumatic Stress Network, Secondary Traumatic Stress Committee. 2011. "Secondary Traumatic Stress: A Fact Sheet for Child-Serving Professionals." Los Angeles, CA, and Durham, NC: National Center for Child Traumatic Stress. https://www.nctsn.org/sites/default/files/resources/fact-sheet/secondary_traumatic_stress_child_serving_professionals.pdf

National Professional Development Center on ASD. 2019. "Components of the Autism Focused Intervention Resources and Modules (AFIRM)." Chapel Hill, NC: The University of North Carolina at Chapel Hill, Frank Porter Graham Child Development Institute, National Professional Development Center on Autism Spectrum Disorder. https://afirm.fpg.unc.edu/sites/afirm.fpg.unc.edu/files/imce/documents/Components%20of%20the%20Autism%20Focused.pdf

National Professional Development Center on Inclusion. 2011. "Research Synthesis Points on Practices That Support Inclusion." Chapel Hill, NC: The University of North Carolina at Chapel Hill, FPG Child Development Institute, National Professional Development Center on Inclusion. https://npdci.fpg.unc.edu/sites/npdci.fpg.unc.edu/files/resources/NPDCI-ResearchSynthesisPointsInclusivePractices-2011_0.pdf

National Scientific Council on the Developing Child. 2010. "Persistent Fear and Anxiety Can Affect Young Children's Learning and Development." Working Paper No. 9. Center on the Developing Child, Harvard University. https://developingchild.harvard.edu/resources/persistent-fear-and-anxiety-can-affect-young-childrens-learning-and-development/

National Scientific Council on the Developing Child 2014. "Excessive Stress Disrupts the Architecture of the Developing Brain." Working Paper No. 3. Updated Edition. Center on the Developing Child, Harvard University. https://developingchild.harvard.edu/wp-content/uploads/2005/05/Stress_Disrupts_Architecture_Developing_Brain-1.pdf

National Wellness Institute. n.d. "The Six Dimensions of Wellness." National Wellness Institute. https://nationalwellness.org/resources/six-dimensions-of-wellness/

Nelson, Catherine, et al. 2007. "Keys to Play: A Strategy to Increase the Social Interactions of Young Children with Autism and Their Typically Developing Peers." *Education and Training in Developmental Disabilities* 42(2): 165–181.

Nelson, Helen, Garth Kendall, and Linda Shields. 2013. "Children's Social/Emotional Characteristics at Entry to School Nurses." *The Journal of Child Health Care* 17(3): 317–331.

Odom, Samuel L., Virginia Buysse, and Elena Soukakou. 2011. "Inclusion for Young Children with Disabilities: A Quarter Century of Research Perspectives." *Journal of Early Intervention* 33(4): 344–356.

Odom, Samuel L., Thomas B. Parrish, and Christine Hikido. 2001. "The Costs of Inclusive and Traditional Special Education Preschool Programs." *Journal of Special Education Leadership* 14(1): 33–41.

Odom, Samuel L., et al. 2000. "Approaches to Understanding the Ecology of Early Childhood Environments for Children with Disabilities." In *Behavioral Observation: Technology and Applications in Developmental Disabilities*. Baltimore, MD: Paul H. Brookes.

Odom, Samuel L., et al. 2001. "The Costs of Preschool Inclusion." *Topics in Early Childhood Special Education* 21(1): 46–55.

Odom, Samuel L., et al. 2004. "Preschool Inclusion in the United States: A Review of Research from an Ecological Systems Perspective." *Journal of Research in Special Educational Needs* 4(1): 17–49.

Odom, Samuel L., et al. 2006. "Social Acceptance and Social Rejection of Young Children with Disabilities in Inclusive Classes." *Journal of Educational Psychology* 98(4): 807–823.

Office of Special Education Programs. n.d.a. *At a Glance: An Introduction to Part C of the Individuals with Disabilities Education Act (IDEA)*. https://collab.osepideasthatwork.org/system/files/at_a_glance_an_introduction_to_part_c_1.pdf

Office of Special Education Programs. n.d.b. "Let's Get Started: Part B Section 619—At a Glance." OSEP Collaboration Spaces. https://collab.osepideasthatwork.org/welcome-world-part-b-section-619/lets-get-started

Office of Special Education Programs. 2020. *IDEA Part B Child Count and Education Environments for School Year 2019–2020*. https://www2.ed.gov/programs/osepidea/618-data/collection-documentation/data-documentation-files/part-b/child-count-and-educational-environment/idea-partb-childcountandedenvironment-2019-20.pdf

Overton, Sheri, and John L. Rausch. 2002. "Peer Relationships as Support for Children with Disabilities: An Analysis of Mothers' Goals and Indicators for Friendship." *Focus on Autism and Other Developmental Disabilities* 17(1): 11–29.

Peer, Justin, and Stephen Hillman. 2014. "Stress and Resilience for Parents of Children with Intellectual and Developmental Disabilities: A Review of Key Factors and Recommendations for Practitioners." *Journal of Policy and Practice in Intellectual Disabilities* 11(2): 92–98.

Prellwitz, Maria, and Lisa Skär. 2007. "Usability of Playgrounds for Children with Different Abilities." *Occupational Therapy International* 14(3): 144–155.

Pub. L. 93-112. 1973. Rehabilitation Act of 1973, §504.

Rafferty, Yvonne, and Kenneth W. Griffin. 2005. "Benefits and Risks of Reverse Inclusion for Preschoolers with and without Disabilities: Perspectives of Parents and Providers." *Journal of Early Intervention* 27(3): 173–192.

Rafferty, Yvonne, Vincenza Piscitelli, and Caroline Boettcher. 2003. "The Impact of Inclusion on Language Development and Social Competence Among Preschoolers with Disabilities." *Exceptional Children* 69(4): 467–479.

Rakap, Salih, and Asiye Parlak-Rakap. 2011. "Effectiveness of Embedded Instruction in Early Childhood Special Education: A Literature Review." *European Early Childhood Education Research Journal* 19(1): 79–96.

Rausch, Alissa, Jaclyn Joseph, and Elizabeth Steed. 2019. "Dis/ability Critical Race Studies (DisCrit) for Inclusion in Early Childhood Education: Ethical Considerations of Implicit and Explicit Bias." *Zero to Three* 40(1): 43–51.

Reardon, Sean F., et al. 2019. "Is Separate Still Unequal? New Evidence on School Segregation and Racial Academic Achievement Gaps." CEPA Working Paper No. 19–06. Stanford Center for Education Policy Analysis. https://cepa.stanford.edu/sites/default/files/wp19-06-v092019.pdf

Rebhorn, Theresa. n.d. "Developing Your Child's IEP." Center for Parent Information and Resources. https://www.parentcenterhub.org/pa12/

Response to Intervention Action Network. n.d. "What Is RTI?" RTI Action Network. http://www.rtinetwork.org/learn/what/whatisrti

Rideout, Victoria J., and Vikki S. Katz. 2016. *Opportunity for All? Technology and Learning in Lower-Income Families.* New York: The Joan Ganz Cooney Center at Sesame Workshop. https://www.joanganzcooneycenter.org/wp-content/uploads/2016/01/jgcc_opportunityforall.pdf

Ripat, Jacquie, and Pam Becker. 2012. "Playground Usability: What Do Playground Users Say?" *Occupational Therapy International* 19(3): 144–153.

Roeser, Robert W., Ellen Skinner, Jeffry Beers, and Patricia A. Jennings. 2012. "Mindfulness Training and Teachers' Professional Development: An Emerging Area of Research and Practice." *Child Development Perspectives* 6(2): 167–173.

Roseberry-McKibbin, Celeste. 2002. *Assessment of Bilingual Learners: Language Difference or Disorder?* Rockville, MD: American Speech-Language Hearing Association.

Rozin, Paul, and Edward B. Royzman. 2001. "Negativity Bias, Negativity Dominance, and Contagion." *Personality and Social Psychology Review* 5(4): 296–320.

Rubin, Kenneth H., William Bukowski, and Jeffrey Parker. 1998. "Peer Interactions, Relationships, and Groups." In *Handbook of Child Psychology: Social, Emotional, and Personality Development.* Hoboken, NJ: John Wiley and Sons.

Ryan, Ruth. 1994. "Posttraumatic Stress Disorder in Persons with Developmental Disabilities." *Community Mental Health Journal* 30(1): 45–54.

Sam, Ann M., et al. 2019. "Visual Cues: Introduction and Practice." Autism Focused Intervention Resources and Modules. FPG Child Development Institute, University of North Carolina at Chapel Hill. https://afirm.fpg.unc.edu/visual-cues-introduction-practice

Sandall, Susan, and Ilene Schwartz. 2008. *Building Blocks for Teaching Preschoolers with Special Needs.* 2nd edition. Baltimore, MD: Paul H. Brookes.

Sandall, Susan, et al.. 2005. *DEC Recommended Practices: A Comprehensive Guide.* Longmont, CO: Sopris West Educational Services.

Sandall, Susan, et al. 2019. *Building Blocks for Teaching Preschoolers with Special Needs.* 3rd edition. Baltimore, MD: Paul H. Brookes.

Schwartz, Ilene S., Samuel L. Odom, and Susan R. Sandall. 1999. "Including Young Children with Special Needs." *Child Care Information Exchange* 130(6): 74–78.

Shippen, Margaret E., et al. 2005. "Preservice Teachers' Perceptions of Including Students with Disabilities." *Teacher Education and Special Education* 28(2): 92–99.

Shonkoff, Jack P., and Deborah A. Phillips, eds. 2000. *From Neurons to Neighborhoods: The Science of Early Childhood Development.* National Research Council and Institute of Medicine. Washington DC: National Academies Press.

Siegler, Robert S. 1996. *Emerging Minds: The Process of Change in Children's Thinking.* New York, NY: Oxford University Press.

Skiba, Russell J., et al. 2005. "Unproven Links: Can Poverty Explain Ethnic Disproportionality in Special Education?" *Journal of Special Education* 39(3): 130–144.

Skiba, Russell J., et al. 2006. "Disparate Access: The Disproportionality of African American Students with Disabilities Across Educational Environments." *Exceptional Children* 72(4): 411–442.

Smith, Barbara, and Lise Fox. 2003. *Systems of Service Delivery: A Synthesis of Evidence Relevant to Young Children at Risk of or Who Have Challenging Behavior.* Tampa, FL: Center for Evidence-Based Practice: Young Children with Challenging Behavior, University of South Florida.

Smith, Leah. n.d. "#Abelism." Center for Disability Rights. http://cdrnys.org/blog/uncategorized/ableism/

Snow, Kathie. 2016. "People First Language." Disability is Natural. https://nebula.wsimg.com/1c1af57f9319dbf909ec52462367fa88?AccessKeyId= 9D6F6082FE5EE52C3DC6&disposition=0&alloworigin=1

Snyder, Patricia A., Bruce Thompson, and David Sexton. 1993. "Congruence in Maternal and Professional Early Intervention Assessments of Young Children with Disabilities." Paper presented at the annual meeting of the Southwest Educational Research Association, Austin, TX.

Snyder, Patricia, et al. 2015. "Naturalistic Instructional Approaches in Early Learning: A Systematic Review of the Empirical Literature." Journal of Early Intervention 37(1): 69–97.

Soukakou, Elena P. 2012. "Measuring Quality in Inclusive Preschool Classrooms: Development and Validation of the Inclusive Classroom Profile (ICP)." *Early Childhood Research Quarterly* 27(3): 478–488.

SRI International. 1993. *The National Longitudinal Transition Study: A Summary of Findings.* Menlo Park, CA: SRI International.

Staats, Cheryl, Kelly Capatosto, Robin A. Wright, and Danya Contractor. 2015. *State of the Science: Implicit Bias Review 2015.* Columbus, OH: Kirwan Institute for the Study of Race and Ethnicity, The Ohio State University.

Stanford University. n.d. "Race and Ethnicity." Gendered Innovations in Science, Health and Medicine, Engineering, and Environment, Stanford University. https://genderedinnovations.stanford.edu/terms/race.html

Stanton-Chapman, Tina L., and Martha E. Snell. 2011. "Promoting Turn-Taking Skills in Preschool Children with Disabilities: The Effects of a Peer-Based Social Communication Intervention." *Early Childhood Research Quarterly* 26(3): 303–319.

Stegelin, Dolores A. 2018. *Preschool Suspension and Expulsion: Defining the Issues.* Greenville, SC: Institute for Child Success.

Steinbrenner, Jessica R., et al. 2020. *Evidence-Based Practices for Children, Youth, and Young Adults with Autism Spectrum Disorder.* University of North Carolina, Frank Porter Graham Child Development Institute, National Clearinghouse on Autism Evidence and Practice Review Team.

Stoiber, Karen, Meribeth Gettinger, and Donna Goetz. 1998. "Exploring Factors Influencing Parents' and Early Childhood Practitioners' Beliefs About Inclusion." *Early Childhood Research Quarterly* 13(1): 107–124.

Strain, Phillip S. 1983. "Generalization of Autistic Children's Social Behavior Change: Effects of Developmentally Integrated and Segregated Settings." *Analysis and Intervention in Developmental Disabilities* 3(1): 23–34.

Strain, Phillip S. 2014. "Inclusion for Preschool Children with Disabilities: What We Know and What We Should Be Doing." https://ectacenter.org/~pdfs/topics/inclusion/research/STRAIN_what_we_know.pdf

Strain, Phillip S., and Edward H. Bovey II. 2011. "Randomized, Controlled Trial of the LEAP Model of Early Intervention for Young Children with Autism Spectrum Disorders." *Topics in Early Childhood Special Education* 31(3): 133–154.

Strain, Phillip S., and Edward H. Bovey II. 2015. "The Power of Preschool Peers to Influence Social Outcomes for Children with Special Needs." In *The Power of Peers in the Classroom: Enhancing Learning and Social Skills*. New York: Guilford Press.

Strain, Phillip S., and Marilyn Hoyson. 2000. "The Need for Longitudinal, Intensive Social Skill Intervention: LEAP Follow-Up Outcomes for Children with Autism." *Topics in Early Childhood Special Education* 20(2): 116–122.

Strain, Phillip S., et al. 2009. "LEAP Preschool: Lessons Learned over 28 Years of Inclusive Services for Young Children with Autism." *Young Exceptional Children Monograph Series* 11: 49–68.

Substance Abuse and Mental Health Services Administration. 2014. *SAMHSA's Concept of Trauma and Guidance for a Trauma-Informed Approach*. HHS Publication No. (SMA) 14-4884. Rockville, MD: Substance Abuse and Mental Health Services Administration. https://ncsacw.samhsa.gov/userfiles/files/SAMHSA_Trauma.pdf

Sullivan, Patricia M., and John F. Knutson. 1998. "The Association Between Child Maltreatment and Disabilities in a Hospital-Based Epidemiologic Study." *Child Abuse and Neglect* 22(4): 271–288.

Sullivan, Patricia M., and John F. Knutson. 2000. "Maltreatment and Disabilities: A Population-Based Epidemiological Study." *Child Abuse and Neglect* 24(10): 1257–1273.

Suprayogi, Muhamad N., and Martin Valcke. 2016. "Differentiated Instruction in Primary Schools: Implementation and Challenges in Indonesia." *International Scientific Research Journal* 72(6): 2–18.

Tertell, Elizabeth A., Susan Klein, and Janet Jewett. Eds. 1998. *When Teachers Reflect: Journeys toward Effective, Inclusive Practice*. Washington, DC: National Association for the Education of Young Children.

Turnbull, Ann, et al. 2010. *Families, Professionals, and Exceptionality: Positive Outcomes through Partnerships and Trust*. 6th edition. Upper Saddle River, NJ: Merrill Prentice Hall.

University of Massachusetts Lowell. 2019. "Diversity Peer Educators: Info and Glossary, Fall 2019." Lowell, MA: University of Massachusetts. https://www.uml.edu/student-services/Multicultural/Resources/Glossary.aspx

University of Michigan Health. 2021. "Sensory Processing Disorder." University of Michigan Health. https://www.uofmhealth.org/health-library/te7831

US Census Bureau. 2020. "Child Population: Number of Children (in Millions) Ages 0–17 in the United States by Age, 1950–2020 and Projected 2021–2050." ChildStats.gov. https://www.childstats.gov/americaschildren/tables/pop1.asp

US Census Bureau. 2019. National Survey of Children's Health: 2019 Screener Data and Input Files. US Census Bureau. https://www.census.gov/programs-surveys/nsch/data/datasets.html

US Commission on Civil Rights. 2019. *Beyond Suspensions: Examining School Discipline Policies and Connections to the School-to-Prison Pipeline for Students of Color with Disabilities*. Washington, DC: US Commission on Civil Rights. https://www.usccr.gov/files/pubs/2019/07-23-Beyond-Suspensions.pdf

US Department of Education. 2020. *42nd Annual Report to Congress on the Implementation of the Individuals with Disabilities Education Act, 2020*. Washington, DC: Office of Special Education and Rehabilitative Services, US Department of Education. https://www.sattlerpublisher.com/42ndIDEA.pdf

US Department of Education, Office for Civil Rights. 2014. *Civil Rights Data Collection, Data Snapshot: Early Childhood Education*. Issue brief no. 2. https://www2.ed.gov/about/offices/list/ocr/docs/crdc-early-learning-snapshot.pdf

US Department of Health and Human Services. 2014. *Birth to 5: Watch Me Thrive! A Compendium of Screening Measures for Young Children*. Washington, DC: US Department of Health and Human Services. https://www.acf.hhs.gov/sites/default/files/documents/ecd/screening_compendium_march2014.pdf

US Department of Health and Human Services and US Department of Education. 2015. "Policy Statement on Inclusion of Children with Disabilities in Early Childhood Programs." Washington, DC: US Department of Health and Human Services and US Department of Education. https://www2. ed.gov/policy/speced/guid/earlylearning/joint-statement-full-text.pdf

Virginia Department of Education. 2018. *Virginia Guidelines for Early Childhood Inclusion*. Richmond, VA: Division of Special Education and Student Services, Office of Special Education and Instructional Services, Virginia Department of Education. https://ttaconline.org/Document/zxblhX_YCJOKW9RFGcsYls8GP00pSKNw/early-childhood-inclusion-guid-doc.pdf

Voorhees, Mary D., et al. 2013. "A Demonstration of Individualized Positive Behavior Support Interventions by Head Start Staff to Address Children's Challenging Behavior." *Research and Practice for Persons with Severe Disabilities* 38(3): 173–185.

Vygotsky, Lev S. 1978. *Mind in Society: The Development of Higher Psychological Processes*. Cambridge, MA: Harvard University Press.

Waxman, Hersh C., Beverly Alford, and Danielle Brown. 2013. "Individualized Instruction." In *International Guide to Student Achievement*. New York: Routledge.

Webster-Stratton, Carolyn, and Mary Hammond. 1997. "Treating Children with Early-Onset Conduct Problems: A Comparison of Child and Parent Training Interventions." *Journal of Consulting and Clinical Psychology* 65(1): 93–109.

Weglarz-Ward, Jenna M., and Rosa M. Santos. 2018. "Parent and Professional Perceptions of Inclusion in Childcare: A Literature Review." *Infants and Young Children* 31(2): 128–143.

Weglarz-Ward, Jenna M., Rosa M. Santos, and Jennifer Timmer. 2019. "Factors that Support and Hinder Including Infants with Disabilities in Child Care." *Early Childhood Education Journal* 47: 163–173.

Weiland, C. 2016. Impacts of the Boston prekindergarten program on the school readiness of young children with special needs. *Developmental Psychology* 52(11), 1763–1776.

WestEd Center for Child and Family Studies for the Child Development Division, California Department of Education. 2009. *Preschool English Learners: Principles and Practices to Promote Language, Literacy, and Learning: A Resource Guide*. 2nd edition. Sacramento, CA: Department of Education, State of California.

WestEd Center for Prevention and Early Intervention. 2015. *Developmental and Behavioral Screening Guide for Early Care and Education Providers*. San Francisco: WestEd.

Whitaker, Robert C., Brandon D. Becker, Allison N. Herman, and Rachel A. Gooze. 2013. "The Physical and Mental Health of Head Start Staff: The Pennsylvania Head Start Staff Wellness Survey, 2012." *Preventing Chronic Disease* 10: e181.

Whittingham, Koa. 2014. "Parents of Children with Disabilities, Mindfulness and Acceptance: A Review and a Call for Research." *Mindfulness* 5: 704–709.

Wijeysinghe, Charmaine L., Pat Griffin, and Barbara Love. 1997. "Racism Curriculum Design." In *Teaching for Diversity and Social Justice: A Sourcebook*. New York: Routledge.

Wolery, Mark, Melinda J. Ault, and Patricia M. Doyle. 1992. *Teaching Students with Moderate to Severe Disabilities: Use of Response Prompting Strategies*. New York: Longman.

Workgroup on Principles and Practices in Natural Environments. 2008. "Agreed Upon Mission and Key Principles for Providing Early Intervention Services in Natural Environments." https://ectacenter.org/~pdfs/topics/families/Finalmissionandprinciples3_11_08.pdf

Yu, SeonYeong. 2019. "Head Start Teachers' Attitudes and Perceived Competence Toward Inclusion." *Journal of Early Intervention* 41(1): 30–43.

Zeanah, Charles H., and Paula D. Zeanah. 2001. "Towards a Definition of Infant Mental Health." *Zero to Three* 22(1): 13–20.

Zeanah, Paula D., Brian Stafford, Geoffrey Nagle, and Thomas Rice. 2005. "Addressing Social-Emotional Development and Infant Mental Health in Early Childhood Systems." Building State Early Childhood Comprehensive Systems Series, No. 12. Los Angeles, CA: National Center for Infant and Early Childhood Health Policy.

Zeng, Songtian, Catherine Corr, Courtney O'Grady, and Yiyang Guan. 2019. "Adverse Childhood Experiences and Preschool Suspension Expulsion: A Population Study." *Child Abuse and Neglect* 97: 104149.

Zero to Three. 2016. "Infant–Early Childhood Mental Health." Zero to Three. https://www.zerotothree.org/resources/110-infant-early-childhood-mental-health

Zero to Three. 2020. *State of Babies Yearbook 2020*. Washington, DC: Zero to Three.

Zoran, Annmarie Gorenc. 2004. "No Teacher Left Behind: Early Language Learning and Students with Disabilities." *Learning Languages* 9(2): 18–21.

Index

20 USC 1400, 35
504 Plan, 45, 211

A

ABC observation, 159
Ableism, 24, 186, 211
Access, 11–13, 18, 100–101, 107, 211
Accessibility, 102–104, 111–119, 211
Accommodations, 18, 61, 107, 141–146, 211
Acquisition, 90, 211
Activity matrix, 94–95, 211, 230
Activity simplification, 142–143
Adaptability, 19
Adaptations, 95, 111–119, 138, 141–146, 190, 211, 232
Adult support, 142, 145–146
Adverse childhood experiences, 175–177, 212
Advocating for inclusion in early childhood, 208–209
Alcoholics Anonymous, 207
American Academy of Pediatrics, 76
American Association of Mental Deficiency, 5
American Indian and Alaska Native populations, 189
American Psychiatric Association, 212–213
Americans with Disabilities Act, 16–17
Antecedents, 159, 212
Appropriate identification, 39
Asking for help, 199–200
Assessing behaviors, 152
Assessment, 36, 67–83, 91, 133, 212
Assistive technology, 12–13, 18, 37, 60, 110–111, 190, 212
At risk, 35–37, 212
Attention deficit hyperactivity disorder, 48–50, 98–100, 212
Attitudes and beliefs, 24–25
Auditory cues, 140

Augmentative and alternative communication, 108–109, 212
Authentic learning, 91, 94
Autism spectrum disorder, 24, 39, 212

B

Barriers to inclusion, 16, 22–25, 107
Barton Lab, 138, 219
Before an evaluation, 58–59
Behavior has meaning, 153–155
Behavior hypothesis statements, 160, 212
Behavior support plan, 96, 152, 158–174, 213
    behavior hypothesis statements, 160
    consequence strategies, 160
    emotional literacy, 161–168
    emotional regulation, 161–168
    friendship skills, 152, 168–173
    long-term strategies, 160
    prevention strategies, 160
    problem-solving skills, 173–174
    replacement skills, 160
Behavior targets, 96
Benefits in implementation of inclusion, 20–22
Big Feelings Box, 165–166
Bipartisan Policy Center, 36
Body sensations, 161, 165
Braille, 60, 110, 140, 190
Building trust, 119–122, 129, 187–188
Bullying, 176

C

Celebrating effort, 172–173
Center for Applied Special Technology, 100–101, 222
Center for Parent Information and Resources, 37, 39, 57, 63, 228

Center on the Developing Child, 176, 222

Centers for Disease Control and Prevention, 68, 70–71, 77–78, 212, 221, 175–176, 195

Cerebral palsy, 104, 121–122, 213

Challenging behaviors, 151–155

Challenging conversations, 54–56

Child abuse and neglect, 35, 77, 176

Child Care and Development Block Grant, 17

Child Care Aware of America, 198, 228, 236

Child Find, 32, 36, 39, 213

Child outcomes, 41–42, 80–81

Child preferences, 142, 144

Child protective services, 77, 175

Child reevaluation, 33

Childhelp National Child Abuse Hotline, 77, 207

Children of color
    expulsion/suspension rates higher than White children, 183
    less developmental screening for, 76
    less likely to receive services, 36

Children with disabilities
    at increased risk for abuse, 175
    benefits of inclusion, 17–18
    importance of friendship, 169
    in the US, 11–12
    negative associations, 4–6, 24–25
    planning for social engagement, 149

Children's books
    Glad Monster, Sad Monster by Ed Emberley & Anna Miranda, 164
    If You Give a Mouse a Cookie by Laura Numeroff, 87
    On Monday When It Rained by Cherryl Kachenmeister, 164
    When Sophie Gets Angry—Really, Really Angry by Molly Bang, 164

Children's Bureau, 175

Children's Equity Project, 36, 183

Choice boards, 139–140

Circle time, 106, 125, 171

Clarity, 122–124

Classroom rules, 128–129, 231

Clear expectations, 127–129

Cleveland Clinic, 214

Cognitive development, 69

Collaboration, 13, 20, 101, 213
    coteaching model, 23
    itinerant model, 23
    transdisciplinary team approach, 84–89
    with mental health experts, 178–179

Collaborative observation, 73–74

Collaborative play, 171

Collaborative problem solving, 133

Communicating expectations, 135–136

Communication boards, 108, 145, 213

Communication skills, 90

Community parent resource centers, 35, 63

Compassion fatigue, 197

Compassionate curiosity, 155

Confidentiality, 57

CONNECT, 57, 216–217, 228, 232

Consent, 58, 213

Consequence strategies, 159–160, 213

Consistency, 122–125

Coregulation, 161, 213

Cost of caring, 197

Coteaching model of collaboration, 23

COVID-19, 27, 53, 82, 147–150, 196

Cross-sector, 213

Culturally responsive practices, 51–53, 78, 94, 180–193, 213–214

Culture, 121, 181, 213
    challenging behaviors and, 142
    embracing diversity, 180–193
    families and, 51–53, 78, 94
    recognizing our own biases, 184–186

Curriculum, 58–59, 80, 142, 214

Curriculum modifications, 132, 141–146, 148

D

Daily schedules, 123–124

Data collection, 38

Deaf-blindness, 39, 60

Deep breathing, 166–167, 201–202

Depression, 195, 205

Describing behavior, 54

Development delays, 24, 35–36, 39

Developmental disabilities, 68

Developmental milestones, 68–70, 214

Developmental monitoring, 76

Developmental screening. *See* Screening

Developmentally appropriate assessment, 81

Differentiated instruction, 133–134, 214

Disability, 39, 182–183

Disaster Distress Helpline, 207

Discrimination, 16–17, 76

Dispute resolution, 61–63

Distance learning, 53, 82, 126, 147–150, 166, 175, 196

Division of Early Childhood of the Council for Exceptional Children (DEC), 11–12, 79, 83, 85, 134–135, 211–212, 216–218, 221, 225

Down syndrome, 214

Dual language learners, 46, 60
    culturally and linguistically responsive practices, 94
    ECTA resources, 89
    embracing diversity of, 190–193
    evaluation in home language, 78–79
    families, 52–53
    misunderstood behaviors, 188–189
    resources, 156
    suggestions for working with, 189–190

Due process, 62–63

E

Early care and education, 11–12, 20, 85

Early childhood educators
    as advocates for inclusion, 208–209
    benefits of inclusion, 19–20
    mental-health supports, 207–208
    reflections on culture for, 186
    self-care, 194–209
    turnover, 196
    wellness, 198–206

Early childhood special education, 7–8, 11–12, 15, 20, 31, 38–41, 45–47, 67–68, 84–89

Early Childhood Technical Assistance (ECTA) Center, 2, 35, 41–55, 57–58, 61, 71, 83, 89, 102, 110, 119, 129, 131, 148, 212–214, 219, 221

Early intervention, 7–8, 31–54, 67–68, 84–89, 214

Electronic communication devices, 108, 145

Eligibility determination, 32–33

Embedded instruction, 214
    acquisition, 90
    fluency, 90
    generalization, 90
    how we teach, 94–96
    maintenance, 90
    opportunities, 84, 89–96, 125
    steps, 96
    what we teach, 92–93
    when we teach, 93–94

Emotional disturbance, 39

Emotional labor, 197

Emotional literacy, 161–168, 214
    practice describing feelings, 163
    practice identifying feeling cues, 163–164
    promoting, 152
    read books about emotions, 164–168
    talk about body sensations, 163
    talk about emotions, 162
    talk about facial expressions, 162–163

Emotional regulation, 161–168, 214
    practice describing feelings, 163
    practice identifying feeling cues, 163–164
    promoting, 152
    read books about emotions, 164–168
    talk about body sensations, 163
    talk about emotions, 162
    talk about facial expressions, 162–163

Empathy, 19, 65–66, 197

Engagement, 101, 107

English language learners. *See* Dual language learners

Environmental support, 142–143

Equality, 186, 214

Equitable learning opportunities, 185–188, 215

Equity, 36, 76, 186–188, 190–193, 214

Ethnicity, 215

Evaluation, 32, 36, 39, 67–83

Evidence-based practices, 131, 156, 215

Executive functions, 189, 215

Expression, 101

Expulsion rates

    children of color, 183–184

    children with disabilities, 21, 183–184

F

Fading, 215

Families

    asking about child preferences, 144

    benefits of embedded instruction, 90–91

    building trust, 129

    collaborative observation, 73–74

    culture and, 51–53

    embracing diversity of, 190–193

    engaging at a distance, 53

    engaging for equity, 185–188

    evaluation and, 78–79

    functional assessment, 82–83

    having challenging conversations, 54–57

    involving, 8, 13, 15

    parent rights under IDEA, 57–63

    part of transdisciplinary team, 85

    participation, 41

    questions for reflection, 66

    relationship-based practices, 50–53

    resistance, 75

    sharing observations with, 75–76

    supporting during transitions, 46

    supporting parental competence, 56

    supporting routines when learning at home, 126

    understanding their perspective, 63–66

    understanding their perspective, 75–76

    when they deny services, 61

    when you suspect a child needs services and
        support, 54–63

    working with, 48–66

Federal Department of Education, 17

Federal legislation, 14–17

Feeling Faces cards (NCPMI), 163, 234

Fidelity, 215

Filing a complaint, 62–63

FindTreatment.gov, 207

First-then boards, 139–140

Flexibility, 27, 147

Flow, 141–142, 215

Fluency, 90, 215

Formal assessment, 81

Frank Porter Graham Child Development Institute
    (FPG), 137, 212, 215, 221

Free and appropriate public education, 14–15, 39,
    215

Friendship skills, 152, 168–173

Functional behavior assessment, 81–82, 158–160,
    215

Functional outcomes, 42

Funding, 13–15

G

Generalization, 90, 215

Grounding strategies, 201–202

Grouping children, 135

Growth mindset, 202–204

"Guide to Disability Rights Laws" (US Dept. of
    Justice), 204

H

Head Start, 2, 17, 21, 85, 93, 95, 152–153, 170, 177,
    191, 194–198, 203

Healthy social-emotional development, 152

Hearing impairment, 39

Hearing officer, 63

Heavy work, 118, 168

Home visit, 31, 73–74, 216

Homelessness, 37

How we teach, 94–96

Hypothesis statements, 160, 216

I

Identity-first language, 6–7

Implicit bias, 183–185, 188, 216

Inclusion, 8–14, 216
    barriers to, 22–25
    breakdowns in implementation, 20–22
    family stories, 25–28
    federal legislation, 14–17
    questions for reflections, 28
    research about the benefits, 17–20

Inclusive Classroom Profile, 102

Inclusive learning environments, 8, 98–129
    access, 100–101
    participation, 101
    physical environment, 102–119
    reflection questions, 129
    social environment, 119–122
    support, 101
    temporal environment, 122–129

Inclusive teaching practices, 130–150
    curriculum modifications, 141–146
    from a distance, 147–150
    multitiered systems of support, 132–133
    planning for highly individualized teaching, 133–141
    response to intervention, 132

Inclusive, equitable, and culturally responsive practices, 8, 94

Individual teacher model, 23

Individualized education plans (IEPs), 15, 20, 26, 33, 40, 58–61, 79–97, 134, 216

Individualized family service plans (IFSPs), 15, 31, 33, 36, 58–61, 79–97, 134, 216

Individualized instruction, 13, 80, 101–102, 101–102, 216
    identifying the right teaching practice, 134–135
    measuring progress, 140–141
    observe the child, 134
    planning for, 133–141
    scaffolding learning, 135–137
    supporting the child, 135–139
    using prompts and visuals, 138–139

Individuals with Disabilities Education Act (IDEA), 14–15, 18, 21, 24, 32, 35–41, 45, 57–63, 78–79, 213, 224

Part B, 34–41, 43

Part C, 34–41, 43, 81

Infant and early childhood mental health, 178–179, 216

Informal assessment, 81

Informed consent, 58

Intellectual disability, 39

Intentional opportunities for relationships, 121–122

Interaction Institute for Social Change, 187

Interdisciplinary team, 84–89, 217

International Children's Digital Library, 192, 235

Intersectionality, 182–183

Invisible support, 142, 146

IRIS Center, 211–221, 225

Itinerant model of collaboration, 23

Itinerant teachers, 23, 84–89, 217

J

Journaling, 204–205

Just right supports, 186–187

K

Kaiser Permanente, 175

Kids Count Data Center, 11

Knowledge and skills vs. attitudes and beliefs, 24–25

Kozlowski, R. V., vii–vii, 29–31, 48–50, 57, 62, 64–65, 67–68, 87, 98–100, 130–131, 155–156, 169–170

L

Language and communication development, 42, 69

Large, bright materials, 110–119

Learning bags, 147–148

Learning cycle, 80–81, 89–96, 217
    acquisition, 90
    fluency, 90
    generalization, 90

how we teach, 94–96
maintenance, 90
the "how" of, 94–96
what we teach, 92–93
when we teach, 93–94
Learning spaces, 105
Learning targets, 92–93
Least restrictive environment, 15, 40, 217
Least-to-most prompts, 138, 217
Length of daily activities, 125
Linguistically responsive practices, 180–181
dual language learners, 188–190
embracing diversity, 190–193
Local education agencies, 45
Long-term strategies, 160
Low birth weight, 35

M

Mainstreaming, 21
Maintenance, 90, 217
Making It Work, 189, 235
The Mask of Motherhood (Maushart), 48–49
Materials, 106, 142–143
Mediation, 62, 217
Medically fragile, 217
Mental grounding, 202
Mental health supports, 207–208
Mentoring, 101, 217
Mentors, 199
Merriam-Webster, 181, 218
Mindfulness, 204–207
Modeling tasks, 137, 145, 217
by peers, 17–18
friendship skills, 170
prosocial behaviors, 170–171
Modifications, 61, 95, 141–146, 218
Modifying the response, 107–109
Monitoring progress, 92
Most-to-least prompts, 138, 218

Movement and physical development, 70, 106
managing emotions, 167–168
Multidisciplinary team, 19–20, 218
Multiple disabilities, 39
Multitiered systems of support (MTSS), 132–133, 156, 188, 218
"My Teacher Wants to Know" (NCPMI), 53, 238

N

National Association for Children of Addiction, 207
National Association for the Education of Young Children, 11–12, 70, 79–80, 142, 181, 183, 185, 187–188, 211, 214–218, 221
National Center for Learning Disabilities, 76
National Center on Parent, Family, and Community Engagement, 54
National Center on Pyramid Model Innovations, 127–129, 156–158, 161, 169, 173–174, 177, 211–221, 234
National Center on Response to Intervention, 133
National Domestic Violence Hotline, 207
National Professional Development Center on Autism Spectrum Disorder, 137, 218
National Scientific Council on the Developing Child, 176
National Survey of Children's Health, 176
National Wellness Institute, 199, 204, 236
Natural environments, 37, 40, 81
Negativity bias, 121
North Carolina Division of Child Development and Early Education, 2
Nutritional deficiencies, 35

O

Observation, 71–76, 218
collaborative, 73–74
in the early childhood education environment, 71–73

questions for use, 72
    sharing with families, 75–76
Office of Head Start, 45, 52, 227, 236
Office of Special Education Programs, 11, 14, 20–21, 24, 35, 37–39, 41–42, 63, 224, 227
Olfactory cues, 140
One-to-one supports, 133
Ongoing assessment, 81, 91
Ongoing evaluation, 13
Opportunities for challenge, 137
Opportunities for choice, 137
Optimal positioning, 107
Orthopedic impairment, 39
Other health impairments, 39
Our Youngest Learners (Education Trust et al.), 76
Outcomes, 41–42

P

PACER Simon Technology Center, 110, 228, 231
Parent Center Hub. *See* Center for Parent Information and Resources, 37
Parent Helpline, 207
Parent rights, 57–63
    before the evaluation, 58–59
    dispute resolution, 61
    during the IFSP/IEP meeting, 59–61
    formal approaches to dispute resolution, 62–63
    informal approaches to dispute resolution, 61–62
Parent training and information centers, 35, 63
Participation, 12–13, 18, 101, 137, 218
Peer relationships, 17–18, 142, 146
Peer-mediated intervention, 137, 218
People-first language, 6–7, 218
Personalized instruction. *See* Individualized instruction
Physical environment, 102–119, 218
Physical grounding, 201–202
Picture cards, 145
Picture Exchange Communication System, 108, 190, 218

Placement, 219
Positive behavioral interventions and supports (PBIS), 133, 156, 219
Poverty, 152, 186, 197
Practice-based coaching, 203, 219
Practices, 219
    evidence-based, 131
    inclusive teaching, 130–150
    reflecting on your own, 203–204
Predictability, 122–125, 177
Prenatal drug exposure, 35
Prevention Strategies, 160
Prior written notice, 57, 219
Priority skills, 91
Problem-solving skills, 152, 173–174
Procedural safeguards notice, 58, 219
Procedural safeguards, 38, 41
Professional development, 13, 20, 23–24, 37, 101
Professional learning communities, 203
Progress monitoring, 33, 133, 140–141
Prompts, 132, 138–140, 219
Providing services, 33
Pull-out programs, 219
    vs. transdisciplinary team approach, 86–87
The Pyramid Model for Supporting Social Emotional Competence in Infants and Young Children, 127–129, 133, 156–158, 161, 174, 176–178, 219, 234

Q

Quality rating and improvement systems (QRIS), 13
Questions for parents, 91
Questions for reflection
    culturally and linguistically responsive practices, 186, 193
    fostering social-emotional development, 179
    inclusion, 28
    inclusive learning environments, 129
    inclusive teaching practices, 150
    screening, evaluation, and assessment, 83
    understanding early intervention and special education, 29

working on IFSP/IEP goals, 97
    working with families, 66
Questions for use in observations, 72

R

Race, 197, 219
Racial disparity, 36, 186, 220
    implicit bias, 183
    in developmental screening, 76
    pay disparities for early childhood educators,
        197
Recorded books, 190
Referrals, 32, 220
Reflecting, 56–57, 203–204
Rehabilitation Act of 1973, 211
Reinforcements, 136
Related services, 220
Relationship-based practices, 50–53
Reliability, 220
    assessment, 79–83
    evaluation, 78–79
    of parents' observations, 73–74
    screening, 76–78
Religious organizations
    exempt from ADA, 16–17
Repetition and practice, 137
Replacement skills, 160, 220
Representation, 101
Research about the benefits of inclusion, 17
    benefits for children with disabilities, 17–18
    benefits for children without disabilities, 19
    benefits for early childhood professionals,
        19–20
    cost benefits, 20
Research-based early intervention services, 37
Resilience, 9–11, 153
Response prompts, 138, 220
Response to intervention, 133, 220
Reverse inclusion, 23
Risk taking, 104–105

Role-play, 172
Routines to the Third Power (Routines3) (Strain &
    Bovey), 124–125
Routines, 116, 122–126
RTI Action Network, 220

S

Safety, 104–105
Sand and water play, 111–112
Scaffolding, 132, 135–137, 188, 220
Screen reader software, 220
Screening, 67–83, 133
    assessment, 79–82
    developmental milestones, 68–70
    evaluation, 78–79
    observation, 71–74
    obtaining parental permission, 77–79
    reflection questions, 83
    resources, 77–78
    sharing observations with families, 75–76
Scripted stories. See Social stories
Self-care, 194–209
Self-contained classrooms, 20–25, 220
Self-regulation, 80, 105, 220
Sensory input, 105–106
Sensory integration disorder. See Sensory
    processing disorder
Sensory processing disorder, 49, 108, 111–115,
    220–221
Sensory reinforcers, 140, 221
Service coordination, 221
Setting events, 221
Sign language, 86–87, 108, 115, 145,
    189–190
SMART approach, 92
"Snack Talks," 136
Social environment, 102, 119–122
Social exclusion, 3, 176
Social stories, 115–116, 136, 172, 221, 232
Social-emotional development, 42, 69
    behavior has meaning, 153–155

behavior support plans, 158–174

collaborating with mental health professionals, 178–179

embedded learning, 90

fostering, 151–179

frameworks, 156–158

functional behavior assessment, 158–174

healthy social-emotional development defined, 152

inclusive classrooms, 17–19

reflection questions, 179

social stories, 115–116, 136

supporting from a distance, 166

teaching social-emotional skills, 155–156

toxic stress, 175–178

trauma, 175–178

Special education

and early intervention, 31–34

child and family outcomes, 41–54

Child Find, 32

child reevaluation, 34

eligibility determination, 32–33

evaluation, 32

IDEA Parts B and C, 34–41

IFSP/IEP meeting, 33

IFSP/IEP review, 34

progress monitoring, 33

providing services, 33

referral, 32

reflection questions, 47

transition from EI to ECSE, 34

transitions, 43–47

understanding, 29–47

Special equipment, 142, 145

Special health-care needs, 221

Specialized services, 221

Specialized supports, 13

Specially designed instruction, 221

Specific learning disability, 39

Speech or language impairment, 24, 39

Spinal muscular atrophy, 147

Stabilizing materials, 107, 109–110, 117

State complaint procedures, 38

State interagency coordinating councils, 38

Stereotypes, 19, 183

Strength-based approach, 188, 221

Stress, 174–178, 194–198, 204–206

StrongHearts Native Helpline, 208

Substance Abuse and Mental Health Services Administration, 207, 222

Suicide Prevention Lifeline, 208

Supervision and monitoring, 38

Supporting parental competence, 56

Supports, 12–13, 101, 133, 186–187, 221

Suspension rates

children of color, 183–184

children with disabilities, 21, 183–184

System of least prompts. *See* Least-to-most prompts

T

Teaching cycle, 80–81, 94–96

Temporal environment, 102, 122–129, 221

Terminology, 3–7, 40, 71–72, 141

Toxic stress, 174–178, 222

Transdisciplinary team approach, 84–89

Transitions, 34, 43–47, 89, 116, 125–127, 177, 232

Trauma, 39, 52, 222

adverse childhood experiences, 175–177

historical, 76, 216

racial and income disparities, 176

signs in early childhood, 177

vicarious, 197, 222

Trauma-informed care, 177–178, 222

Triggers, 76, 159, 212

Tucker Turtle Takes Time to Tuck and Think (NCPMI), 169, 235

U

Universal design for learning, 12–13, 100–101, 107–108, 222

US Department of Education, 12, 11, 14, 20–21, 35, 38, 183

US Department of Health and Human Services, 12, 183, 220, 222

V

Validity, 222

Visual impairment, 39, 60, 104–105, 110–119

Visual supports, 132, 136, 138–140, 149, 170, 190, 222, 232

Voice output devices, 190

W

We Carry Kevan, 147, 233

Wellness, 198–206

Wiggle seats, 140

Work samples, 72, 222

Z

Zone of proximal development, 93, 135, 222